M000222821

Also from Pronghorn Press:

Rodeo Time in Sheridan Wyo
A History of the Sheridan-Wyo Rodeo
by Tom Ringley

My Cowboy Hat
Still Fits

My Life as a Rodeo Star

Abe Morris

Cover Photo: Dan Hubbell
August 1991, Douglas, Wyoming
NFR Bull # 91 Terminator
Ike Sankey Rodeo Company

Cover Design: Antelope Design
Published by Pronghorn Press

www.pronghornpress.org

I made a lot of fans during my rodeo career. It did not take me long to realize that Justin Abraham Morris was the biggest rodeo fan that I would ever have.

It was for this reason and several others that I decided to dedicate this book to my son.

Forward

I met Abraham Jackson Morris, Jr. on the field of battle, or at least the man versus beast kind of battle called bull riding. We would practice riding bulls in the icy confines of the OK Corral (aka High Plains Bar and Arena) in Laramie. The harsh climate of Wyoming creates a certain element of camaraderie in and of itself in a sort of "us against the environment" kind of way. Add bulls intent on harm—or at best not the least concerned when they cause it—to the mix, and you create a bond that easily transcends any differences in background, religion, politics or race. I appreciated then Abe's competitiveness, infectious laugh and willingness to lend a hand.

I learned a great deal more about him when I moved into Orr Hall at the University of Wyoming. There, coincidentally, he was the Resident Assistant (aka Boss) of the fifth floor to which I was assigned. I was a hellion. Though I never drank at the time (thank God for Abe), we were constantly inventing ways to keep ourselves dutifully occupied by playing jokes on fellow dormmates, hosting wheelchair races around the floor and stealing people's clothes from the community shower to test their ingenuity in getting back to their rooms. Abe could always strike a careful balance between keeping order on the floor and preventing damage; and allowing us to have some fun and enjoy the experience. There, I learned to appreciate his tolerance, wisdom and respect for others.

During the latter part of my junior and senior years, Abe and three of us shared a house our friend and fellow bull rider Gerry Strom's mother had bought at Gerry's behest, for a rental property. There were four of us and two bedrooms. Brad Morris and I shared one bedroom and Hap Kellogg and Abe shared the other. Hap and I were still in college and Abe had recently graduated. Brad had dropped out to work and rodeo.

Brad and I spent all of our spare time chasing girls and carousing. During my senior year Hap and I went on a pre-planned two week drunk. Often Brad and I would work for Abe, who was the Banquet Manager at the Holiday Inn, usually for the food, sometimes the money and always to help Abe. I began to appreciate his meticulous nature, impeccable, and I do mean outstanding, memory for details and his singular dedication to reach his goals.

Growing up in Wyoming you didn't see very many African-Americans and those you did, you tended to judge individually as you did all people. No one considered the color of the hand reaching to drag you out of a snowbank, you were just grateful for the hand. All of us had obtained our PRCA cards and at various times were traveling "down the road" trying to win some money. It was one such trip in the winter when Abe, Chris Horton and I walked into a Monroe, Louisiana bar, and I learned his trek was much more difficult than my own. Abe was not welcome in that bar and we made a hasty exit. At Myrtis Dightman's bar in Houston, Texas, when we were the only white guys in the joint, I at least got some sense of his situation, though there were no incidents. It was there that I learned about Abe's courage, intelligence and individualism and what it took for him to have moved here from the East.

As I watched Abe in his work at a group home in Laramie, Wyoming, for "at risk" teenagers— a largely thankless counseling job where he affected many lives in a positive and reaffirming manner— I was motivated to try and make a positive impact myself. Later, when he turned his efforts to the financial world, I saw the same kind of resolve that had won him many titles in the rodeo arena win him accolades in the sales arena. There I saw his humanity, charity and ability to grow and transform.

As we drove through the Colorado mountains in December 2002 on our way to the National Finals Rodeo in Las Vegas, Nevada, and we swapped stories of our struggles to remain in contact with our beloved children through difficult personal travails with their mothers, I came to know his deep love and determination for a good life for his son, Justin. He has dedicated himself to that end and I know his son appreciates his father's love and dedication.

As for Abe the writer, I am certain he will meet with the same success through the same successful methods he has honed over the years. I enjoy reading the stories he writes for various publications and I have enjoyed reading this book. I have learned a great deal from Abe through the years and even a thing or two about myself from his book because, alas, I trust his memory far more than my own.

I know you will enjoy his stories as much as he and his friends enjoyed the journey.

Shaw Sullivan
Founder and CEO of *Bull Riders Only*

So You Wanna Be a Bull Rider

What in the world would possess you to decide that you wanted to become a bull rider? I was asked this question numerous times during my professional bull riding career. I never wavered in my response and the answer was always the same. My cousins Gene, Jimmy Lee, and Willie Ed Walker all got me started riding bulls. They started me out on roping calves and then it was a gradual promotion to the big bulls. They refused to let me get on anything that they knew that I could not ride or an animal that they thought had the potential to hurt me.

There are many different ingredients that go into making a successful and qualified ride on a bucking bull. A classic ride is like dancing in sync with a great partner—in order to be successful, you must move together in time and always counterbalance your partner's moves. Unfortunately, the bull is not always committed to this "dance" in the same way as the rider. Nonetheless, if you lose your form, then you will lose points with the judges and can "buck off." Thus, a bull rider must have a lot of athletic ability.

The most essential ingredient for a bull rider is that they must have a lot of "heart"...or be a little crazy. First and foremost, a bull rider has to have the courage to get on a very unpredictable animal that is fixed on dislodging them from his back any way possible and that is also willing to cause them bodily harm, or even death.

When a bull is bucking, a rider must squeeze tightly with his knees and legs to hang on. It is virtually impossible to get a hold of a stout bull on the first jump out of the bucking chute and then maintain that position with your feet. At the same time you have to be loose and fluid with your upper body in order to counteract the moves of your bull. A common saying of the bull riders is, "be loose and cool." A bull rider cannot afford to be stiff.

Another essential ingredient is good equipment. A bull rider needs a pair of snug fitting boots.

They also need a pair of spurs that fit snugly but are not anchored down too tightly. There should be a little bit of give and movement in the spurs. They should use a pair with rowels (the round disk with points that spins) that will rotate about a quarter of a turn. When I was a young bull rider, the concept was to use rowels that were locked down tight and would not turn at all. As I got older, the scientific theory changed. So of course, like all of the other bull riders, I adapted. The spur rowels were a little thinner in the sixties and the seventies. In the decade of the eighties and the nineties we started using rowels that were a little larger and slightly thicker. They also got a little fancier.

The rowel will help the bull rider grab some of the bull's loose hide. The spurs are not designed to cut. If they cut a bull, they would not serve their purpose and the stock contractor would get very upset if a rider left cuts and marks on one of his prized bucking bulls. The idea is to get a solid "hold" to help pull yourself back into position.

Having good solid spur holds was a part of my riding style. Other bull riders rode with their knees and more of a balanced style. Tuff Hedeman, a three-time PRCA World Champion Bull Rider and Terry Don West, the 1996 and 2003 PRCA World Champion Bull Rider rode with that style and did just fine. Both of those guys were excellent at getting out over bulls and "posting." (Posting is the term used in English-style riding where the rider stands in the stirrups, moving up and down, countering the horse's steps in the trot).

Charles Sampson, the 1982 World Champion Bull Rider, rode with that style. Charles was great at getting out over rank bucking bulls with his upper body in order to get away from their power. A bull rider tends to get in trouble when he doesn't stay up close to his bull rope. Getting moved back is what gets you in "bad shape" and then you are going to buck off. It is simply a combination of physics and mechanics. Charles combined both styles and it was very rare that a bucking bull could force his feet out and away from their sides. Charles always was able to maintain deep solid holds with his feet and spurs.

The angle of the spurs will depend on how well the rider can turn their toes out to try and get a hold. Personally, I never had any trouble turning out my toes. This is one of the reasons that a lot of bull riders tuck their riding pants into the tops of their boots. I had to. If I didn't, I would regularly catch my Wrangler jeans in my spurs and tear them. Some bull riders didn't turn their toes out very well and therefore did not necessarily need to tuck them in. For me tucking in my jeans was not a fad, it was a necessity.

The next major piece of equipment is a flat braided bull rope. The bull rope has a twelve inch long hand hold braided into it. The bull rider's hand is laid flat on the bull's back with the little finger as close to the center of the bull's back as possible. The hand is placed snug and squarely against one side of the handhold. Being a right handed rider, I would place my hand to the left side or the "block" of the handhold.

What causes a bull rider to "hang up" (his hand catches in the bull rope) is bucking off to the side opposite the hand that you ride with. Whenever a right-handed bull rider bucks off to the right side, his hand will usually slide out of the extra length of the handhold. When he bucks off to the left, there is no room in the handhold for the hand to slide.

Thus the bull rider "hangs up" and is still bound to the moving animal.

A bull rider wears a leather glove with a long wrist. He will either tie or tape the glove on tightly right before he competes and will always wait until the last minute to put his glove on so that his hand doesn't sweat.

Just as in other sports, a bull rider needs to warm up and stretch his muscles. It is especially important to stretch your groin muscles before competing. Many bull riders (myself included) have pulled their groin muscles riding bulls. The groin muscle is attached to your knee and if you tear it, it's extremely painful. If a bull rider pulls a groin muscle, it is usually the one in the leg opposite his riding hand.

Once you injure a groin the best cure is to rest it and let it heal. It can be a very troublesome and nagging injury. If you try to come back too soon it only gets worse. In the quest for his eighth and final World Championship, Don Gay sat out an entire season in order to let his groins heal before hitting the rodeo trail again.

Before their turn in the competition bull riders put their bull rope around the middle of the bull, right behind the front legs. The bull rope has an adjustment loop with a long tail. The tail is threaded through the loop and the rope is wrapped around the bull. There are a cowbells on the rope that are meant to be an added irritation to the bull.

Once the rider sits down over their bull, he loosens up the rope and shakes it a little so that the bells will slide to the middle of the bull's belly. Then he asks his partner to pull his rope taut. While his partner holds on to the tail of the rope, the rider will rub some powdered rosin into the tail of his rope and then the handhold. This is done in order to warm up the rope and make the rosin stickier and the rope easier to hang on to.

All the while, the bull rider rests his feet on the inside slats of the chute. He is very careful not to stick his spurs into the bull, which could cause him to buck or lunge forward in the chute. This can also result in the bull rider getting jerked down in the bucking chute and getting crushed by a mean and angry bull.

Next the rider places his hand in the handhold and gets his friend to pull and snug the rope around the bull. He has to make sure that the rope is tight. If not, when the rider pulls on it for leverage, it will slide off to one side or the other. Most of the time it takes two guys to pull a rope tight enough for a contestant. One will pull from the top and another will pull the rope from underneath the bull's belly.

After the rope is tight enough, the rider takes the tail of it from his friends and lays it across his open hand. Then he takes a wrap behind his hand and lays the tail back across his palm. Some bull riders will run the tail between their ring finger and their pinky. This makes it a lot easier to hold on to your bull rope. It also increases your chances of hanging up on your bull; if you buck off away from your riding hand after you do a "split tail wrap," you are almost guaranteed to hang up.

The bullfighters that work in tandem in the arena like to know before a rider nods his head if he has taken a split tail, knowing before the bull takes his initial jump out of the bucking chutes that there is a good chance that the rider may hang up and drag.

Right before a bull rider nods his head for the gate to open, he wants to get up as close as possible to his riding hand. The theory is to try and sit on your riding hand.

A bull's initial move on leaving the bucking chute is to raise up his front end. A rider needs to be down low and tight or else he will get "beaten out of the bucking chutes." If you sit up straight on the first jump out of the bucking chute you should immediately buck off.

After the bull hits the ground with his front feet, he will kick up and out. Some of the great bucking bulls like Bodacious and Rocky Raccoon were known to kick over the back of the bucking chutes. Cowboys who knew this would make sure that they got down from the back of the chute and therefore out of harm's way. Good bucking bulls really come up high in the front end and then kick over their heads with their hind legs. The best bucking bulls spin.

Most spinning bulls are attempting to buck the rider off to the outside of the spin. This is aided by centrifugal force which pushes the rider to the outside of the spin. Only a few bulls spin with the intention of pulling a rider down into what the bull riders refer to as the "well" which is the inside of the circle the bull is spinning. I would say that about ninety-five percent of the bulls that spin are trying to buck you off to the outside.

Bull riders are very good about sharing information about the bucking tendencies of different bulls. If a rider is getting on a "well-y" bull, then he will do all that he can not to get sucked down into the center of the spin. A mistake can prove costly and can lead to serious injury.

The technique for a rider is to reach forward with his free hand as the bull rises in the front end. The bull rider wants to stay low and arch his back. Then as the bull kicks up his back feet, the bull rider sits up straight and throws out his chest and whips his free arm back slightly behind his head. Then he repeats the process over again.

Riding bulls is about finesse and balance. It is more about timing and balance than overall strength. Gary Leffew, the 1970 World Champion Bull Rider who is considered the Guru of bull riding, always talks about constantly reaching forward and moving your free arm to regain a "base" position.

A rider must be very careful not to sling his arm too far because it will rotate his hips outward and cause him to buck off. It must be a controlled swing and not a violent swing of the free arm. The free arm cannot go past an imaginary line or it will cause the rider to be tipped out of shape.

A bull rider needs to keep his free arm in the air for the entire eight seconds of his ride. If he touches either himself, his bull rope or his bull with his free hand during the eight seconds, he will be disqualified.

A rider likes to find the "sweet spot" and get tapped off. Once he is there, it is extremely hard for a good spinning bull to buck him off. If a bull is spinning into a rider's hand, then the cowboy needs to lift his free arm over his cowboy hat and throw it in the direction of the spin. You always want to keep your momentum moving so that you can stay in time with the animal.

You always want to wait on your bull. If you move ahead, you'll get out of shape by what is known as "over riding." If a bull rider tries to anticipate the moves of the bull, it is known as "setting a trap." Bull riders know better than to do this but we all do it. It is human nature to try whatever it takes to be successful and make a qualified ride. For example: Say that a bull has a reputation for turning back to the right just one or two jumps out of the bucking chutes, and is consistently bucking everyone off when he turns back. A rider would cheat a little bit and ease his weight to the right to anticipate the turn back.

Bucking bulls are a lot more intelligent than people give them credit for. A bull may spin to the right fifteen or twenty trips in a row. Then, because he felt some "hot shot" bull rider trying to anticipate his move to the right, he will instead turn back and spin to the left for the first time. This scenario happens on a regular basis in the rodeo world.

Some bull riders prefer bulls that spin into their hands, while others prefer to have them go away from their riding hand. It seems like most bull riders have a tendency to master bulls that spin into their hands. Even the great bucking bulls have figured out to spin away from a guy's riding hand. Number 007 Red Rock and #61 Little Yellow Jacket are two great bucking bulls that fit this category.

Personally I didn't care which way my bulls spun as long as I had a good seat when they turned back. Back in the day when I was gung-ho I vowed to spur every bull that I got on, no matter which direction that he spun. Bull riders are not required to spur during the ride. If they do, they will receive a few extra points from the judges.

A good bull rider must constantly be moving his feet. A bucking bull usually blows your feet out of line. You have to constantly shuffle them forward towards the bull rope area. A rider should not be overly concerned about positioning when a bull turns back. If you have a good solid position, then the bull is simply going to take you with him when and if he turns back to spin. Riding bulls is difficult enough without trying to spur as well. It takes a lot of skill, adds more risk and increases the chances of bucking off. As I got older, I mellowed out and became a lot more cautious and conservative. I bucked off of a lot of good bulls because I spurred them when I had no business pulling a foot.

A bull ride lasts for eight seconds and will be judged accordingly for style points. The rider is scored by two official judges: From one to twenty-five points on how well he rides and one to twenty-five points on how well his animal performs. The highest possible result is a perfect one hundred point ride. Any score in the eighty or ninety point range is considered to be very outstanding.

Long sleeve shirts are a necessary part of the attire when competing in the rodeo arena and also afford some protection to the arms and elbows during the rough and tumble efforts of a rodeo cowboy. It was not until the decade of the late 1980s that some bull riders started to wear the protective vests. Now they're mandatory.

Cowboy hats are also part of the attire. Nowadays, some of the bull riders have opted to wear a helmet during competition. Most of those who wear helmets have already suffered a serious head injury. They aren't ready to retire from bull riding so they wear a helmet and continue their careers.

Charles Sampson was the first bull rider who wore a helmet in competition. This was after he suffered a serious head injury in Landover, Maryland in September 1983. He received special permission from the PRCA to wear a lacrosse helmet during the 1983 National Finals Rodeo.

You don't see very many big people riding bulls. It's rare to find a talented bull rider who is over six-foot-two. The larger people have a difficult time getting back into position. The bigger guys are usually steer wrestlers or calf ropers. Most bull riders are shorter than six feet and weigh less than a hundred and seventy pounds. I would say that the average bull rider is five-foot-seven and weighs about one hundred and fifty pounds. The smaller guys can shift and control their weight much more easily. During a ride a bull rider can very quickly get out of shape and must make a recovery. It helps to have low sense of gravity.

Not only does size play a major role in bull riding but so do the mental aspects. Considering all of the odds, a rider must believe that he can successfully make a qualified ride on the best bucking bulls. Otherwise, he is defeated before he even nods his head. Positive mental attitude is a must. He must often compete while in severe pain and be able to rebound to the same level of competition after suffering a serious injury in the arena.

Before competition, athletes will mentally psyche themselves up to prepare for battle. Bull riders are no different. They mentally put themselves into the game and go through a routine of visualization, of seeing themselves making a successful ride and coming out on top of a bucking bull.

Bulls buck because they do not want you on their backs. The flank strap only encourages bulls to buck. The flank is a ticklish area near the hind legs of the animal and does not harm the animal in any way. If it were to cause either pain or discomfort, the animal would not perform. The pain and discomfort theory is a myth created by people who have never really been around rodeo livestock. If one were to grab that area of the animal's body, then it would cause the animal to kick out. Horses do the same thing and so the bucking horses also have the flank strap.

Average bucking bulls are smaller and more athletic these days. During my era there were a few rank bulls. Now, because of all the interest in the extreme sport of bull riding and all of the breeding programs, there a lot of rank bulls. In the '70s, '80s and '90s there was an abundance of eighteen to nineteen hundred pound bulls. Now stock contractors have figured out that they can get more of the smaller bulls on a semi-trailer. Many contractors are paid by the number of trips per bull. The more bulls, then more trips and more trips means more money in the bank account. The contractors get more bang for the buck (literally!).

Bucking traits are passed from one generation of bulls to the next. The great bucking bulls are constantly producing more calves that also buck well. Stock contractors have discovered that the cows of great bucking bulls also pass along these bucking traits.

A cowboy who is truly terrified or scared of bulls has no business getting on them. He's sure to end up getting hurt. Those of us who ride them have a great deal of respect for bucking bulls; for what they can potentially do to us as well as respect for their athletic ability. Bull riders have a saying that, "it is not *if* you are going to get hurt, the real question is *when* and *how badly.*

Deep down inside, all bull riders are afraid of bulls. But you must learn to control, as well as channel, your fear. Any bull rider who tells you that he's not a bit afraid to ride bulls is not telling the truth. How can you not be afraid of such massive creatures that have the potential of seriously injuring, crippling, or even killing you? Gene Walker said many times, "the safest place is on their backs. When you're on their backs, they can't hurt you."

A good bull rider has to have an unbelievable amount of try and fortitude. There are many times that a bull rider felt out of shape or that he was on the verge of bucking off only to grit it out and be scored 80 or 90 points and win a big fat check. Bull riders often say "don't quit until the back of your head hits the ground."

The sports writers voted bull riding as the most dangerous sporting event in North America and sadly, we have lost some friends such as Johnny Bottoms, Jeff Crockett, Lane Frost, Glen Keeley, Mike

Mason, Sean Murphy, Mick Whitely and Brent Thurman along the way.

As a little kid growing up in New Jersey I would watch all of the TV westerns such as *Bonanza, Rawhide, Wagon Train, Wyatt Earp, the Rifleman, the Virginian, Gunsmoke, the Big Valley, Death Valley Days, Have Gun Will Travel, High Chaparral, Lancer, Maverick, My Friend Flicka, Roy Rogers, the Lone Ranger* and *Stoney Burke* and dream of living out West.

I was fortunate enough to be able to live out my childhood dreams. How many people can say that during their lifetime? I couldn't wait to go out West and compete against the big boys. I didn't want to be the "big fish in the little pond" and stay on the East Coast.

If I had to live my life over again, I would want to be a professional rodeo cowboy. I've traveled all over the United States and met a lot of good people and rodeo fans. It led me to success and recognition in other business related fields. I was and will always be a novelty in the sport of rodeo.

Abe Morris

1

In The Beginning

My rodeo career started in 1964 at the age of eight, riding roping calves on a summer afternoon at the Cowtown Rodeo arena in Woodstown, New Jersey, which is in Salem County. Salem County in South Jersey in those days had a lot of agriculture, dairy farms, wooded areas and open space.

When I was growing up Cowtown had a thriving livestock auction, flea market and rodeo. There was also a State Police barracks, horse racing track and a golf driving range. The flea market and livestock auction were the places to hang out on Tuesdays and the rodeo was the place to hang out on Saturdays. The flea market has become so popular that it has now expanded to Saturdays. It's very well known in the tri-state area of Pennsylvania, Delaware and New Jersey, which is geographically known as the Delaware Valley.

Because of the livestock auction, there was never a shortage of different animals in the barn. Someone was always leaving cows, steers, sheep and calves in the barn, if only for a few days.

My first day, there were some boys and also two girls getting on the calves. The first calf that I got on was a gray Brahma with big floppy ears. He bucked me off. Then there was one particular black calf branded #1. The girls refused to get on the feisty black calf and I, being a young and gung-ho little kid, volunteered to ride him. Whenever the two girls, Kathy Harris and Mary Ann Rogers, would ride, Charlie Driver, a cowboy from Florida, would hold onto the back of their belts and run along beside the bucking calves. When the girls bucked off, he would prevent them from hitting the ground. Charlie did not do that for me or the other boys.

I got on the black calf and when I bucked off, the calf stomped and pounced on me a couple of times before going on about his business. I took in a deep breath and was set to let out a huge wail when Charlie Driver picked what was left of me up out of the dirt. When I saw all of those people on the back of the bucking chutes I squelched my tears and instead let out a huge sigh. I refused to burst out crying, especially in front of those girls.

I am right handed and that little black calf stomped on my right arm a couple of times. He hurt it pretty badly and it was even bleeding. I could not lift my right arm and that evening I had to eat dinner left handed. At least there weren't any girls present to see that!

Before I even started kindergarten, I went to Cowtown to spend the whole summer with my cousins. Gene, David, Jimmy Lee and Willie Ed Walker were all older and tougher than I was. I really didn't have anyone my age to play with and my father, Reverend Abraham J. Morris, Sr., was afraid that I would grow up to be a "sissy." So he sent me off to the school of hard knocks, hoping that my cousins would toughen me up.

When I first started hanging around my cousins, they were all into riding ponies. Of course I was afraid of the little creatures. Finally, they convinced me to get on and, without any instructions, they hit the pony on the rear end and away we went. All I could do was hold on tight and they sure got a kick out of me straddling this runaway pony for dear life. I was too afraid to fall off and finally I figured out how to make him stop.

Although they didn't bother to teach me, through trial and error I figured out how to make the pony stop, start and go either left or right. Then it became fun and I didn't want to get off. My cousins lost interest when it was clear that I was enjoying myself and then got mad at me because I wouldn't get off.

All of my cousins, except for David, aspired to be rodeo cowboys. I made it very clear from the beginning that I wanted nothing to do with rodeo, cowboys and especially bulls. I did not want to be associated with a bunch of smelly animals. Undaunted, my cousins continued to push and prod me, to convince me to do the things that they did. They would even bribe me with quarters to get on certain calves. In those days you could buy a lot with a quarter—a soda and a candy bar. And it worked. I was cheap entertainment for them. They would get their laughs watching me getting thrown in every direction and I would get those quarters to buy my treats.

There was not an official Mutton Bustin' event when we were growing up. We were all very mischievous kids. We were always in the barn and kept our eyes out for any new possible mounts. As soon as the owners left we would go out to the barn to see if the animals were small enough for us kids to get on.

Most of the time I hung out with Willie Ed. He was only three years older than I was and always treated me like a little brother because he was the youngest in his family and didn't have a little brother of his own. He was always making me get on first because as he was growing up, his brothers did that to him.

The barn in Cowtown was located about one-eighth of a mile

off of Route 40. It also was only about fifty yards from the Walkers' house. Needless to say, in the summer with the windows open a bunch of bellowing calves could keep you awake all night.

The barn had the perfect layout for us kids to ride in. There was a chute located near the front that opened up to a long narrow alley with a livestock scale for weighing at the far end. On one side there was a solid cinderblock and concrete wall. On the other side were six different holding pens for livestock. A pen at the front of the barn was connected to the chute. An air conditioner was built into the wall for the administration office and we always had to be careful because it was right there when we opened the chute gate to let the animals out. It was a little scary because if you bucked off into the wall, you were definitely going to get hurt.

It worked out perfectly for us. We would herd the animals into the holding pen and then cut them out, one by one, and guide them into the bucking chute. We would then ride the animal down the alley. Most of the time they would buck straight down the alley and if you made it all the way to the scales, then it was considered to be a qualified ride and you could jump off.

Sunday was the best day to ride. There was always a lot of activity going on in Cowtown on the other six days and too much of a chance of getting caught with so many people around. Whenever a strange vehicle came down the road, we would frantically hurry to put the animals back in their original pens and run out of the back of the barn. We had a routine already in place: we would sneak in the back door of the Walkers' house and then be seen nonchalantly walking out the front door of the house and sitting around the picnic table, acting as if we were just enjoying a lazy summer day. As soon as the intruder would leave, we would go back out to the barn and continue with our riding sessions.

We always did our riding during the daylight hours because we knew we couldn't risk turning the lights on in the barn. Somebody would be bound to notice. There were a couple of times when we didn't have time to get the animals returned to their original pens. We just opened the chute gate and then ran out the back. I'm sure that people were baffled as to how their steer or other animal got in to the alley. They had come out to check on their animal to make sure that it had enough food and water and somehow it would be loose in the alley. I suspect they believed it sure was a good thing they'd come out as maybe they'd accidentally left the gate unlatched during their last visit.

Quite often livestock, having been transported long distances, would be dropped off at Cowtown for a few days of rest. We loved the sight of a semi-trailer loaded with a bunch of steers or calves backing up to the loading dock. Like a pack of hungry wolves, we waited impatiently as our fresh mounts were being unloaded.

Many times livestock owners would bring their animals to Cowtown on Sunday or Monday to be sold in the auction on the following Tuesday. We were always on the lookout for something in the barn to get on. There were also many occasions when someone would purchase an animal on Tuesday and for some reason have to leave it there for a few days. If we happened to spot potential practice candidates, we would check back on late Tuesday evening or first thing on Wednesday morning to see if they were still there. Just as soon as the coast was clear and the administrative staff had gone home for the day, we would gather up our riding gear and head out to the barn for another impromptu practice session.

I had a good friend, Eddie Shorter, who lived a mile down the road in Sharptown and I would always call him on the telephone whenever there was something in the barn that we could ride. As we were growing up we were all in agreement that Eddie had more talent than any of the rest of us. I don't ever remember Eddie getting bucked off before he made it to the scales at the end of the alley.

But after a few years of riding junior bulls, Eddie lost his heart and quit riding bulls altogether. We were all very disappointed because

Eddie and I had talked about going down the road together to a lot of the major rodeos out West when we were older. We all knew that Eddie had the potential to be a world-class bull rider and, barring injury, would have had a very successful professional rodeo career.

The amazing thing about all of our riding sessions is that never once did we get caught and none of us ever got injured except for a few scrapes and bruises.

We didn't limit ourselves to animals in the big barn. There were many occasions that animals were left overnight in the smaller calf barn next door. We would even ride the pigs and sheep that were left in the calf barn. Anything that was large enough for us kids to ride was fair game. The pens in the calf barn were very small and did not have access to food and water. So we would herd the animals down to the cow barn where they could get ridden. Just in case any adults would question our motives, we would just say that we were looking out for the welfare of the animals and moving them so that they would have some food and water.

The ground in the alley of the barn was extremely solid and hard. One fond memory I have was of riding a big fat Hereford steer who landed extremely hard on his two front feet. It was another of those situations where Willie Ed forced me to get on first, saying that he would get on after I did. But, as usual, when his turn came, he didn't.

This steer jolted me every jump but I still made a qualified ride on him. Afterward, I got off and complained of severe chest pains. Willie Ed and Ken Wells, a cowboy and horseman from Montana who was staying in Cowtown for that summer, laughed at me pretty hard. I was in serious pain and because they kept laughing, I got mad and told Uncle Little Bit (Willie) and Aunt Etta Bell (my dad's sister) that it was Willie Ed's fault that my chest was hurting so bad.

I did not live this down for several years. To this day Willie Ed will tease me about whining to him that my chest hurt. He will also talk about how I got him in trouble with his dad for getting me hurt. Uncle Little Bit really yelled at Willie Ed and told him he was going to get me hurt if he wasn't careful.

My Uncle Willie was nicknamed Little Bit because he was so much smaller than his identical twin brother. He was always threatening to beat me with the thick leather strap that he used on his own boys whenever they got out of line. But he liked me and never did. Growing up I always thought that his real name was Little Bit because no one ever called him Willie. It was years later that I found out that his real name was William Rogers Walker.

Howard "Stoney" Harris and his son Howard Harris, III, were the owners of Cowtown. They started the weekly Cowtown Rodeo in 1956. The rodeo is still every Saturday night from late May until late September and is the longest running weekly rodeo in the nation.

The Junior Bull Riding event was not initiated until the summer of 1966. Even before Junior Bull Riding became a regular event at the old Cowtown Rodeo arena as a part of the entertainment, Willie Ed once rode a full-grown buffalo named Agnes during the weekly rodeo performance. Agnes was a very amiable and docile animal and Willie Ed was about nine years old at the time. Agnes was loaded into the regular bucking chutes just like the other animals. Howard Harris, III, had asked Willie Ed to do this. I'm sure that he probably gave him a couple of dollars just to get on the buffalo. The buffalo didn't buck but the crowd sure got a kick out of the two of them streaking across the rodeo arena. Willie Ed had been riding ponies for most of his life so he'd already developed an excellent sense of balance. He grabbed a bunch of Agnes's hair with both hands and just held on tight. This was a precursor to the Mutton Bustin' Contest that started in the 1990s.

In those days there was no such thing as a bucking barrel, bucking machine or mechanical bull. But at Cowtown there was a dummy that was suspended across the old rodeo arena on a cable that was pulled out during the Bull Riding event. He was kind of like a piñata. He was dressed just like a rodeo clown and really frustrated the bulls because no matter how hard they hit him, he always came back for more punishment.

Willie Ed had this harebrained idea that we could practice our riding skills on this dummy. So we would pull it out into the middle of the rodeo arena during the weekdays. Then we would sit on the dummy's shoulders and the person on the ground would jerk the dummy around and try to buck us off. We were only allowed to hold on with one hand, just as though we were riding a bronc or a bull, and it seemed a very long way to the ground.

I could never buck Willie Ed off because whenever he felt himself losing his balance, he would always cheat and double grab with his free hand. I didn't have sense enough to double grab and would land on my head or shoulders every time that I attempted to ride the dummy. We would even wear our spurs and by the time that the Saturday rodeo performance would roll around, the shirt on the dummy would be all torn up from Willie Ed and me spurring him during the week.

Stoney Harris gave my cousin Gene a horse named Shorty to break and everyday Gene would be seen riding that horse. He was a small but very pretty palomino, thus the name. On one occasion I got a little too close to Shorty and he stepped on my foot. I cried, so Genie told me to step on the horse's foot to get even. I stepped on Shorty's foot not knowing that the horse never felt a thing—at least I felt a little better!

Stoney was also a well-known horse trader who would buy ponies on a regular basis and let us kids ride and break them. After a few weeks, he would run them through the livestock auction on Tuesday evenings, sell them for a profit and then turn around and buy more ponies. Just about the time we would get attached to one of them, they would be sold and gone.

On one occasion, Willie Ed told me that Stoney had given him a pony. He said this to try and make me jealous. I responded by telling him that I was going to go and ask Stoney for a pony for myself. Willie Ed told me not to, but I did anyway. I said, "Mr. Harris can I have a pony?" He looked at me as if I were crazy and did not even respond. Meanwhile, Willie Ed had run into the house to hide so that it wouldn't seem like he'd put me up to another one of his practical jokes. His older brothers had played tricks on him and so Willie Ed would, in turn, play tricks on me.

I started attending the rodeo on a regular basis my first summer in Cowtown. Our Uncle Little Bit worked for Stoney and Howard Harris and held a regular assignment at the rodeo. The Harrises were good employers and a class act to work for. On Saturdays he worked to help sort and load the steers and calves. During the week he would work on the premises or in the barns. On Wednesdays and Thursdays he drove a wagon and a team of white mules to clean up after the Flea Market.

I would go to the rodeo with my cousins Barbara Jean and Christine, who were older than the boys in the Walker family. We would be joined by our cousins Vera, Sara, Cindy and Johnny Harp who lived right next door to the Walkers. Their father, John T. Harp, was married to Carrie Danner and he was a brother of Uncle Little Bit. Uncle Little Bit got us into the rodeo for free and so we all sat in the same area every week.

The only time that I spent any time with the girls was on Saturday night during the rodeo. Otherwise I tried to hang out with the boys. John T. was a big, strong man and he and I got along very well right from the start. He decided that Abraham was too long of a name to have to say on a regular basis and so he nicknamed me "Ham."

By this time Genie was riding big bulls. It was thrilling to watch Genie ride in the rodeos week after week. He was very talented and soon became a favorite with the fans. Howard Harris had told him as a little boy that he was going to start him riding bulls and keep all the money that he won in order to send him off to college someday. I fondly remember sitting in the grandstand, week after week, and in unison we would be yelling, "Ride 'em Genie! Ride 'em Genie!" It was like a chorus line and we were very loud. Little did we all know at the time that this tradition of riding bulls was going to be passed down from one family member to the next. At the time, I had no inclination or desire to someday be on the other side of that fence riding bulls myself.

2

Junior Bulls

There was no Junior Bull Riding event held in Cowtown during the summer of 1964 and 1965. Finally, in the summer of 1966 Howard Harris started having Junior Bull Riding for us kids as a regular event at the Cowtown Rodeo. We had been looking forward to this for a long time. It was the perfect scenario for the stock contractor "to separate the men from the boys" and the future bucking bulls from the slaughterhouse batch. By this time Howard's two sons, Grant and Andy, were ripe and they wanted to get some rodeo experience under their belts. Grant, at thirteen, was three years older than Andy, who was a year older than I was. So in July 1966, Junior Bull Riding became a regular event for the three of us.

The first week I didn't compete because I had to have permission from my parents. My father was a Baptist minister and surely had not anticipated that his son would want to get involved with the rodeos. I'm sure that he had no idea that sending me to Cowtown would eventually lead to me wanting to ride bulls. So when I asked his permission to ride he said, "Yes" rather than saying, "No" and the two of us having a big debate about the issue. He must have been hoping to end the discussion by giving in right away. I'm sure that he figured that when push came to shove, I would just chicken out and not follow through with getting on a bull in front of a large rodeo grandstand filled with people.

The big day finally arrived. It was July 9, 1966. All of the animals designated to be used in the rodeo performance that evening were at the rodeo grounds several hours before the 7:30 p.m. start. We would pick our bulls that afternoon. My cousins knew the patterns of all of the junior bulls and so they told me that I was going to get on this white Brahma bull. The bull had red eyes, a big hump on his back and a pair of short horns. He was the easiest and most docile bull in the herd. He would not act up in the bucking chute and would just "crow hop" across the rodeo arena. Also, after the ride was over, he would not chase after you and would just go on about his business back to the catch pen.

Slowly, I eased down the fence in order to pet the bull that was lying on the ground. I was trying to get an idea of his temperament. Willie Ed said, "You better pet him because you are going to have to ride him later and he may buck you off."

"Get your ropes boys," yelled George Freas, a longtime Cowtown Rodeo employee. My bull was the last one to be loaded into the bucking chutes. Jimmy Lee and Willie Ed could not assist me during the Junior Bull Riding event because they were busy getting themselves prepared to compete, so David helped me get ready. I didn't have any equipment, so they gave me a hand-me-down bull rope that had probably been originally used by Genie. But I did have a cowboy hat—a-hand-me-down, as well. I didn't even have cowboy boots so I rode in my loafers.

Of course I was a nervous wreck. The Junior Bull Riding was the first event. This would allow us kids to get it over with and then get out of the way. It was very dangerous behind the bucking chutes and after the Junior Bulls, we were under strict orders to hit the rodeo grandstand ASAP. After the bulls were loaded, David and I were standing on the back of the bucking chute. He asked me to hold out my hand and then to hold out one of my fingers as well. It was quivering and I could not keep it still.

I had no idea why he would ask me to do such a silly thing right before I was about to risk my life and climb on the back of my first bull. He never did tell me why he had asked me to hold out my hand right before I competed.

One by one, the riders came out and one by one, each was bucked off. There had been no qualified rides. We were only required to ride for six seconds, as opposed to the usual eight seconds for the men.

Finally it was my turn. Ted Bailey, the rodeo announcer said, "Next to go in chute number nine will be Abraham Morris." As I settled down on my bull, I heard Howard Harris yell out to me, "Come on Abraham, you ride better than the rest of these boys." I asked David to pull my bull rope tight with my hand flat against the bull's back. Then I eased up to my rope, squeezed tight with my legs and said, "Outside."

I remember the chute gate swinging open and the bull took his initial first jump out of the chute. I was immediately thrown back as his forward movement sent me off balance. After that I completely blacked out and don't remember anything that happened for the next few seconds. All I remember is that somehow I ended up hanging on to his left side and kind of up on his neck. But this was after the whistle had already sounded.

No one had ever explained to me how to jump off of a bull. We had always been more concerned with staying *on* to make a qualified ride. I didn't know that because I was a right-handed rider, I was supposed to dismount on the right side of the bull. I was used to riding ponies and I always mounted and dismounted on the left side. Somehow I splattered on to the ground and hurt my knee in the process. It was a good thing that I didn't have to jump up and run. I started the long walk back to the bucking chutes. And I was even limping, just like a real cowboy!

Kaye Kirby, who competed after I did, was the only other contestant to make a qualified ride that evening. Kaye won first and ten dollars and I ended up winning second and seven-fifty, a good prize since we didn't have an entry fee to pay. Kaye, who was fifteen at the time, was right on the verge of starting to enter the big Bull Riding like his older brother, Sandy. He was planning to take the money that he could win in the Junior Bull Riding and use it to pay the fifteen dollar entry fee needed for the big bulls. But Howard told him no. He said that he could compete in one event or the other, but not both.

Needless to say, I was pretty ecstatic to win some money! I forgot all about my sore knee and had a smile pasted on my face that lit up the whole arena. I think that Willie Ed was even happier than I was. We gathered up our equipment and got out from behind the bucking chute area. When we returned to the Walkers' house, Willie Ed ran ahead of me and into the house yelling to everyone that I'd just won second place in the Junior Bull Riding. I tried to keep up with him but my knee was still hurting and I was limping pretty badly.

I could not wait to go over to the office after the rodeo was over to collect my money. I was on cloud nine for the next few days. I figured that if I could earn that kind of money for six seconds of work, why would I want to go out and work for a living? At that moment, I knew that I wanted to become a professional bull rider.

When I told my dad that I'd won second place in the rodeo, he was not very pleased. He promptly told me that was the end of my rodeo career and that I was not ever going to ride bulls again. I started crying and said, "If you didn't want me to ride bulls, then you shouldn't have given me permission to ride in the first place." After a few days he finally relented and said, "Okay, but, the first time that you get hurt don't come crying to me."

After that, no matter what kind of pain I was in, I never said a word to my dad about it.

The next week I was back at it again. That time I bucked off of a big black bull with a white face. The next week I rode thet same red eyed white junior bull again and this time I won third place and five dollars. I also earned a little money helping Jack Bitter and his crew clean up the Flea Market area for the annual Salem County Fair which was held the first week of August.

Jack Bitter was a short, stout man who would get down into the bucking chutes with us junior bull riders. He tried to keep the smaller animals as stable as humanly possible in those large chutes. Whenever a bull was acting up, he would always calmly tell you, "I got you, I got you. Don't get off, stay right where you are." He was very dependable. Jack did all that he could to keep us young kids from getting hurt in the bucking chutes. He was the junior bull riders' best friend for a couple of decades at the Cowtown Rodeo.

I saved my money and my parents took me out and I bought my very first pair of cowboy boots. Then Willie Ed gave me my first pair of bull riding spurs. These were a pair of shiny bright Kelly spurs. At that time they were considered to be the top of the line. And just think, I was *given* a pair! My cousins were always looking out for me. During my entire rodeo career I only owned two pairs of spurs. I lost one of my Kelly spurs in the summer of 1974. I bought a pair of Bob Blackwood spurs in 1974 from someone while I was attending the University of Wyoming, and used them for the rest of my career.

I competed in the Junior Bull Riding event a total of five times that summer. I was forced to relinquish my money bull at the request of George Freas to his granddaughter, Robbie Coleman, who also wanted to start riding junior bulls. I chose a little black bull that had a lot more spunk. I stayed away from the top bulls such as a bull named Ralph and another one named Woolly Booger. Woolly Booger was to grow up and become #2046 Brown Mule, one of the five best bulls to ever come out of the Cowtown Rodeo armada. His name was later changed to Cowtown and his number was shortened to #12 after he was sold to another stock contractor out West.

Jimmy Lee, Willie Ed and Kaye, the top junior bull riders at that time, fought over the best bulls. I knew that I had no business getting on the good ones but I hoped that in the future, I would be talented enough to be able to match them, jump for jump.

Number 2046 Brown Mule was the same bull that bucked off World Champion Bull Rider George Paul in the first go-round of the National Finals Rodeo in 1968. George Paul had successfully ridden a total of seventy-nine bulls in a row until Cowtown broke his consecutive string of qualified rides. This is an all time PRCA record that will never be broken. This should give you an idea of the quality of bucking bulls that came out of Cowtown, New Jersey.

There was another exceptional junior bull that bucked very hard and jumped pretty high in the air. Willie Ed had decided that he was going to attempt to ride him. There was, of course, a big build up for this particular ride. Howard Harris had a lot of confidence that Willie Ed could succeed. Believing that there would be too much crowd noise to hear the whistle, Howard told Willie Ed not to get off the bull until he told him to.

True to his prediction, the crowd noise was unbelievable and none of us heard the whistle. Willie Ed made a brilliant and successful ride on the bull that was going to grow up and become known as #59 Dr. Spock. He was a very docile brown cross-bred Brahma bull with a big ol' hump on his back. This was probably my favorite bull that ever came out of Cowtown. He would leap way up into the air and spin. He was a very showy bull and he was seldom ridden. After he bucked off his rider he would always immediately head for the out gate and completely ignore anybody who got in his way. Any bull that doesn't try to mangle you after a ride is a good bull in my book.

We kids couldn't afford the dry rosin used on the bull ropes by the men. I figured out that it was a derivative of pine sap so I found a freshly cut board at home at Cream Valley Dairy where we lived in Woodstown and where Dad was the manager of the milk processing plant. I put a whole gob of that stuff on my Bull Riding glove. I needed all the help that I could get to compete on the better bulls. The first time I bucked off of the little black bull I got hung up. I had never been hung up before but I didn't panic. Somehow my hand came free and I escaped unscathed. The very next week I got on the same bull again and I got hung up again. Only this time, my hand came out of the glove and my glove stayed dangling in the bull rope. At least my glove didn't get bucked off!

During one of the rodeos I ran into Mrs. Cook, the elementary school nurse from Mary S. Shoemaker School and she was shocked to see me competing in the rodeo. She told me that I'd better not ever come into her office complaining of even the slightest little headache if I was going to be out there riding in those rodeos. So after that I made it a point not to have to go in to see the school nurse for anything.

After Eddie Shorter decided to quit riding bulls, he convinced me to quit in 1970. Junior Bull Riding was not held every week. We had heard a rumor that it was going to start on a certain Saturday. Eddie and I ducked off and went to Sharptown about the time the rodeo was going to start. Since the Junior Bull Riding was always the first event we figured that it would be over by the time we got back.

Well, they fooled us. Junior Bull Riding was not held until about the third or fourth event on that particular evening. We showed up at the rodeo just as the event was ready to start. I promptly told Genie and Howard that I had retired from bull riding. They would not take "no" for an answer. I remember saying to Genie, "If I get hurt then you and Howard are going to have to pay my doctor bills."

Because they were short of contestants, Genie and Howard made me ride twice. I was announced as the 1969 and reigning Junior Bull Riding Champion of Cowtown even though no official records were kept. I could have been, but to be honest, I really don't remember. I ended up winning first and second on those two bulls. Then afterward, Genie and Howard wanted to claim my money saying that if it weren't for them, I never would have even gotten on in the first place. When I went to collect my prize money, I got upset because I was only allowed to collect the money for first place and the rodeo secretary would not pay me for my second place finish, as well.

During my Junior Bull Riding career I never had to worry about extra help in preparation for my rides. By this time we were competing in the new rodeo arena that was only about a hundred yards off of Route 40. Willie Ed, who was riding the big bulls by then, was always there without fail to pull my bull rope and offer me encouragement.

1970 was the last year that I competed in the Junior Bull Riding event. One of the reasons that I quit was that I was the "star" on our one hundred and twenty-five pound Midget Football League team, the Woodstown Pirates. I was the fastest player on the team. My teammates would tease me and say that the reason that I was so fast was because I spent so much time running away from all those bulls. I figured that I owed it to myself as well as my team members not to get hurt riding bulls. I ended up setting a record for kick-off return yardage in my midget football career that, to this day, hasn't been broken.

3

Big Bulls

I started entering the big bull riding event at the age of sixteen in September 1972. For a couple of years I was too old for the junior bulls and too young for the big bulls so I just hung out at the rodeos and was a fulltime spectator. I was not supposed to be behind the bucking chutes, but I was always back there until one of the cowboys would yell at me to get out and go sit in the grandstand.

By then I had become pretty good friends with Tony Bouldin who was also about my age. His nickname was "Spaz" and he was known as a wild and crazy acting guy. Tony was the adopted brother of Freddie and Stanley Thomas. Freddie and Stanley were two black cowboys from Woodstown who had also become involved in rodeo. Stanley and I had played on the same Little League baseball team and he was Kaye Kirby's best friend.

Tony was about my size and complexion. Sometimes people accidentally mistook him for me. I'm not sure how he got his nickname. It was probably because he had a temper and loved to fight. He was a very feisty character and tough as nails. Spaz eventually signed up for the U.S. Marines. I've lost track and have no idea what ever happened to him.

We had planned to enter the Bull Riding for some time but we kept putting it off week after week after week. It was a well-known fact that whenever Howard Harris had a road show, he would take the "A" string of bulls with him and buck out the "B" and "C" strings at Cowtown. Otherwise he would buck the "A" string every week at Cowtown. We were just waiting for this opportunity so we could enter the big Bull Riding on the "B" and "C" bulls. So were several other wannabe bull riders. Whenever Howard would go on the road, the wannabe bull riders would come out of the woodwork and the entries would increase in the Bull Riding at Cowtown.

Howard was fast building up a reputation as having one of the best bucking bull strings in the nation. Most were born and raised right there on the Cowtown ranch. They would generally only get bucked once a week during the summer and then they could relax the rest of the time. Eight seconds worth of work each week. Many of his bulls only had to work two or three seconds a week. What a lifestyle.

Howard was not an easy person to get along with, especially if he sensed that you were afraid of his bulls. And rightfully so—they were considered rank. A lot of the bull riders were intimidated by his snarly attitude towards them. For lack of conviction, many of the riders were already bucked off even before they nodded their heads.

Tony and I picked one such weekend to start our big bull riding careers. Well, Howard fooled all of us. After we had entered the Bull Riding on Friday afternoon, we were very dismayed to go to the bull pen that evening and see that Howard had taken the "B" string on the road and had left the "A" string to get back at all of us wannabes.

We immediately knew that we had gotten in over our heads. But it was too late.

I was particularly afraid of #214 Surprise. He was a National Finals Rodeo bull that Howard had named when he had bucked off Doug Brown from Silverton, Oregon, the 1969 World Champion Bull Rider. When he bucked off Doug Brown in a rodeo in New York, the bull did not have a name. Howard's reaction was, "Surprise, surprise, surprise" and that name stuck.

Surprise would turn back right in the gate. And I do mean right in the gate. His first initial move was one jump and then a hard spin to the left. He was a big mean dark brown brindle bull. (Brindle is a color combination consisting of tiger-like stripes. There are a lot of brindle colored bulls in professional rodeo.) Also, Surprise had these huge baseball bats for horns and he could and would use them if you bucked off and he could find you before you could get up and get away.

The stock was drawn that same night. Otherwise I would have had a long sleepless night thinking that I might draw Surprise, #20 Stag, #4+40 Punt, #11 Heartache, #102 Rocky Raccoon, #O28 Loup Garou, #000 Mr. Yoast, #C2 Deepwater, #C13 Top Cat, #C1 Lizard or some other rank bull. Lucky for me, I drew around all of the bad boys and was going to have to get on #27 Hardcore. Spaz was not so lucky and drew the biggest bull in the whole herd, #-10 Playboy.

I remember before the Bull Riding started John Risoli from South Plainfield, New Jersey, started razzing me saying, "Aren't you too small to be entering this big Bull Riding?" So I smarted off to him, "They don't judge you on your size, they judge you on how well you ride." Spaz and I both bucked off but we had now taken a major step and joined the men.

The next week I entered again. It was the last rodeo of the season on Saturday September 2, 1972 and I drew #208 Beep Beep. The bull took about two jumps and then turned back to the left. I was definitely in over my head and was bucked off again. But I was already looking forward to the next rodeo season and competing against the men and the big bulls.

4

My First Season Competing Against the Big Boys

During the off season I got all prepared for the next rodeo season by purchasing a lot of new rodeo equipment. I got a brand new manila grass bull rope from Booger Bryant of Hagerman, New Mexico. At that time Booger Bryant was one of the top bull rope braiders in the nation. He passed away from cancer during the 1980s. His son, Blu Bryant, is now a world-class bull rider who finished second for the PRCA world title in 1998.

Grass is what everyone used in those days. The newer synthetic poly (polypropylene) ropes didn't hit the scene until the 1980s. No one uses grass ropes anymore. They didn't last very long and wouldn't maintain their body.

I also bought a green rigging (equipment) bag with my nameplate already on it, a new glove, a bull rope bag, a bull rope pad, and new bull bells from a company called Custommade Leather Goods.

I would sit on my bed, put on my glove and take out my new bull rope. I would place my hand in the handhold and take my wrap. I'd slide up close to my rope to pretend and visualize over and over that I was riding bulls. I would even put on my boots and my spurs and check them over and over again to make sure that they would feel right when it came time to compete again.

Traditionally, practice sessions started the first Sunday in April each year. It was a great opportunity for Howard Harris, III to crack out his new young bulls and see which ones had the great bucking potential he was looking for. It was also a great opportunity for the cowboys to get rid of the winter rust and cobwebs as well. And even the veteran bulls needed to kick up their heels and strut their stuff again during this time of the year.

Most of the rank bulls got a free roll because no one dared to get on them right off of the bat. Usually it was a couple of weeks before anyone would start getting on the "A" string. The bad boys would rest all spring because no one was going to get on them until the rodeo season started and they were forced to mount them out.

During my early years in Cowtown, practice was held across the Highway in the horse barn. This was in the 1960s, before Jimmy Lee and Willie Ed were competing on junior bulls. Danny Dent, a rodeo clown and bullfighter from Vero Beach, Florida, owned a trained Brahma bull named Poncho that he kept in the horse barn during the summer months. One night, Danny and Willie Ed put me on Poncho. I was being a smart alec, so they threatened to make the big bull jump over a portable hurdle while I was still on him. Poncho weighed over seventeen hundred pounds and I was only seven years old and scared to death.

Danny led Poncho towards the apparatus on a dead run and I

held on for dear life. The bull went up and I went down. I was afraid he was going to land on me and I'm sure he would have killed me if he'd stepped on me. I crashed down hard and I was mad at both of them because they laughed at me. This was typical of Willie Ed: he was always putting me on something just so he could get his kicks.

Practice in the horse barn was discontinued in the late 1960s. It was an enclosed barn but there was no heat. It was a very scary place to practice because there were no fences.

My rodeo season came to an abrupt end at the first spring practice session of the season when I was sixteen years old and a junior in high school. It was on Palm Sunday, April 15, 1972. I got on a bull, #131 Darrell.

The bull was named after Darrell Barron (from Texas) who spent a summer at Cowtown trying to fill his permit. (The PRCA requires a cowboy to buy a permit and then win a thousand dollars before he can become a full-fledged member.) Darrell was on the rodeo team at the University of Southern Colorado in Pueblo. He now works for U.S. Smokeless Tobacco Company and is the bucking chute boss at the Wrangler National Finals Rodeo and the Cheyenne Frontier Days Rodeo.

Darrell (the bull!) had big Cadillac type horns and when he bucked, he would swing his head violently with each jump. I nodded and soon afterward got into bad shape. But instead of throwing in the towel and just letting him buck me off, I ended up hanging on to the side. Somehow I ended up near his head and he hit me right above my ankle with one of those big horns. Immediately, I knew that my leg had been broken, and it turned out to be both my tibia and fibula. When I hit the ground, I somehow managed to maneuver my body so that I wound end up sitting on my rear end.

I sat on the ground, watching in disbelief as my foot quivered due to the shock. I was sitting upright and my foot was lying off to the side, just as though it had been completely detached from my ankle. It was pretty sickening. Everyone could see that it was broken because of its weird position. Irene Harris (Howard's wife) said, "He broke his leg. You better go out there and get him before that bull comes back."

A few of the cowboys scurried out to haul me off to safety. As they picked me up, my foot twisted then dangled. It really didn't hurt very much at all. That's the wonderful thing about shock. It gives you some time before the pain sets in. They helped me out of the arena and then sat me down. Jimmy Lee took me to the hospital. Soon afterward he left and went back to practice. I felt so alone. Big tears just poured out of my eyes.

It was Sunday and there was no way to contact my dad and mom because there wasn't a telephone at the church. Dad was the minister at the Friendship Baptist Church in Brotmanville, New Jersey. After a couple of hours, my Uncle James Pope (my mom's brother) came down to Salem County Memorial Hospital to see me. There was nothing that the hospital could do for me without my parents' consent. It was dark and late by the time Dad and Mom arrived and I was still in the emergency room. By then I was in a lot of pain.

They prepared me for surgery to reset the two bones in my lower leg. My dad said that after surgery, the hospital staff couldn't wake me up again. So instead of wheeling me off to a room, I was taken down to the Intensive Care Unit. Apparently the staff tried to downplay my situation but my dad told me the next day that it was pretty serious.

Dad and Mom had stayed at the hospital until about two a.m. They refused to leave until I responded to my name. Dad said that I sat up when they called me. I don't remember a thing. When I woke up the next morning, I was hoping that it was all just a bad dream. But when I reached for my leg and felt that huge plaster cast, my hopes were dashed.

The next day Dad said, "They almost lost you last night." At first I had no clue what he was talking about. For some reason the terminology just didn't register. Sodium pentothal, which is rarely used anymore, had been used on me.

My leg really hurt me after it was reset. It hurt a lot more after it was set than it did when I broke it. I had a full plaster cast on my right leg clear up to my groin area. It was bulky and heavy. When I stood up with my crutches for the first time, it felt just like someone was trying to pull my leg off. It was a very strange sensation. When Willie Ed came to visit me at the hospital, he scolded me for getting on that bull in the first place. If Willie Ed had been at practice, he would not have allowed me to get on #131 Darrell. He said, "Boy, you didn't have any business getting on that head slinging bull with those big ol' Cadillac horns just for practice."

Until I broke my leg, I had perfect attendance at Woodstown High School. I ended up missing the rest of the school year. I was pretty bummed. I was assigned tutors for some of my classes so that I could complete the 11th grade along with the rest of my classmates. For others, I would do my assignments and give them to my sister Patricia, and she would take them to school for me. I had been blessed with intelligence and had very good grades.

The summer was long, hot and humid. We didn't have air conditioning and we lived in the country. I spent a lot of time sitting in front of a floor fan in an attempt to cool off my hot, itching, encased leg. I used a wire coat hanger to reach places to scratch under my cast which I had to wear for twelve weeks.

Despite the heat and the bulky cast, it was hard for me to keep still so I would attempt to ride my sister Rosalyn's bike. I was okay as long as I kept my weight positioned to the left side. I would hold my cast in the air on the right side and push myself along using my good left leg. A couple of times I got off balance and fell on my right side and the cast. One time I crashed pretty hard and it hurt badly enough that I quit trying to ride the bike.

In July, my full cast was removed and replaced with a half cast just below the knee. This was called a "walking cast." There was a rubber disk set at the base of my foot to help me to start putting weight on my leg and walking again. It would also allow me to bend my knee. My leg was covered with a bunch of thick hair and dead skin. It was very, very gross to look at. My leg looked like it belonged to Wolfman. And due to the lack of exercise, my calf muscle had shrunk. My leg started bending and I had NO control over it. It was weird. It had been imobilized for so long that it hurt to move it at all.

After I got the walking cast, I could ride Rosalyn's bicycle and pedal just fine with my bad leg. I'm sure that the extra exercise was good therapy. I also played on my crutches and spun, simulating the motion of a bucking and spinning bull in action. I had to wear that cast for eight more weeks.

During those twenty weeks in the cast, Willie Ed started calling me "Crip." I know it was just in good fun but I didn't like the nickname. Nickname or not, he and Jimmy Lee would still look out for me. Either Willie Ed, Jimmy Lee or Rosemary (Willie Ed's wife) would pick me up every Saturday afternoon and take me to the rodeo.

Willie Ed had married the previous year. At the time we were living in Monroeville. We had moved in the summer of 1971. Uncle Little Bit had died from cancer in October of 1971. The Walkers had moved from Cowtown to Clayton, New Jersey, in the summer of 1972. Monroeville was only six miles and Clayton was about twenty miles from Woodstown. I could continue to attend high school in Woodstown.

My parents still allowed me to go to the rodeos, so I sat in the grandstand for the rest of the summer. One very frightening experience that summer was in the Bull Riding event. Grant Harris made a fantastic ride on a wild jumping, spinning brown bull, #209 Haint, who had big horns with splinters on the ends of them.

After the whistle he hung up and got kicked in the head. I immediately thought that he was dead. I told myself right then and there that if he were dead, I was never going to get on another bull again. I remember Jimmy Lee—who had also become a topnotch bareback rider as well as bullfighter—picking up and dragging Grant's limp unconscious body out of harm's way. It was a very scary scene for all of us to watch. Fortunately, Grant was okay. I don't believe that he even went to the hospital.

Most of the time I would pass on any offers to go to other rodeos. My cousins were gracious enough to invite me along because they knew how depressing it was to sit around the house all day long. Sometimes, I traveled to a few rodeos, not enjoying being cooped up in a car for several hours at a time. A couple of times we went to a non-RCA sanctioned rodeo in Round Top, New York on Friday nights or another one in Freehold, New Jersey on Sunday afternoons.

One Friday night, Jerome "Buck" Howard from Woodstown, who had recently started competing in rodeos, was not very pleased with the score the rodeo judges had given him in the Bareback Riding. Buck was a year older than me. Buck didn't compete in the Bull Riding event, but had been entering the Bareback Riding event at Cowtown. On this particular night in Round Top, he was entered in the Bull Riding event for the first time. Buck said, "Wait until the Bull Riding, because I am going to give my bull some Pittsburgh." He had never even been on a bull before and rode this one just like a bronc rider and spurred him every jump.

After that, Buck started entering the Bull Riding event at Cowtown and became one of the top bull riders on the East coast for several years. For a number of years we would still talk about "Pittsburgh" whenever we referred to spurring bulls. "Pittsburgh" became our battle cry. That little statement became very famous and was used quite often among our group of Cowtown rodeo buddies.

5

The
Madison Square Garden
Rodeo

Howard Harris, III and his Cowtown Rodeo brought the sport back to Madison Square Garden in 1971 after several years of absence. I was fortunate enough to attend the rodeo there in the fall of 1972.

It was there that I saw one of the worst hang ups of my entire rodeo career. Andy Harris was about seventeen at the time and he was mounting out bulls that, for one reason or another, the contestant was turning out. There are a lot of reasons a contestant will opt to "turn out" a bull without getting on it. It could be that he's drawn a bad bull and feels he can't win any money or he's changed his mind and doesn't want to invest in an airline ticket to fly all the way to New York City to compete. He'd be responsible for paying his entry fees and a small fine for turning out his livestock since, obviously, the rodeo producers would prefer that he be there to ride.

Andy got on an NFR bull #4+40 Punt. He was one of the bad cats of the "A" string who'd had a free roll during the entire spring practice sessions. No one in their right mind was going to get on him just for practice because chances were very good that he was going to buck you off and Punt had a reputation as a sinister bull who enjoyed mauling downed cowboys. He was a very big, pretty and proud black and white spotted bull with a huge head and big, thick horns that had been cut off short and looked like two large sledge hammers. Everyone was afraid of him and even when the helpers were working the bulls or loading them into the bucking chutes, Punt was one to watch out for because he was always trying to hurt someone.

Andy was wearing a red and white checkered shirt, which the crew on the Cowtown labor list would wear at all of the "away" rodeos. Andy rode left-handed and Punt usually spun to the right. I remember Andy saying on several occasions, "You have to get in there," when referring to bulls that spun. He meant that the rider had to lean and move his upper body over to the inside of the spin to combat the centrifugal force.

On that particular occasion, either Andy made too big of a move to "get in there" or Punt felt him move and proceeded to drop him into the well.

About three seconds into the ride, Andy bucked off and hung up. Punt wanted him pretty badly and kept spinning in an attempt to get to him. He also was swinging his head and hooking at Andy at the same time. Andy was okay until Punt reached and somehow got a horn behind his rib cage and back. Then, in one nasty heave ho, he threw Andy up onto his head and right in between the crosshairs of those two sledgehammer horns.

It got worse. Punt still continued to buck and spin and fling Andy into the air. Andy was at the bull's mercy. It was a very horrifying scene. Because Andy was hung up, his hand, which was still in the bull rope, had turned over so that his thumb was now flat against the bull's back. Whenever a bull rider completes his wrap, he positions his thumb over his index and middle fingers to help secure his grip. If his hand turns over, then it becomes literally impossible to open it with his thumb locked down over his fingers.

Andy was flailing in the air and looked like a rag doll without a bone in his body. It was kind of like paddle ball—that toy that little kids play with that has a rubber ball on a long rubber band string attached to a wooden paddle. No matter how hard Punt hit Andy in his back, he would come right back to him only to be hit again and again.

The bullfighters were pretty much helpless because every time they would make a move to get in and rescue Andy, Punt would just keep on spinning. At one point one of the bullfighters attempted to grab Andy's foot, but even that move proved fruitless. It was pretty obvious that Punt was mad and was not going to slow down. He continued to work on Andy for what seemed like forever. Finally, Andy's hand somehow came free. Punt had gradually beaten Andy out of his bull rope. Then, to the amazement of all who witnessed it, Andy simply walked away as if nothing had ever happened.

Years later, about 1984, I saw some taped footage of a similar type of hang up involving Randy Queen from Harrah, Oklahoma, at Tucson, Arizona. He had drawn the infamous #O18 Cowtown (originally Brindle Velvet from Cowtown) who was the 1985 PRCA Bucking Bull of the Year. Randy also bucked off in the well, hung up and was thrown up on to #O18's head. It just so happened that Wrangler was sponsoring one of their Bull Fighting tour events so there were several top bullfighters on hand that day. They tried in vain to rescue Randy but the bull was intent on working on the cowboy who was positioned up on his head. Again, they were all pretty much helpless as #O18 kept spinning and bucking with Randy on his head.

Number O18 had a notorious reputation for completely ignoring the rodeo bullfighters and clowns and going after the guy who has just attempted to ride him. Rickey Lindsey from Huntsville, Texas rode him for a lot of points one year at the National Western Stock Show and Rodeo in Denver, Colorado, and made the remark afterward that, "Sometimes a guy is just too afraid to buck off!"

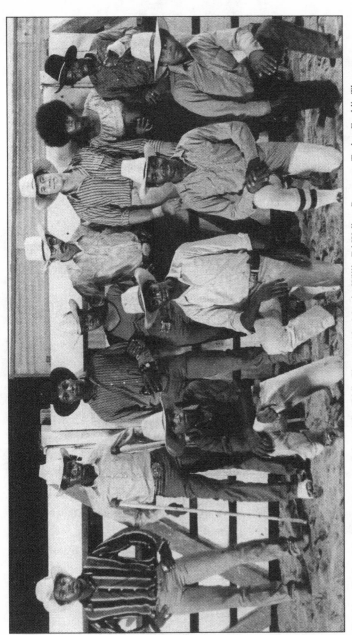

Cowtown Rodeo July 1973   Back row, left to right: Eddie Shorter, Abe Morris, Willie Ed Walker, Rosemary Taylor, Freddie Thomas, Stanley Thomas, *Unknown*, Gene Walker   Front Row: Buck Howard, Tony Bouldin, Jimmy Lee Walker, Roland Shorter, Jr.   *Photo:Al STone*

6

Return to High School

About a week before I was to return to school in September
1973 for my senior year, my second cast was cut off. It was on a
Saturday morning at Salem County Memorial Hospital. When I saw my
leg I told my dad that, "I hardly have much of any leg left now." My
thigh and calf muscles had deteriorated to almost nothing. I was very
embarrassed and knew that it would be a long road of exercising and
therapy before they would be built up again to their original size. The
hospital employee that used a saw to cut off my cast knicked me a
couple of times and my leg was bleeding.

The doctor told me that my leg would swell up due to the
sudden changes. He gave me a couple of ace bandages to wrap it with,
just in case it started to swell. That night I went to the rodeo
without the ace bandages and afterward realized that my leg had swollen

pretty badly. My ankle also swelled and never did return to its normal size. To this day both my ankles are larger than normal due to the fact that they were stepped on several times during my rodeo career.

It was very hard on me when I returned to high school and I was still on crutches. I was putting weight on my leg but I still needed my crutches in order to get around. I used them for about two months after my cast was cut off.

Formerly an outgoing and popular student I now became withdrawn. I wouldn't ride the school bus or go in to the cafeteria at lunchtime. Instead, I rode to and from school with my mom, who worked as a Teacher's Aide at the Mary S. Shoemaker elementary school in Woodstown.

One of my classmates was particularly hard on me. It was difficult enough to have to go through the entire summer vacation with a cast on my leg. But then to be teased and tormented by a very inconsiderate kid only made my situation worse.

He was a lot bigger than me and played on the football team. I knew that I couldn't beat him in a fight, so I just had to endure the teasing. He would hold up his hand and bend the middle and ring fingers and say that, "If you mess with the bull then you get the horns."

One day in History class during another one of his teasing sessions, I'd had enough. "Go ahead and tease me," I said, "but one of these days you'll read about me." To that he responded, "Yeah, we'll read about you, alright, but it will be in the obituaries."

Several years later in July of 1989, when Lane Frost was killed at the Cheyenne Frontier Days Rodeo, I remembered that little incident from high school. By that time I'd received a lot of media coverage in the newspapers, so I photocopied some of the best articles and sent them to that guy as a reminder of what I had said. But the fact that Lane had just been killed struck a nerve in me and I didn't care if my old classmate would be offended by my newspaper articles or the accompanying letter.

Our Senior Class trip in December was to Florida and to Disney World. One day a bunch of my classmates played touch football on the beach in Daytona. The frustration of sitting on the sidelines watching instead of playing summed up the first part of my senior year.

7

Philadelphia Spectrum Bull Riding

The event was held in October of 1973 in conjunction with a major horse show. I was still on crutches because I still couldn't walk. Jimmy Lee or Willie Ed gave me a ride to the event each night. They were always good about making sure that all of the friends and family members had a ride to the popular events.

The Bull Riding was a major success. We also enjoyed the horse show jumping events and we all started pulling for a horse by the name of Idle Dice and his rider Rodney Jenkins. They were both very impressive and took home first place.

There was a lot of animosity between the bull riders in the RCA and the IRA (later changed to IPRA). The International Rodeo Association was a much smaller organization than the RCA, which later became the PRCA (Professional Rodeo Cowboys Association). The

PRCA was and always will be known as the elite rodeo association in the United States. There are talented cowboys in both groups but the PRCA always had a much larger talent pool. More cowboys eventually go to the PRCA from the IPRA rather than in the opposite direction.

Because of the competition between the two groups, all of the IRA bull riders who had entered the event were scheduled to compete on the same evening. That was done so there wouldn't be any conflicts during the prestigious event that might spill over into the horse show. People who were involved in horse show events were known to be very financially well off and Howard Harris did not want rowdy cowboys ruining the first time event.

That was the first time that I met Larry Mahan, who was the World All Around Champion six times in the PRCA. Larry was one of my rodeo heroes and I had always looked forward to meeting him. Even though I was a little nervous, I hobbled over to him and shook his hand. Larry was very nice to me. He gave me an autograph that I still have in my photo album. He showed up at that event with an author named Douglas Kent Hall who had written a book titled, *Let 'er Buck!*

The Bull Riding was very good. Jerome Robinson from Brandon, Nebraska, rode #C13 Top Cat and won first place. I think that was the first time Top Cat had ever been ridden. Jimmy Myers from Thorofare, New Jersey, rode #63 Charlie and made a jam up spurring ride to win second. Other memorable rides were Stanley Thomas from Woodstown, New Jersey on bull #O28 Loup Garou and Freckles Brown from Soper, Oklahoma, on bull #102 Rocky Raccoon.

8

Capital Centre Rodeo
Landover, Maryland

In late May of 1974 and 1975 Cowtown Rodeo produced a big rodeo at the Capital Centre in Landover, Maryland. It was the home of the NBA Washington Bullets (now Wizards).

These turned out to be outstanding rodeos. A lot of the "toughs" from out West entered the events. This was one of the first times that I saw a lot of the World Champions and the top fifteen cowboys who regularly qualified for the NFR (National Finals Rodeo.) There was a huge instant replay screen set up above the arena. It was pretty cool because it allowed the contestants to review their runs and rides right after they'd finished.

During the first performance, Donnie Graham from Troup,

Texas, was bucked off of #20 Stag. A.J. Swaim from Bremerton, Washington, was bucked off of #102 Rocky Raccoon. Larry Mahan rode #O28 Loup Garou and Barry Brown from Opelika, Alabama, rode #C13 Top Cat. Donnie Gay of Mesquite, Texas, rode #C1 Lizard and touched the bull with his free hand and still got a score from the rodeo judges.

The bull riders were so impressed with the performance and quality of Howard Harris' bulls that they said that he could put on a performance at the NFR all by himself. He would need fifteen top notch, world class bucking bulls in order to accomplish this feat and he already had a whole herd of outstanding bucking bulls.

John Davis from Homedale, Idaho, won the Bull Riding event with a super ride on #C1 Lizard. Years later, in January 1982, I gave him a ride from Laramie, Wyoming, to the airport in Denver, Colorado, and told him his winning score and that he had worn a bright green shirt when he rode Lizard that night. He confirmed this and was absolutely astonished that I could remember these minute details after all of those years. My memory for the details prompted Andy Harris to nickname me "Mister Rodeo" because of my memory of rodeo history and facts.

During one of the rodeo performances, a cowboy named Ken Painter from Carneys Point, New Jersey, was quickly dispensed with by his bull. It happened so fast that the bull exited the rodeo arena via the out gate before the eight seconds whistle had sounded. As a result, the bull had taken Ken's bull rope back to the stripping chute. This was very embarrassing. The stripping chute is where the helpers removed the flank straps. In the case of the bucking horse events, they would also remove the bareback rigging or the saddle, as well.

The bull rope is tied on in a loose fitting way so that when the cowboy releases his grip, the bull rope will be pulled off the animal by the weight of the bells. The helpers, in anticipation of the next bull, had opened the rear sliding gate to the stripping chute and closed the front exit's sliding gate. No one knew that there was another bucking bull on his way out of the rodeo arena.

Ken had gone into the stripping chute to retrieve his bull rope that was, by then, laying on the ground. All of a sudden there was a lot of yelling and commotion in the alleyway. People were yelling, "Heads up, heads up." A huge and mean Charalois cross bull, #000 Mr. Yoast, came crashing into the stripping chute. Mr. Yoast had not noticed or expected anyone to be in there with him. I'm sure that the bull was more surprised than anyone else but there was no way out for poor ol' Ken.

Normally, one of the workers would immediately slam the rear sliding gate in order to hold the bull in place until the flank strap was removed. In this case they couldn't. The massive Mr. Yoast was now straddling Ken who was crouched down underneath him. Everyone knew that Ken was about to be seriously injured or even trampled to death. But Ken, to the disbelief of all who witnessed this bizarre scene, crawled out the back of the stripping chute right between Mr. Yoast's hind legs. Ken didn't even get kicked. Unbelievable!

During the 1970s the new breed of young cowboys—like many other young men at that time— wore their hair a little longer. This did not sit very well with Howard Harris, who classified them as "hippies." Howard came from the "old school" which still had heroes like John Wayne and Hoss Cartwright. Butch Kirby, who was then living in Texas, showed up in Landover with some very long hair. The Kirby boys were all Howard's nephews—or "Chunky" as he was referred to by his close friends. He didn't approve of Butch and his long hair and made that very clear to him.

Butch sat down on his bull, #022 Lots of Shadows, and was warming up his bull rope for his ride. Lots of Shadows was a good bull and Butch would surely place on him as long as he paid attention and did things properly. Realizing that Butch would be concentrating on taking care of business, Sandy and Howard picked that opportunity to strike. Sandy grabbed a bunch of Butch's hair, which was sticking out from underneath his cowboy hat. As Sandy held the hair out away from Butch's neck, Howard took a disposable cigarette lighter and burned it.

Butch still made a good ride on the hard spinning Lots of Shadows and placed in the rodeo. Afterward, he was very angry with his brother Sandy and his uncle Howard for burning off some of his hair.

Another memorable incident occurred in the Steer Wrestling event. Fred Larson from Sheridan, Wyoming, bulldogged a white steer branded #50. Number 50 was really a bull but no one knew it. We all knew that he would surely hook you and he always acted like a bull. He was small enough to be just the right size for steer wrestling, so Howard Harris used him. The livestock handlers always had a difficult time loading him into the chutes because he would charge and hook you whenever he got a shot, just like a bull.

The steer wrestlers always drew for their animals, just like the riding events. Those animals were also branded with a number and they had to be loaded in a certain order according to which cowboy had drawn them. In the timed events, the cowboys would all compete in a certain order and their stock had to be loaded and placed in that order.

After Fred had successfully thrown his steer to the turf, he got up off of the ground and started to walk away, as usual. Well, #50 had other things on his mind. He did not appreciate being thrown around like some old *corriente* steer. So, he got up and charged after the unsuspecting cowboy. Fred Larson was about six foot six and weighed about two hundred and fifty pounds. He had very long legs.

When #50 hit Fred from behind, instead of knocking him to the ground, he ended up running underneath him. Fred was lifted up and the next thing we knew, he was riding that steer down the middle of the rodeo arena. The flabbergasted cowboy threw both hands up in the air as he was carried off.

Everyone who saw this happen was very, very amused. So were the people who were in charge of the giant instant replay screen. It was replayed over and over again throughout the remaining rodeo performances. *Rodeo Bloopers* didn't exist at that time or it surely would have been included on one of their tapes.

A couple of years later, #50 grew up and filled out and was used in the Bull Riding event at Cowtown Rodeo. He turned out to be a decent bucking bull. I even drew and made a qualified ride on him during one of the weekly Saturday night performances. When the whistle blew, I knew enough to get off and run because #50 was still very temperamental and always seemed anxious to punish us for once treating him like a steer.

9

Return to
the School of Hard Knocks

Rodeo practice started again in April 1974. I attended a few of the sessions but refused to get on. I would graduate from high school in a couple of months and didn't want to attend my graduation ceremonies on crutches. I did not care to be ridiculed by my classmates again.

Mentally, I was not ready to get back on bulls. I knew it was critical that when I decided to get on again, I have a nice easy bull so I could start to rebuild up my confidence. About a week before graduation, I drummed up my courage.

By this time Howard had a new crew of young guns from Texas who were staying in Cowtown for the summer. They were working on honing their competitive rodeo skills and also filling their permits. They worked for Howard during the week and then competed in the rodeos on the weekend. They all lived in the old police barracks. It was a win-win situation for everyone. Howard needed people to work on the Cowtown ranch, to mend fences, work livestock, bale hay and various miscellaneous chores. Those guys needed an opportunity to get on as much practice stock as possible. Also, Howard always had a lot of young bulls that needed some trips, so they could figure out what they wanted to do and this allowed Howard to assess the bulls' potential future in the rodeo business.

That particular practice session my cousins picked out a nice little bull for me that they thought that I could get along with okay. It was a big deal for all of us because they not only wanted me to continue riding bulls, but also to be as successful as they had been. Our little gang all knew prior to this practice session that I was going to "crack out again."

Once I sat down on the bull, he showed us all that he wasn't a "nice little bull." He started jumping around in the bucking chutes and banged me up a little. I got shaken and scared and asked my cousins to let me get off and regroup but they figured that if they let me get off, then I might never get on another bull again. So they refused and made me tough it out. I made out okay but it was a shaky start. Afterward, they teased me unmercifully because I had tried to get off in the chutes. For a bull rider, that is considered a huge no-no.

I started practicing and entering the rodeos on Saturdays at Cowtown again. My confidence and heart really were not into riding bulls. I guess that I rode partly because my friends and cousins expected it of me. I entered the Bull Riding every week and bucked off. Sometimes I would ride a good bull through the storm, realize what I had done, then get scared and just open my hand before the buzzer. It was not a lot of fun to "donate" my entry fees, week after week after week. To tell you the truth, I was probably looking for a good excuse to throw in the towel and quit riding bulls altogether.

During another one of the midweek summer practice sessions I wanted to get on a certain bull but Genie insisted on putting me on #100 of the "A" string. I knew that I couldn't ride him with two hands, let alone one, and wanted to stay as far away from him as possible. Sure enough he jumped out, started spinning and I bucked off.

He kicked me in the head and I must have had some kind of a flashback because I uttered the words that would haunt me for several years to come: "Help! Come and get me, I'm broke." No one even budged to come out and offer any assistance. Jimmy Lee would tease me about that for years afterward whenever he felt I was getting out of line and he needed to put me in my place.

One week I didn't enter and was scolded by my cousins. I told them that I was broke but I was really looking for an easy way out. This didn't work because Jimmy Lee, who also had a good job at DuPont's and was a consistent money winner at Cowtown, volunteered to pay my entry fees every single week and never asked for anything in return.

"Skimmer," as he was nicknamed by all of his close friends and relatives, consistently placed in the Bareback and Bull Riding events. Jimmy Lee also had a guaranteed paycheck because he was one of the rodeo bullfighters. I didn't make a qualified ride the rest of the summer.

In August, a few weeks before I was to go to college, I went to the rodeo in North Washington, Pennsylvania. Due to the lack of entries, the Bull Riding event was two go-rounds. I drew #C13 Top Cat who, at that time, was Cowtown's best bull and I also drew #7 Choice. I was way over-matched by Top Cat, a future NFR performer, and he easily flung me off.

Next I got on Choice. I had not been on very many spinning bulls so I thought that in order to ride one, you had to really over compensate to the inside of the spin so that you wouldn't be thrown off to the outside. Choice would usually spin to the left. He turned back to the left and I dove in there, bucked off and was promptly hung up. Jimmy Lee scolded me by saying, "You have to wait on the bull to make a move before you commit."

It was the first time that I'd ever hung up on a big bull. It was a little scary but I didn't panic and was able to quickly get my hand out of the bull rope. It also helped that Choice was a muley (a bull that doesn't have horns) and was not known to try and hurt a cowboy. It turned out to be a big learning experience. In the future I would know better than to make such a big move with my upper body on a spinning bull.

I also remember helping out with the sorting of the rodeo livestock to be used during each performance. One afternoon we were cutting out the bucking horses on foot. I jumped in front of some of the horses to cut them off. One bareback horse named Prairie Creek was scheduled to be bucked that night but he had second thoughts about being separated from the herd. I yelled and violently waved my arms. It didn't faze him at all. He knocked me down flat and ran right over me. After people checked to see if I was okay, they all burst out laughing. I was embarrassed and everyone teased me for the rest of the night and kept calling me "Prairie Creek."

I was scheduled to go to college the last week of August and hoped to build some confidence and momentum before heading out to the University of Wyoming in Laramie. I left pretty empty. But I was very enthused to be going out West because this is something that I had looked forward to for most of my life.

Before I left for Wyoming, my father questioned why I was going so far away from home just to go to college. The reason I had chosen the University of Wyoming was because Genie had attended Casper Junior College in Casper, Wyoming, on a rodeo scholarship. He had competed on the Rodeo Team in the NIRA (National Intercollegiate

Rodeo Association). By this time "Cowtown Gene" Walker had become a world-class bull rider. I had always looked up to him and wanted to follow in his footsteps.

Gene had won his region in the bull riding event and had qualified for the College National Finals Rodeo in Bozeman, Montana. During his tenure in college he had ridden #7 Lizard, owned by Edker Wilson of Sanford, Colorado. Lizard, at the time, was considered the baddest bucking bull on the college rodeo circuit.

Gene had built up quite a reputation during his college rodeo years. The rodeo judges had disqualified Gene for touching Lizard with his free hand during the ride. Those who witnessed the ride said that it was a "travesty of justice" because Gene had never even come close to slapping the bull with his free hand.

Grant Harris followed Gene a few years later and also competed on the Casper College Rodeo Team. So it became a tradition for the guys from Cowtown to attend school in Wyoming.

I was fortunate enough to earn several academic scholarships but I had to use them at a four-year school. I had planned to go to college in Wyoming so the University of Wyoming was my choice.

Because of my lackluster performance during the rodeo season, my dad had a conversation with Genie and told him that he was going to make me quit riding bulls. He was afraid that I was going to get seriously hurt again. Genie talked him out of it because he said that I would just leave home and go out West on my own and continue. My brother Reuben attended the weekly rodeos with me and told me about that conversation. I waited for my dad to approach me with this suggestion but he never did.

10

The University of Wyoming

At UW I lived in Orr Hall with a lot of other black football players. There were several athletes in the dorm and so naturally many students thought I was a football player. Almost every other black male student who lived in Orr Hall played football.

Most of the upper classmen on the football team lived in Orr Hall. The freshmen lived in Crane Hall. This was by design so that the coaches could keep track of them. It also helped to bond them as a team.

The black students made up about five percent of the entire student body population. Ninety-eight percent of the black men at UW were there because of some affiliation with sports. So naturally, most of the students assumed that I was an athlete. The only question was which sport did I participate in. Was it football, basketball or track?

The football players seemed to be put on a pedestal by the other students. They earned their scholarships. They worked extremely hard, went to practice and then study tables in the evenings. I was always impressed with them and I became friends with many of them. After all, football was the money sport and was by far the most popular. There was no doubt that the program carried a few of the other sports which brought very little, if any, income and resources to the University.

The black students and the white students at UW got along very well. Many of the black male students were known to congregate in Orr Hall during the noon hour and on Friday evenings. Most of the time they were very loud and intimidating to the other students.

They never bothered me. They all liked and respected me for having the courage to get on those big mean bulls and I got along very well with all the students, both black and white. I was a very popular guy on campus and a lot of the women in Orr Hall were very receptive.

The legal age for drinking was nineteen at that time. I wouldn't turn nineteen until the summer after my freshman year so I altered my driver's license and was always seen down the street at Snorts Bar, a cowboy bar. It has long since closed its swinging doors on Grand Avenue and is the current location of a Kinko's Copy Center.

As far as consuming alcohol goes, I was and still am a total lightweight. Most of my friends have never seen me drunk. I would probably drink only two beers during a night out on the town. The other cowboys liked me and were always buying me beers so I never had to take any money into the bar.

Without fail, I was usually the only black person in the bar. But once people got to know me, I was always very comfortable. I never once had a bad experience in a Laramie bar because some old redneck wanted to display his racial bias and bigotry.

I would walk over to the college football games alone. I would simply stroll across the bottom aisle and the cowboys would start to yell my name and I would always sit with them.

The football team was not a powerhouse in the original Western Athletic Conference. The actions and antics of the UW students at some of the games were absolutely zany. I would laugh my head off. There were times when there was more excitement in the grandstands in the fourth quarter than out on the field.

When I showed up at UW my roommate, Terry Wiekhorst, told me that a very well known magazine had ranked the top ten party schools in the nation. Then as an asterisk they had added, "We did not include the University of Wyoming in this survey because it is unfair to rank amateurs with a professional." This was a black eye for the administration and the officials at the University.

Another story from my college days is that one year Laramie had a major blizzard and classes were canceled. The UW students got on the telephone to find out which saloons still had some beer in their stock pile. Then they jumped into their four-wheel drives and went from bar to bar to purchase beer. Eventually there was no beer available in the entire city because the roads in and out of Laramie were closed for a few days.

During my tenure at UW, there were a few well-known professors on the roster. I played basketball with John Edgar Wideman who taught English and was a world-renowned author. Dr. Wideman, a Rhodes scholar, was a great master of the hardwood as well.

When I changed my major and enrolled in the business college, I found out that many of my professors had written their own classroom books. I had an anthropology class that was taught by Dr. George Gill who was world-renowned in his field. Bart Mears was a famous geologist.

Overall, I felt that Laramie and the state of Wyoming were very accommodating to me during the entire time that I was a resident.

I was a very shy freshman. In Orr Hall I was intimidated by the football players. Those guys were a lot bigger than the high school football players that I'd been around. Immediately, I put away my cowboy hat and tried to fit in as a typical college student.

In addition to the academic scholarships, I was awarded a rodeo scholarship after my junior year to help pay for my education. It didn't cost me anything for the first four years to go to college. I changed my major from History to Business and lost a lot of credits so it took me five years to graduate and I had to take out a loan to complete my final year of school.

I didn't look much like your typical rodeo cowboy. I was not sporting a nice trophy belt buckle like most of the other college rodeo students. They had been competing in Little Britches and High School rodeos for several years and had won buckles. Trophy belt buckles have always been a status symbol in the rodeo world. Whenever you meet someone who is a part of the rodeo crowd, the first thing that they do is glance at your buckle to try and get an idea of just how good you are. Some people are pretty nonchalant about peeking at your buckle but the majority are just downright rude about it. It's sad but true, and just a clear cut facet of the rodeo world.

I would never wear my cowboy hat or boots unless I had a purpose such as practice or a rodeo. My daily uniform was Wrangler jeans and a T-shirt. As a result, I was pretty invisible on campus until people got to know me. I remember meeting Lawrence Gaines, my next door dorm neighbor, at the elevator one day. I knew that he was a football player and remarked that he was probably a tackle on the football team. He very quickly put me in my place and told me that he was a running back. The man was huge. My thighs were about the same size as his calves. Later on, he would be drafted in the first round of the NFL by the Detroit Lions. Aaron Kyle, who lived next door to me on the opposite side, was also drafted in the first round by the Dallas Cowboys.

One day I was playing basketball outside and wearing a T-shirt that said "Rodeo, America's #1 Sport." A football player, named Nate Williams, remarked that I shouldn't be wearing a T-shirt talking about a sport that I had absolutely nothing to do with. I told him I was a rodeo cowboy and he burst out laughing and said, "There is no such thing as a black cowboy." Of course I got very defensive and invited him up to my room so I could prove him wrong. Instead, he continued to harass me and figured that I was not telling him the truth.

A few days later I saw Nate and again invited him up to my dorm room. He just blew me off and continued to give me a hard time. Finally one day I stepped out of my room and saw Nate on my floor waiting to catch the elevator. I told him to just wait one minute and I would go and get my photo album. He balked and said, "Man I don't have time to be messing around with you." I finally convinced him to just hold on. I ran to my room, brought my photo album back and handed it to him.

I was totally shocked at his reaction. Nate took my photo album, looked at my bull riding pictures and freaked out. He started running up and down the halls knocking on doors and telling the other football players to look at this crazy little guy riding these great big bulls. I had to chase him down saying, "Hey man, where are you going with my photo album?"

After this little incident I was no longer an unknown on the college campus. I had all of these football players coming out of the woodwork to meet me because they had never met a black cowboy before. It really made me feel good that they had all taken such an interest in me and my rodeo career. They were especially shocked to find out that I was from New Jersey. I guess they thought there were no cowboys from New Jersey, black or white. Later, I was told that I was the first black cowboy ever to attend the University of Wyoming.

Abe Morris

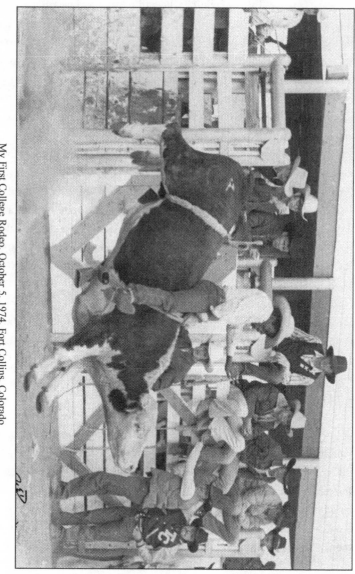

My First College Rodeo, October 5, 1974, Fort Collins, Colorado
#11 Snowmass
Photo: Georgia Reed

My first college rodeo was on October 5, 1974 in Fort Collins, Colorado. I will always remember looking out at the grandstand during that first performance. There was hardly anyone there. I had always envisioned college rodeos in the West as having grandstands packed full of enthusiastic fans. Needless to say, I was a little disappointed.

But I was not disappointed in the talent of those young students. They included several future NFR qualifiers and a host of others who had the talent but for one reason or another did not qualify for the NFR. I was the only black cowboy at the rodeo and I stuck out like a fly in a bowl of milk. I was not used to this kind of an atmosphere because in the past I always had my cousins and other black friends around. It was the first time in my life that one of my cousins was not there to pull my bull rope and offer me some encouragement.

I drew a pretty good bull branded #11 Snowmass. He jumped out and spun to the left and I rode him for about seven seconds before he bucked me off. I surprised a lot of people, including myself, because up until this point in my career it was probably the best ride that I'd ever made. A lot of people thought that I was going to win the Bull Riding. Afterward the bull stepped on me and tore my nicest pair of Wrangler jeans.

My rodeo coach, Dr. Thomas Dunn, had been pretty reserved with me. He came right up to me to see if I was alright and congratulate me for making a good showing at my first college rodeo. In looking back at a photograph of my first ride, all of the contestants in the background had frowns on their faces. They were sizing me up. It's in sharp contrast to my later college rodeo photos where you could see the smiles of acceptance on the other bull riders' faces.

College bull riders out West wore casual shoes to the rodeos and not cowboy boots and nice leather chaps when competing. I hadn't seen that before. Even their riding styles were different. The young bull riders made big sweeping moves with their free arms. I had not seen guys ride bulls like that back East but I liked it, and soon found myself trying to emulate their moves.

Those bull riders also carried an extra pair of jeans in their rigging bags and wore them only when competing. These were termed "riding pants." After their rides they would put their regular clean jeans back on. Just sitting on a horse or a bull always leaves dirty stains where your legs make contact with the animal. Your riding pants were usually an older worn out pair of loose fitting jeans. By using a pair of riding pants, a contestant could avoid messing up their nicer jeans and would use their riding pants several times before washing them.

I didn't make a qualified ride at any of our four fall semester college rodeos but I made a pretty good showing. I was trying to continue the legacy of the good cowboys who came out of the Cowtown Rodeo. Gene, Jimmy Lee and Willie Ed Walker had all turned out to be peak rodeo performers and champions. Jimmy Myers from Thorofare, New Jersey, qualified for the NFR in the Bull Riding in 1969. He later would be the IPRA World Champion Bull Rider as well.

Sandy, Kaye, and Butch Kirby all got their starts in Cowtown. The three brothers all qualified for the NFR in 1975. Sandy qualified in the Bareback Riding and Bull Riding. Kaye qualified in the Bareback Riding and Butch qualified in the Bull Riding events. Sandy and Butch also qualified on several other occasions for the NFR and Butch was crowned the 1978 World Champion Bull Rider. Bobby DelVecchio, originally from the Bronx, New York, who qualified for the NFR in the Bull Riding on several occasions during the 1980s, also got his start in Cowtown. This was the proud heritage that I had to live up to. Believe me it was no easy feat.

In March of 1975, the Laramie River Rendezvous Rodeo was held in the Fieldhouse, right on the UW campus. By far this was the best college rodeo of the season in the Central Rocky Mountain Region. This was what I had imagined a good college rodeo would be like with a huge enthusiastic crowd. The winters in Laramie were always pretty brutal, partially because of the altitude (7,200 feet above sea level) combined with the relentless Wyoming wind. Due to cabin fever, students and residents alike were always looking for a good excuse to get out of the house and that rodeo fit the bill.

I drew up in the slack on Saturday morning and I had bull #329 Bad Actor of the Korkow Rodeo Company from South Dakota. Whenever there is an abundance of entries, some of the overflow will compete in the slack which is usually in the morning or after the regular rodeo performance.

I was amazed by the number of my fellow students and football players who got up early that morning just to watch me compete. The early morning crowd was pretty subdued until the rodeo announcer said, "Next to go, from the University of Wyoming will be Abe Morris." All of a sudden the place erupted with cheers for the local college student.

Kurt Humphrey was pulling my bull rope and said, "My goodness Abe, did you bring along your own cheering section?" I didn't let them down. I made a good bull ride and the small crowd really showed their appreciation. I also showed mine and in my own way to thank them for coming out and cheering me on.

We all thought that I should have received more points but it makes no sense to argue with the judges. They will remember you the next time you compete and dock your score again.

After the first go-round was completed on Saturday night I checked the judge's scores and had ended up in a tie for tenth place. The top ten bull riders would get to compete again in the finals on Sunday afternoon. I was elated to qualify for the finals at my own college rodeo.

Many of the students knew that I'd done well and were just as happy. Afterward, I went to a big party attended by a lot of the college rodeo groupies. I was having a good old time but decided to leave early because I needed a decent night's sleep so I could do well in the rodeo the following day.

The next day, I went over to check the judges' sheets to see what bull I'd drawn for the finals. I could not find my name. As I was frantically checking the sheets, another cowboy came up behind me and put his hand on my shoulder and gave me the bad news. Trey Reeves, a cowboy who also played football for UW, had been watching for me because he knew I'd be very disappointed. Sometime after the Saturday night performance, the judges had changed their scores and bumped me from the top ten. My heart just sank. I was devastated.

Sitting through the day's competition was the worst time I had to endure at a college rodeo. Several of my fellow students who had gone to the rodeo to watch me compete were also very disappointed. After the rodeo, I had to explain to them the reason why I didn't ride again in the finals. They all felt like I had been cheated. I did, too. Even though the judges had the right to change their scores, I still felt I should have received a higher score to begin with. It was an injustice directed at me and I took it personally.

At one of the college rodeos in Fort Collins, Colorado, there was a very bizarre and scary incident. A local student had entered the Saddle Bronc Riding event. I don't think that he'd been on very many bucking horses. He bucked off pretty hard and when he hit the ground he was knocked unconscious and swallowed his tongue. Bob Romer, "The Bull Dancer" from Texas, was fighting bulls at this rodeo and was in the arena at the time. Bob was frantically working on trying to get this kid's tongue so that he could start breathing again. I had no idea what was happening and I went out into the arena to see what was going on. The kid was blue from lack of oxygen. I thought for sure he was going to die and I didn't want to hang around and watch. I immediately walked away.

Somehow Bob managed to get the kid's mouth pried open and got his tongue out of his airway. In the process, both of Bob's thumbs were cut pretty badly and bleeding. The kid was taken away in an ambulance and survived. Bob had to seek first aid for his bleeding fingers. I knew I would never forget that kid's skin color as he fought to get some air into his lungs. It was very scary.

I did not have a lot of success at the rest of the spring college rodeos. When I returned home to New Jersey, I didn't have a lot of good news to report to my colleagues about my adventures out West.

I also caught a lot of flack because I came back sporting a brand new pair of nice leather chaps. "Everyone out West wears chaps," I told my cousins. Their response was, "You're not out West now and you don't need chaps to ride bulls."

Not willing to let it go I said, "The chaps flash up your rides and can get you extra points from the rodeo judges." Jimmy Lee's response was, "If I want to get some extra points then I'll spur my bulls."

By this time I had purchased my RCA permit and set out with hopes of winning my thousand dollars so I could become a full-fledged member. While attending school in Laramie, I had gotten on a lot of practice bulls. I'd regained a lot of confidence and desire and was putting out a good effort in the rodeos.

On June 17, 1975, my first rodeo that summer at Cowtown, I got on a bull #T2 Teco. He had a reputation for kicking pretty good and was known to have a lot of jerk in his bucking style. I was riding him just fine. About five seconds into the ride, he jerked on me pretty good. A piercing pain shot through my shoulder. I grabbed my shoulder and still rode him for a couple of more jumps and then I just got off. I was in a lot of pain and I thought that my shoulder had been dislocated. I went to the hospital and the X-rays were negative but I had to sit on the sidelines for about three weeks before competing again.

In July 1975 we went to a rodeo in New Alexandria, Pennsylvania. The stock contractor was Matt Dryden from Marianna, Florida. We'd never been to a rodeo before that was produced by the Circle D Rodeo Company so we had no idea what to expect from his string of bucking bulls.

After our arrival, we were met by Barney Faircloth, one of the rodeo judges. He asked, "Where are you boys from?" We stuck our chests and said in unison, "Cowtown." Barney asked if we were entered in the Bull Riding. "Yes," we replied and immediately he told us, "You boys better had brought your riding pants with you."

Later on we found out exactly what Barney meant because that pen of bulls was outstanding. There was not a slouch or dink in the bunch. They all bucked extremely hard. During the rodeo we met a few professional football players from the Pittsburgh Steelers who were attending their summer training camp nearby.

It was there that Stanley Thomas introduced us to the split tail or "suicide wrap." Instead of laying the tail of the rope straight across the palm of your riding hand, you would run it between your ring finger and your pinky. He told us how safe it was and bragged to us that it was impossible to hang up.

Stanley got on NFR bull #HO. He was a blue-colored bull with little nub horns. Stanley's bull spun, bucked extremely well and quickly bucked him off and hung him up. In the process he whacked him right above the eyebrow with one of those little nub horns and knocked him out cold.

The bullfighters had an extremely hard time getting Stanley out of his bull rope. He was literally tied in and all of the pressure was on his riding hand.

To add to this Stanley was a big man at six foot four and over two hundred and ten pounds. He was considered large to be riding bulls. Eventually a few guys, including Buck Howard, left the bucking chutes in an effort to save our friend. Finally, someone got Stanley's hand out of the rope and he was lying on his back on the ground, unconscious.

There was a pool of blood covering Stanley's eye. It looked as if one of his eyes had been knocked out. The reality was that he had split his eyebrow and the blood had run down into his eye and lying there on the ground we couldn't tell the difference.

After Stanley was hauled off in the ambulance, we still had to get on our bulls. I can tell you that whenever a close friend gets hurt and you still have to compete, you just don't feel up to snuff.

None of our little entourage from Cowtown wanted to get on after this horrifying accident. I got on a big Charolais NFR bull #4 Deputy Dawg. He spun hard to the right and slammed me into the ground on my left shoulder. Stanley Thomas, Buck Howard, Mike Castelein, Grant Harris, Andy Harris and myself had traveled to the rodeo in two different vehicles. We all got bucked off. Apparently we'd all left our hearts and our "riding pants" somewhere else on that evening.

Stanley recovered. He ended up getting a few stitches in his eyebrow. He also had been stepped on a few times. Stanley could not compete for a couple of weeks and had to use a cane to get around.

I didn't win anything until the last two rodeos that I competed in at Cowtown. I won second place on a bull named YoYo and I was ecstatic. I had finally won some money on my RCA permit. The very next week I came right back and placed again. I was on a roll. The statement that, "success breeds success" is very true.

The next week I was on my way back to college. Classes at UW always started in late August. I had a hard time visualizing sitting in class during the month of August because school in New Jersey had always started in September.

11

OK Corral

The UW Rodeo Team had made arrangements to use the High
Plains Arena owned by Pete and Hal Burns for rodeo practice sessions.
The OK Corral was kind of a rustic looking place and it had no heat but
that didn't stop us. It was a great deal for us college cowboys because it
didn't cost us anything to practice. We could get on as many bulls as we
wanted. Sometimes the owners would buck a bull more than once if we
asked him to do so. There were several decent bulls for us to get on and
none of them were considered rank. There was one huge bull that they
called General Custer that was the terror of the pen because he was so
much bigger than the other bulls.

There were four bulls that would eventually be selected to
perform at the NFR because of their outstanding bucking ability.
Number J1, #J2, #J3 and #J26 would all end up being hauled by the

Mike Cervi Rodeo Company out of Sterling, Colorado before going to the NFR.

I got on #J2 several times at the OK Corral and then I drew him again at the National Western Stock Show and Rodeo in Denver, Colorado in 1978. I rode him for about seventy points. I drew him again that same year in Phoenix, Arizona, and he bucked me off onto my head. The Prorodeo Sports News put a picture of my crash landing in their April 5, 1978 issue. I also got on #J26 Dynamite at Denver in 1984 and he jerked the bull rope out my hand and bucked me off.

Over the years that I lived in Laramie I would get on a lot of bulls at the OK Corral. Some of the veteran bulls I got on several times, either in practice or in a jackpot. A jackpot is a small competition where all of the contestants pay an entry fee and also a stock charge. The stock charge goes to the owner of the bulls and the rest goes to the winners. The stock is drawn and the riders are judged just like they are at a regular rodeo. Most jackpots would only pay first and second places but it depended on the number of entries.

There was an outstanding bucking bull, #13 Sarge, who was considered to be an eliminator. His performances also merited two NFR selections. I got on this bull about a dozen times counting practice, jackpots and rodeos. I liked to get on him because he really made me bear down and try extremely hard. He never bucked me off.

My years at the OK Corral were filled with successes as well as disappointments, though the successes far outweighed the failures. Once, I was riding a practice bull and he was bucking straight for the turn back fence that had been set up to shorten the arena. He never even slowed down and bucked straight into the panel fence and just kept on going. I managed to get off, but I sustained a nasty gash in my right leg in the process. I still have a huge scar on my shin because of that bull.

During one of the practice sessions I was bucked off pretty

hard. There were three or four girls sitting in the stands who had come out to watch the practice session. For some reason completely unknown to me, they thought that I had no business riding bulls and they laughed very loudly at me. It upset me that they were rude enough to laugh at my misfortune. I told J.D. Hamaker, another rodeo team member, that I wanted to get on another bull.

I was determined to show these girls something. That bull jumped out and turned back and started bucking and spinning to the right, into my riding hand. I made a good solid ride and spurred this bull, #31 White, every single jump. After the whistle I walked over to the grandstand and just glared at those ignorant girls as if to say, *now go ahead and laugh about that ride, too, if you think that me getting on bulls is so funny to watch.* I didn't get a response.

Another time, during a Sunday afternoon jackpot, I bucked off and landed on my head. It was about 1981. It was the first time in my career that I got knocked out cold. It was a very weird feeling. When I came to, I was surrounded by a bunch of people. It felt exactly as if I were waking up at home, in bed. The strange thing about it was that instead of seeing my bed and bed sheets, I was looking at an arena full of dirt. I thought to myself, *this is not my bed.* Afterward, I realized that I had been temporarily unconscious.

During a jackpot around 1981 I was bucked off and stepped on by a bull, #7 Downdraft, who was later selected to go to the NFR. I sustained a cut in a ligament in my knee and ended up wearing a knee brace and being on crutches for about three weeks. I had to make a trip to the Gem City Bone and Joint clinic where I was to become a regular patient. Dr. David Kieffer and I got to visit and know each other very well over the years.

At one of our Sunday jackpots, I drew Sarge, a bull that gave me a shot at first place. Before we could start, a few other bull riders from Colorado showed up and wanted to get in on the jackpot. They were very late and wanted us to redraw the stock so that they could participate. I objected the most because I didn't want to relinquish my good money bull.

Finally, I gave in and drew Andy Capp, a Charolais bull. I was still a little mad because I knew I couldn't win first place on Andy Capp. Usually he would just jump and kick pretty good, but nothing spectacular. Everyone knew that I was upset before I even got on. You could see it in my body language and because I wouldn't say much to anyone. J.D. Hamaker was fighting bulls and told me that he would do his best to get him to turn back and spin. J.D. did an excellent job and Andy Capp had one of his best trips ever. He turned back right out of the gate and spun hard to the right. I made an excellent spurring ride on him and ended up winning first place, after all.

On one occasion, a film crew from WTBS out of Atlanta, Georgia, came to Laramie about 1983 to do a segment on Pete Burns who, at the time, was the UW Rodeo Team coach. Several of the current college students got on bulls, including me, though I had already graduated from college by then. It was aired on their station a few months later.

Overall, I have a lot of fond memories from the OK. It was definitely a place to separate the men from the boys. Some days we practiced and the wind chill factor was below zero. After competing, your riding hand would burn just like it was on fire and you wouldn't have a lot of feeling in it for a while. On days like that, mentally you had to really want to be a bull rider and not just someone who *claimed* they got on bulls. There is a difference. I always had a saying: "You simply can't just hold on to bulls, you have to ride them!"

After I filled my permit and was a full-fledged PRCA member, I was asked to judge several permit bull riding sessions at the OK. This is because the PRCA realized that it was extremely difficult for many up and coming bull riders to be allowed to enter rodeos in the West due to the abundance of bull riders and the many rodeos that didn't accept permits.

The Burns Rodeo Co. and the PRCA conducted permit sessions in which bull riders could earn points to fill their permits. They would compete against other permit holders. It was like the farm system of Major League Baseball. All of the bull riders would have had to qualify in order to be able to compete against the "big boys" in the major rodeos.

During my years in Laramie I spent a lot of time at the OK Corral. Over the years there were several rodeo functions held out there and a lot of good parties, as well. In the early 1980s there were a couple of events in the fall called the Buckfest, which drew a lot of UW students. The place was packed with a lot of screaming, beer-drinking students. It was a blast.

12

Summer of 1976

When I left school in May of 1976, I knew that I would not be returning again until August of 1977. I really didn't like school, although I'd had perfect attendance a few times before I graduated from high school. I'd had perfect attendance in second grade and also from the fourth grade through the seventh. I had already decided during my senior year in high school that I was going to go to college for two years and then sit out one year before returning to finish up. I was burned out on school and ready for a break.

My goal for that summer was to win enough money to fill my permit. I got started right away in May at Cowtown by making a good ride on #T3 Loco. This was in the days when the judges didn't score very high. He jumped and kicked pretty good and then spun to the left. I dressed him up by riding him like the guys did out West and made big sweeping motions with my free arm. I really wowed everyone because no one had ever seen me ride a good spinning bull at Cowtown until that night. I ended up being scored seventy-three points and won second place that week.

I rode very well the whole summer and Howard Harris started calling me "the stylist." He and Genie would chastise me for the methods that I now used to ride my bulls. They both felt that all of that waving with my free arm was totally unnecessary.

This was the country's Bi-Centennial year. Howard Harris and Cowtown Rodeo were awarded the official Bi-Centennial Rodeo of the PRCA to be held in Philadelphia, Pennsylvania. I think that rodeo was held at Franklin Field. Permits were accepted in the Bull Riding event, so I entered.

The rodeo lasted about five days and one of those days was June 24th which happened to be my birthday. I was decked out in a stylish polyester shirt that my sister Janice had made for me. I called them "silk" shirts. Janice was a superb seamstress and she tailored several of my Western shirts for me throughout the years. All I had to do was pick out the material and she would do the rest. I had a whole wardrobe of nice, classy shirts. After that performance on the 24th, I was mauled by my cousins and my friends and they took off my belt and beat me with it twenty times each to commemorate my birthday.

I drew a new bull named Pete that Howard had recently purchased from Pete Clemons from Okeechobee, Florida. Some of the Brahma bulls from Florida had a very distinctive appearance. You could tell just by looking at this bull that he'd come from the deep South. He jumped out and went a little way before turning back to the left and rapidly spinning. I was sitting pretty good until I decided to make a big move with my free hand. I was trying to look real showy on him and it ended up costing me. It tilted me out of shape and I bucked off. I was very upset because that move cost me placing in the rodeo and probably filling my permit, as well. Also, since there were a lot of the "toughs" there from out West, I had wanted to make a great showing for myself at that major rodeo. The toughs would only venture to the East Coast when there was a large purse up for grabs because they needed to weigh the expenses of traveling against the opportunity and potential for a big win.

A lot of the top cowboys from out West entered and it was a very good rodeo. Robert Blandford from Texas won the Bull Riding on #303 Ravioli. Stanley Thomas from Woodstown made a super ride on a bull #O7 Cowboy. He was named Cowboy because his front legs were bow legged just like a real cowboy. He was a son out of #214 Surprise and he looked just like his dad, only smaller. He had inherited the same bucking traits and personality. He would turn back and spin right in the gate and he was also prone to hook you in a heartbeat.

Stanley was disqualified. It was a very controversial decision from the rodeo judge Marty Stein. At first the judge said that Stanley didn't make the eight seconds whistle. Later, he said that "Beamish" (as we had nicknamed Stanley) had touched the bull with his free hand. Neither was even close to being true. It was not a pretty scene afterward.

We had nicknamed Stanley "Beamish" after the television character Stanley Beamish on the *Great American Hero*. Stanley would easily have won the Bull Riding. We all felt that because he was black and a local contestant, the judge preferred to have one of the big name cowboys from out West to win that major rodeo.

In 1976, I completely turned my bull riding career around. I rode very well and was consistent for the entire rodeo season. Cowtown Rodeo decided to award trophy belt buckles to the winners in each event and for All Around Cowboy at the end of the season. The buckles were based on a point system. I ended the year in third place behind Kaye Kirby of Woodstown, New Jersey and T.J. Hawkins from Reidsville, West Virginia. Finishing ahead of my cousins in the point standings proved that my bull riding had come full circle.

Kaye ended up winning the Bareback Riding and Bull Riding buckles as well as All Around Cowboy. He was one of the most talented riding event cowboys ever in the PRCA. He rode his bareback horses right-handed and his bulls left-handed. I only knew of two rodeo cowboys that were talented enough to ride with either hand on an ongoing basis. Butch Knowles was the other.

Kaye bucked off of only one bull at Cowtown during the entire 1976 season. He probably would have qualified for the NFR in 1976 in the Bull Riding event but he bucked off of #17 General Issamo in Albuquerque, New Mexico, in September. He also rode saddle broncs on occasion but he didn't like this event nearly as much as the Bareback and Bull Riding events. He loved the Bareback Riding and qualified for the NFR in 1975.

During his rodeo career I personally saw Kaye ride #2046 Brown Mule (Cowtown), the bull that broke George Paul's consecutive record of qualified rides. Kaye also rode #-10 Playboy during the prime of this great bucking bull's career.

In my opinion Kaye Kirby was one of the most talented bareback riders of all time. He never received the recognition that he truly deserved because he didn't "go hard" like many of the cowboys who lived out West. He didn't like to travel and preferred to stay on the East Coast and therefore cleaned up at Cowtown every week. Kaye would consistently win the Bareback Riding event almost every single week at the Cowtown Rodeo. And he deserved it.

The natural lead for bulls is to the left. This is the reason that most bucking bulls spin to the left. The same concept applies to the human race in that most people are naturally right-handed. Bull riders usually prefer bulls to spin in the same direction of their riding hand. They seem to have a notion that it's easier to ride bulls *into* your hand rather than *away* from your riding hand. Since most bulls tended to spin to the left, Kaye chose to ride bulls with his left hand, even though he was naturally right-handed.

Even the great bucking bull #007 Red Rock, owned by John Growney from California, consistently spun away from the bull rider's hand. That bull was originally retired and came out of retirement and was not successfully ridden in the PRCA until the matches against 1987 World Champion Lane Frost. Another reason that Red Rock was so hard to ride was because he didn't bend his knees when he hit the ground like ninety-nine percent of bucking bulls. The bull riders were left to absorb all of the shock on each jump and were jolted until they bucked off.

During the entire summer of 1976, I did well enough in rodeos that I didn't have to work. I spent most of my summer hanging out with Tony Bouldin. Tony got on a few bulls but his heart was in bareback riding. Freddie and Stanley Thomas got him interested in rodeo. "Spaz" did quite a few odd jobs for Freddie who had gotten on a couple of bareback horses during his brief rodeo career.

We spent a lot of time at Cowtown. Sometimes I would leave home and be gone for a couple of days. I loved my family but I chose to hang around with the rodeo guys at Cowtown.

A neighbor named Al, just down the road in Monroeville, had set up a bucking barrel. It was suspended by four garage door springs. It was wrapped with a few layers of foam rubber and had a sawdust pit below it to cushion your landings. It was wicked, to say the least.

We would go and get on it on a regular basis. On one occasion Freddie, Stanley, Andy and Tony were on hand for a raucous practice session. We bucked Tony so hard that he came off on the right side of the barrel and it jerked him clean underneath it and deposited him on the left side of the sawdust pit. We all laughed so hard that we had to hold on to something so we wouldn't fall down.

Tony got upset because it hurt him. But then again, he was one of the toughest characters that I'd ever known. He would hang up on his bareback horses on a regular basis and still come back for more abuse.

No matter how hard they tried, they could not buck me off of that barrel. But the only way to ride it was to lean way back so that your back would be touching the barrel when it jerked you forward. It got me into some very bad habits. If you lean back on a bucking bull, you will get jerked down onto their heads and seriously injured. After riding that barrel a lot, I would get on my bulls and lean way back. It was a tough habit to break.

In July, Willie Ed convinced most of our group to enter an all black rodeo in Chicago to be produced by Thryl and Mike Latting from Robbins, Illinois. Thryl Latting, an African-American, was a very well-known rodeo producer in the IPRA. I had never before seen or competed in an all black rodeo and I really looked forward to going. Several guys agreed to go with us and then, at the last minute, changed their minds and backed out. As a result, Willie Ed, Roland Shorter, Jr. and I entered the rodeo that was to be held in the Amphitheatre on the South side of Chicago.

Willie Ed was not very pleased that all of the other guys had backed out because of the distance between Woodstown, New Jersey and Chicago, Illinois. When we left for our trip he made it very, very clear that because the other guys had changed their minds, we had better come back with a carload of money to show them what they'd missed.

After we arrived in Chicago and I noticed all of the bars over the windows and doors and heavy duty padlocks, I realized we were in a bad part of the city. I told Willie Ed and Junie (Roland) that I was not leaving our motel room except to get something to eat and to go to the rodeo.

I ended up winning first in the Bull Riding and the payoff was all in cash. I won over five hundred dollars and because I was one of the last contestants to get paid, I received most of my money in smaller denomination bills. I stashed two fat wads of money into my front jeans pockets and said, "Boys, lets get the heck out of Dodge." With those two big knots of money I didn't want to spend any more time in Chicago than I had to. Willie Ed had also won some money. We had fulfilled our mission and immediately left town. After we got back to New Jersey, the guys who'd stayed behind wished they'd gone with us as they'd originally planned.

During one of the Saturday night performances at Cowtown I drew a young and feisty bull. He had only been bucked a few times and he fought in the chutes a little bit. After my bull rope was pulled up tight, he lunged to the front of the bucking chute. This move caught me completely off guard. He then immediately reared up and fell to the back of the chute and pinned me. There was no time for me to react because my hand was tight in the bull rope. Somehow I managed to get my hand out of the rope but he was squeezing my body against the rear sliding gate of the chute and my legs could not reach the ground. Then, realizing exactly where I was, the bull started swinging his head back and trying to hook me with his horns.

Willie Ed and Jack Bitter the flank man got hold of me with their hands under my armpits and they refused to let me slide further down into the chute. Otherwise, it would have become a very dangerous situation. By the time I was able to get out of the chute, that bull had completely opened the snaps on my western shirt with his horns. I was slightly ruffled but unhurt and was able to compete on the same bull a while later with no other problems.

The PRCA rules state that a cowboy must make three honest attempts to get out on an animal. After that, the judges will draw the contestant a re-ride. The judges can also fine a cowboy for not making an honest attempt to make the whistle after the chute gate is opened, though it is extremely rare to see that happen. I've seen some guys look at the ground or open their hands right out of the gate and not get fined.

The other riders really frown on a guy who chickens out and doesn't try.

     That summer I easily won the amount of money necessary to fill my permit. In those days a prospective PRCA member needed to win a total of one thousand dollars in a three year time frame in order to become a full-fledged member. If a contestant came up short, then he would have to start all over again. I filled my permit in the second year that I competed with it.

14

Fall of 1976

My life pretty much came to a standstill after the rodeo season was over because I wasn't working or going to college. My parents were not very happy and encouraged me to go back to school in January of 1977. They were pretty convinced that if I sat out for a whole year, I would never return to school. They cited several examples of kids who had said that they'd go back after a year of sabbatical and then never did. I refused. I knew for sure that I would return to college but I was determined to sit out for the entire school year.

For a few weeks I went on a job search but was not hired. Then one day one of my aunts (my dad's sister) from Florida called and asked him to come down to help out with delivering newspapers temporarily while her husband was sick in the hospital. Right away my dad volunteered me to go instead. So I ended up going to Clewiston, Florida and living near Lake Okeechobee for about five months.

I took along my rodeo equipment just in case I met some cowboys while I was in Florida. I had intentions of competing in a few rodeos but it didn't happen. I would need to purchase my PRCA membership card in order to enter and I didn't do that until I returned to New Jersey in April 1977.

After helping my uncle and aunt deliver newspapers for about a month, I worked in the orange groves picking oranges. It was a very good, eye opening experience. Picking oranges is not a very glamorous job. Orange trees have very nasty thorns that are about an inch and a half long and thick. You needed to wear a long sleeve shirt and thick gloves because the thorns are wicked and you get stuck on a daily basis. I told myself that there was absolutely no way that I wanted to do this kind of manual labor for the rest of my life. If I was not sure about returning to school before, I was sure after picking oranges.

Later, I got a job building cattle pens for a ranch. I was the only black person on the work crew. One of the guys, who considered himself to be a cowboy, found out that I'd said I rode bulls and of course didn't believe me. He said to me very sarcastically, "Yeah, I would just love to see you get on a bull." I calmly told him all he had to do was to purchase a ticket just like the other rodeo fans and he could have his wish.

I had set a goal to buy myself a car in 1977. I was sending money home to my dad on a regular basis and he was depositing it into my savings account for me. I had hoped to have enough money saved during the summer for a down payment. I wanted to have a vehicle when it was time to go back to college. It had been a major disadvantage in Laramie to not have a car. Besides, I could save a lot of money not flying back and forth to school.

When I returned to New Jersey from Florida, I was physically out of shape. I had gained some weight and my stomach even poked out a little. Jimmy Lee ribbed me and told me that I had better get back into shape before the rodeo season got under way if I planned to pick up where I'd left off the previous season. I knew that he was right. I started working out and skipping lunch in order to lose weight. Skimmer even brought his exercise wheel over to my house and gave me explicit instructions to start using it right away. I took his advice because I knew it was for my own good.

I came back in time for the Spring practice sessions. During one of the practice sessions Howard Harris, III, was on a roll and just being his usual and sarcastic self. I got on a few bulls that I had hand picked. I was careful not to get on anything that I thought might hurt me.

I got on #T3 Loco because I had ridden him the previous year and he promptly bucked me off pretty hard. I knew I was very rusty. Later, I picked out a small Brahma with nub horns. Howard was sitting on a horse in the arena. I put my rope on the bull and was going through my pre-ride routine. Howard asked, "Andy, does that bull that Abraham is getting on have any horns?" Andy looked at the bull in the chute and looked back at his father and smiled and shook his head, "No." Howard had been picking on me every time I got on a bull that day. I had learned my lesson the hard way about getting on dangerous bulls just for practice and I was not going to repeat that mistake again.

The bull I was getting on was branded #12W and he didn't have a name yet. Howard had gotten under my skin and he knew it. I scooted up to my bull rope and said "outside." The little bull leaped high into the air for a couple of jumps and then turned back to the right (into my riding hand) and started spinning. He continued to leap high and spin. I had a good seat on him and for some reason I decided to take out my frustrations with Howard on this bucking little son of gun.

I started spurring him with my (outside) left foot. I had never spurred a bull before in my life and was not even sure that I could successfully do it. I was angry. The small crowd was loudly yelling and I could hear them, so the louder they yelled, the harder I spurred.

After a few rounds the yelling was interrupted by Howard telling me to, "Get off, get off!" Stock contractors are noted for not enjoying seeing their good bulls get ridden and spurred. And this was a good young bull having his first trip out of the bucking chutes and the last thing Howard wanted to see was one of his great new prospects get discouraged because he bucked his heart out and got spurred in the process. Bulls are just like people; they also need to build up their confidence.

One of the trademarks of my riding style was that I turned my toes out East and West and got really good deep holds with my spurs. I was also known to really hustle my feet and get new holds during a ride whenever a bull blew my feet out and away from his body. From that day forward I also realized that I could spur bulls with the best bull riders in the world. And for the rest of my career spurring bulls became a good— and sometimes bad—habit of mine. It was good at times because I would try to get a few extra points from the rodeo judges. It was bad at times because sometimes when you spur a bull, it's taking an even bigger risk. If your bull suddenly changes directions and your feet are not in contact with him it can cause you to buck off.

When I strutted out in the arena to retrieve my bull rope Howard snarled at me, "Wait until he gets bigger." At the time I was feeling pretty cocky and I thought by the time he gets bigger, I'll also be a better bull rider. So bring it on.

Everyone raved about my ride for the rest of the practice session. I will admit that I was shocked. I had no idea I could spur a good solid bucking bull like I'd just done. I didn't win any money because it was just practice, but my confidence had been raised several notches.

The first Cowtown Rodeo for the season was held on Saturday, May 31, 1977. I was delighted when I looked at the rodeo program to see #12W listed next to my name in the Bull Riding event. The young bull had another good trip and spun to the right. I ended up winning first place on him. The judges scored me seventy-one points and I won $245.00. During my ride, Jimmy Lee noticed I was weakening and he yelled at me, "Boy, you better hustle!"

Later on he told me that he deserved half of my prize money check because if he hadn't yelled at me, I would have bucked off. Although he was only kidding, I agreed with him because for some unknown reason, during that ride I had just gotten tired all of a sudden.

That bull was named #12W Bunny. He was a son out of #-10 Playboy and he went on to become one of the five best bucking bulls to ever come out of Cowtown. He grew up be a big solid and stout bull. He didn't ever get as big as his father, though. He was selected to buck at the NFR on a few occasions. He was featured in a highlight film clip from the National Finals Rodeo in December 1978. Bunny had leaped way up into the air which was his typical bucking style. He jerked Randy Magers from Comanche, Texas, down. They butted heads and Randy was knocked out cold. Even though he landed on his head, Butch Kirby, who was also at the NFR, said that the next day both of Randy's ankles were sprained and swollen, too.

Bunny was a very docile bull. He would not hook and would even let you pet him just like another bull, #C9 Andy. I once saw Chris Risoli sit on #C9 Andy in the bull pen at a rodeo in North Washington, Pennsylvania. He didn't even budge. Bunny was later purchased by a Canadian rodeo contractor along with a bucking mate, #514 Hagar.

That bull's original name was "Hagar the Horrible." He was named after a cartoon character because of his Viking-like horns. Hagar had been selected to go the NFR one year as a fighting bull. Fighting bulls were used on the Wrangler Bullfighting Tour to decide the PRCA World Champion Bullfighter. Hagar had a big set of horns that curved back right into the bull rider's lap. The following year he turned into a rank little son of a gun. He was again selected to go to the NFR but this time as a bucking bull. The bull riders at the Finals were not very thrilled when they saw the set of horns on Hagar. He would turn back, spin right in the gate and flash those horns right in the face of his rider. Hagar was a master at using those big horns.

The following year Hagar was again selected to buck at the NFR but only under certain conditions. Howard Harris had to cut back his horns because the PRCA Bull Riding director, Bryan McDonald, considered his horns to be very dangerous. Grant Harris was not very pleased because he had to severely trim Hagar's trademark horns.

Jimmy Lee said that one summer he bucked off of Hagar as he turned back and was spinning right in the gate. He landed on his back and saw Hagar's feet pass over his head. "Skimmer" said that he knew that that head and those big horns would soon follow in an attempt to scoop him up. He couldn't move fast enough and prepared himself for a mauling. T.J. Hawkins, who was then fighting bulls as well as still riding them, had diverted Hagar's focus away from Jimmy Lee and now had Hagar's undivided attention. "Skimmer" lifted his head only long enough to see that T.J. had one hand on each one of Hagar's horns as he was being carried across the rodeo arena like he was in the bucket on a small tractor. Jimmy Lee said he quickly turned from bull rider to bullfighter as he jumped up and ran after Hagar in order to rescue his friend, T.J..

Bunny and Hagar were always seen together whenever they were in the pasture in Canada. Tourists and kids could sit on Bunny's back and have their pictures taken. Dale Johansen set the all time

Canadian high marked bull ride of ninety-four points on Hagar in 1989 in Wainwright, Alberta, Canada.

Bunny became one of the most dreaded bucking bulls during his rodeo career at Cowtown and later in Canadian rodeos. He regularly jerked cowboys down and then would butt them in the head as he leaped back into the air again. There was no malice on his part. It was just the way that he had learned to buck and rid himself of cowboys. Otherwise he wouldn't hurt a flea. He would always ignore the downed cowboy and head straight for the out gate.

1977 turned out to be another successful year for me on the East Coast. I regularly placed and won money in the Bull Riding at Cowtown and the other Northeastern Circuit rodeos. I also worked at Cowtown during the week. This gave me two different sources of income on a steady basis. It had been a usual summer job for me for four different years. I did manual labor throughout the week and worked in the livestock auction on Tuesdays. On Wednesdays and Thursdays we cleaned up the trash that was left behind after the Flea Market.

In June 1977, I purchased my first car. It was a 1973 yellowish-gold Chevy Malibu. It was a very nice looking vehicle and it ran very well. Willie Ed nicknamed it "Old Yeller." The first week in July, I won the Bull Riding at Lake Luzerne, New York. This was a weekly PRCA rodeo held on Friday nights at the Painted Pony Ranch during the summer months. They also held a big rodeo during the Fourth of July weekend celebrations. Although I had heard a lot about it over the years, it was the first time I had ever entered a rodeo at Lake Luzerne.

I placed at Cowtown on Saturday night and then won first in the Bull Riding on Sunday afternoon in New York. I didn't see my family until Monday afternoon at a big family barbecue at Uncle James and Aunt Shirley Pope's house in Woodstown. My dad asked, "Skaber, how did you do at those rodeos?" (Skaber is my nickname.) I gave him the good news and he remarked that if I kept it up, I would have my new car paid off in no time. My dad, who was still a little skeptical about me riding bulls, was so proud of me. That made me feel even better.

The summer rodeo season ended all too soon for me. I had become the first cowboy to successfully ride two really good bulls. Number 12W Bunny was not ridden for the rest of the season. I also successfully rode #131W Eveready, who also had not had a qualified eight second ride on him. Both bulls were selected to perform at the NFR in their future rodeo careers.

In August I left home and went to a few rodeos on the East Coast and then ended up in North Washington, Pennsylvania for a couple of days. From there my cousin Cindy (Harp) Brandjord and I ventured back out west to Wyoming to attend college. Cindy had enrolled at Casper Junior College in Casper, Wyoming and I was returning to Laramie and UW for my junior year. My parents were so proud that I was heading back to school. To me it was not a big deal because I'd known all along that I was going to follow through and return to college.

15

Return to
the University of Wyoming

I was living in Orr Hall again. I received a really good reception from my fellow students when I returned to Laramie. I'd always been popular and well-liked and my friends were glad to see me. I was very glad to see them. Returning to school with my PRCA membership card and a car were two major goals that I had set for myself and I was very proud. I had a whole different attitude and walk when I strolled around campus this time.

When I'd left school, I had been a history major. During my year away I realized that the only thing I could do with a history degree was to teach. I knew that I didn't want to be a history teacher. So I decided to change my major to business. As a result I lost a lot of credit hours. That meant it was going to take me an extra year to graduate.

I had been told by several people that their college years were some of the most enjoyable times of their lives. I preferred to live on campus because I resumed my previous routine of playing basketball and working out in the weight room. Also, living in the dorms provided me with the opportunity to meet and associate with a lot more of my fellow students. I couldn't cook and really didn't have the time so it was very convenient to live on campus and eat in the Washakie Center student cafeteria.

When I graduated from High School I had been one of the shortest, skinniest boys in my class. I was tired of looking like a wimp and I had been going to the weight room on a regular basis in order to bulk up and gain some weight. Also I wanted to be in great physical shape for the demanding trials and tribulations of bull riding.

Our first college rodeo was held in Riverton, Wyoming. I drew bull #00 of the Harry Vold Rodeo Company from Fowler, Colorado. I wore one of my prized "silk" shirts made by my sister, Janice. I wanted to show everyone that I was a much improved bull rider since they had last seen me compete. Number 00 was a big white spinning bull with flat horns. I had seen him buck previously and knew that if I could ride him, I would surely place in the rodeo.

I went through my pre-ride routine and psyched myself up for the ride and did a lot of strutting and jumping around. When I finally sat down on my bull, I was completely drained. When I started warming up my bull rope I tried to pump myself up again but to no avail. I had worn myself out with all of the moving around and I had nothing left in the tank.

Number 00 had a good trip and bucked me off. I was very disappointed. I made a decision right then and there that I would never again wear myself out by bouncing around so much before a ride. In the future I would do my physical warm up and then sit down and relax so I would be physically as well as mentally prepared.

During the rodeo, a bright young bull riding star named Jeff Chadwick was making an excellent ride on bull #14W. He was a big, tall, slab sided, brown brindle bull who had a very long set of horns. The bull was bucking and spinning away from Jeff's riding hand and he had a good seat. All of a sudden we all heard a loud "crack." The bull had reached back with his horns and literally had knocked Jeff about a foot off of his bull rope. Undaunted, Jeff continued to try to make the whistle but bucked off. I was amazed both by the heart of that bull rider and the concept that a bull could just beat a cowboy off of his back with his horns. A few years later PRCA Bull Riding director, Bryan McDonald, permanently banned #14W from the PRCA because he was just too dangerous.

Also, during that rodeo one of my fellow rodeo team members, Doug Carr, fell in love with my shiny maroon shirt with the mushrooms. He asked where I had purchased it and I told him that my sister had made it for me. He responded by telling me, "I'll own that shirt!" I pretty much ignored him until I returned to my dorm room in Laramie and opened up my garment bag to discover that my pretty shirt was indeed gone. To this day I don't know how Doug managed to get his hands on my shirt, but a couple of weeks later I went over to his trailer house and his roommates Howard and Gary Huxtable, also UW Rodeo Team members, gave it back to me.

During the fall season I still had not broken the ice and at least placed at a college rodeo. The only requirement to letter in the sport of rodeo was to place in a college rodeo.

A major highlight of the fall was attending college football games. I've always loved to laugh. Hanging around other rodeo team members such as Kurt Humphrey, Mike True, Steve True, Jeff Ketcham and Guy Givens always kept me in stitches. It was a tradition for the college students to go to the bars on Wednesdays, Fridays and Saturdays.

After the fall semester, I was back in New Jersey for the

Christmas and semester break. As usual, I went to Cowtown on a Tuesday. Because of the Flea Market it was still a popular place to hang out.

The Harp family lived in one home there and Roland and Vera Shorter lived in another. It seemed as if the Shorters had called an impromptu gathering at their home as Willie Ed, Jimmy Lee and Gene Walker showed up. Gene had just returned from a trip abroad filming *The Black Stallion*. He had played a role as an Arab before the shipwreck that set the black stallion free. Gene had also led one of the horses onto the race track during the big match race near the end of the movie. Stanley and Freddie Thomas, Buck Howard, Andy Harris, Mark and Ike Redd, Eddie Shorter, Kaye Kirby, Johnny Harp and I all converged on the Shorters' home.

We were all saying, "The gang, the gang is all here." It had been years since we'd all gotten together for any type of an occasion. We decided we'd better have a drink and a toast to the Cowtown Cowboys. Before we could toast, Stanley Thomas made a very profound statement that none of us paid much attention to until less than two weeks later. He said, "Y'all had better enjoy this moment because in ten years some of you guys are not going to be around."

Kaye Kirby was found dead about ten days later.

Genie gave me permission to wear one of his trophy belt buckles because I didn't have one. Jimmy Lee had most recently worn the buckle won by Genie at an NIRA College Rodeo. Jimmy Lee had won his own buckle in the Bareback Riding event during the summer of 1977. Genie wanted to know how soon he would get his buckle back. I told him, "As soon as possible." I wanted very badly to win my own trophy belt buckle. Later that evening several of us went to the Turnpike Inn in Carney's Point, New Jersey, where we would hang out on Saturday nights after every rodeo performance.

Afterward, Stanley Thomas gave me a ride to my parent's house in Monroeville. I said goodbye to everyone and told Kaye that I would see him in Denver at the National Western Stock Show and Rodeo. It would be the first time that I was eligible to enter that prestigious rodeo. Little did I know that Kaye wouldn't make it to Denver and that I would never see him again. His funeral was on the same day as my airline flight back to Wyoming and I was not even able to attend.

I always cried whenever I left home. This time, some of those tears were also for a friend who, without a doubt, was the greatest bareback rider to ever come out of Cowtown.

16

1978

At Denver, I rode #J2 and even though he was an NFR bull, he spun kind of sluggish and slow. I spurred him and was only scored about seventy-two points. Next I got on Bernis Johnson's #47 Rainbow. He was a big Charolais and former NFR bucking bull. He crowded his head and neck into the back corner of the bucking chute before I nodded my head. Concerned, I asked Bernis if he would leave the chute okay from this awkward position. He assured me that it was fine and so I said, "Outside." He ended up falling on me right out of the chute. I was given a re-ride.

It's a little frightening to have a bull fall on you. They are extremely heavy animals and can easily break your leg. Plus, once they fall on you, they usually thrash around and kick until they can get up again. This just adds insult to injury.

My re-ride bull spun hard to the left and bucked me off. Brian Claypool, an NFR qualifier in the Saddle Bronc Riding as well as the Bull Riding events from Saskatoon, Saskatchewan, Canada, complimented me on my ride and said that I had a lot of try. I told him that, "I hate for bulls to spin to the left and away from my riding hand." Brian told me something I never would forget. He said, "Bulls that spin away from your hand are actually easier to ride because you can reach out over them and stay down a lot easier."

Over the spring semester break I caught a ride to Phoenix with Theresa Brown, a UW student from Thermopolis, Wyoming, and her roommate Tammy Abreu. Theresa's mom was not too fond of the idea of me staying at their home so I ended up staying at the YMCA for a week. I caught the bus to a rodeo in Globe, Arizona. From there I jumped in with Rob Erickson, a former UW student from Glendive, Montana, and John McDonald from Red Bluff, California. We all spent the night in Globe. On our way back to Phoenix, we stayed with a lady who lived in Tempe, Arizona. The next morning when I woke up, I didn't know where I was. I had been moving around and sleeping in so many strange places that I didn't recognize my surroundings. It was a very weird feeling. I rose up and looked around the strange bedroom and then it dawned on me. Only then could I lie back down and relax and go back to sleep.

I competed in the rodeo in Phoenix. I bucked off of #J2 of the Cervi Rodeo Co. and landed on my head. The picture was published in the April 5, 1978 issue of the *Rodeo Sports News*. I looked just like an ostrich that had stuck its head into the ground. It was amazing that I didn't break my neck.

After the rodeo I met up again with Theresa and Tammy for our ride back to Laramie. A rodeo fan saw us walking across the parking lot and ran over to me and said, "Hey man, that was an excellent run that you made tonight in the Calf Roping event, but you need to work on your Bull Riding." He had mistaken me for Sylvester Mayfield from New Mexico, another black cowboy who had made an excellent run in the Calf Roping event on that same evening.

Apparently, that overzealous rodeo fan had not made the distinction that we were two different people. It was probably because at the time there were only a handful of black cowboys on the PRCA circuit. Theresa and Tammy sure got a kick out of the fan's remark. They couldn't wait to get back to the University of Wyoming to tell the other rodeo team members about my bull ride and the fan's comment following the rodeo in Phoenix.

The annual Laramie River Rendezvous College Rodeo was scheduled for March in the UW Fieldhouse. In anticipation of the event, the Rodeo Team set up a display case on the main floor of the Wyoming Student Union with all of the championship trophy belt buckles that were going to be handed out at the conclusion of the final performance. I would walk by the display case going to and from my classes and drool over them and hope I could win and eventually wear one. The University of Wyoming awarded the nicest buckles, by far, in the Central Rocky Mountain Region of the NIRA. Since I had never won a buckle, I especially wanted to win one of those B-K trophy belt buckles.

A fellow student named Jeffrey Fry, who was an English major, lived on my floor in Orr Hall. His class assignment for the semester was to write a story about another student who he thought was interesting. He approached me and asked if I would be interested in doing an interview because I had a unique story to share. The story was going to be printed in *The Branding Iron,* the official school newspaper, which was published five times a week.

After we did the story, the school paper decided to run my story to coincide with the college rodeo. The college rodeo was to start on Friday evening and my story was published in *The Branding Iron* on that Thursday, March 30th. When I walked into the cafeteria on Thursday morning, a student named Larry Singletary saw me coming and reached for the newspaper laying on the table. I immediately knew that my story was in it. Larry blurted out, "A whole page, a whole page," in reference to the article about me. The story was entitled, *A $7.50 Prize and This Cowboy Was Hooked.*

I received a lot of compliments all day long from my fellow students. My response to each of them was that I didn't write the article and that the real credit should go to Jeffrey. Being a little shy, I sometimes I wanted to hide because I felt as if everyone was staring at me all day long. I know that a lot of the students were trying to figure out just who the black guy on campus was who rode bulls because I would never dress like a cowboy in my daily activities. I also was a regular at the Corbett Gym on campus and played basketball weekly after class. A lot of the guys that I played with had no idea that I was a rodeo cowboy. Besides, I wasn't sure I wanted the publicity before the rodeo. If I didn't do well, the notoriety from the story would be hard to live down.

The stock for the rodeo was drawn by lottery on Thursday evening. Andy Hamaker, a rodeo team member, called me on the telephone to tell me what bull I would have to get on during the Friday night performance. I immediately told him I didn't want to know because I had already gone through enough pressure for one day. I also had to study for an important exam on Friday morning and I needed to concentrate on that first.

Finally, the pressure got to me and I just had to get out of Orr Hall for the evening. I decided to go over to the Coe Library in order to study. Usually, I studied in my dorm room since I had a room to myself. But the phone was ringing and people were dropping by. I needed a little privacy.

I found myself a very secluded place in the library and settled in for a session of uninterrupted study. As usual, there were several current issues of *The Branding Iron* lying around on the tables. As I was sitting there, I noticed that two other students kept looking at me. I pretended to ignore them. They would look at the article with my pictures and then look over at me again. After several moments they pointed across the room at me as if to say, "There he is." I couldn't even go to the library to hide and escape the pressure.

The next day, right after my exam, I went straight to the rodeo office in the Student Union to check the draw. Next to my name I saw #00, the same bull that had bucked me off in Riverton at the college rodeo the previous fall.

During those two days I was complimented again and again by a lot of my fellow students on the newspaper article. Many people wanted to know when I would be competing in the rodeo. They assured me that they would be coming over to the Fieldhouse to watch me ride. All during the day, the football players continued to urge me on. Most of the football players who lived on campus were living in Orr Hall. They all wanted to see me, "do it up," as they kept telling me throughout the day.

That evening I put on one of my "Flash Gordon" polyester shirts, a brown shirt with patches of white on it. A couple of my friends in Orr Hall wanted to walk over to the Fieldhouse with me.

When the elevator doors opened, the lobby was full of football players. As I stepped off the elevator in full cowboy attire, a big war hoop came up from the guys sitting in the lobby. "Abe, Abe, Abe. Are you going to do it up tonight? We're all going to come over to the Fieldhouse to check you out."

I acknowledged them and as I was leaving one of the girls called out. "Hey Abe Morris, just because you had a big article in the newspaper now you think that you're a superstar, don't you?" My first thought was "Why is Tina Nelson cutting me down like this?" Apparently she thought that all the celebrity stuff was going to my head.

I thought I'd done a pretty good job of handling all of the media attention. In fact, I had even tried to hide out in the library.

As I was walking out of the door I turned to her and took off my hat and tipped it saying, "My cowboy hat still fits!" I put my hat back on and strode out the door. I heard a huge roar erupt from the impromptu audience behind me in the lobby.

I was a very, very nervous person when I arrived at the rodeo. I realized that I couldn't hide but I really didn't want to associate or talk with anyone. I knew that every one of my moves would be watched by my peers as well as the Laramie rodeo fans. They all knew about the newspaper article and I had a lot to live up to. I didn't want to let them down but more importantly, I didn't want to let myself down. There was an extreme amount of pressure on me to perform well.

I set down my rigging bag with my rodeo equipment in it and did a few stretches and exercises to loosen up. I knew that I had to get away again, so I looked for the most secluded place that I could find to sit down and still be able to see the rodeo action. I went up to an area of the second floor of the Fieldhouse where no else was and sat down by myself. I had a view directly above the bucking chutes on the northwest side. Every now and then I would see one of the rodeo cowboys behind the bucking chutes point up at me as they were talking to other cowboys.

After awhile, I was joined by Jerry LaValley from Claremore, Oklahoma, a rodeo team member who also was on the UW wrestling team. He had to compete that evening in the Bull Riding event and figured I had the right notion in mind when I decided that I just wanted to be left alone for awhile. I needed to be able to relax and concentrate. I didn't want to work myself up again like I did the previous time when I'd drawn this bull and he bucked me off.

My cousin, Cindy (Harp) Brandjord had come down from Casper to watch the rodeo and was sitting in the stands. We'd already decided that if I made the whistle I would throw my cowboy hat to her in the grandstand. I'd never before thrown my cowboy hat after making a qualified ride.

I still had a mental block about riding bulls that spun away from my riding hand. I had asked Miles Hare, a PRCA World Champion Bullfighter from Gordon, Nebraska, to turn my bull back and entice him to spin to the right. Number 00 was known to spin in either direction and I figured that I would have a lot better chance of riding him if he spun to the right and into my hand. Miles encouraged me not to worry about it and said, "You can handle him no matter which direction that he spins." He sure had more confidence about my bull riding skills than I did.

Scott McClain was the first bull rider and he successfully rode #33 Panda Bear, the 1976 PRCA Bucking Bull of the Year that was owned by Bill Milnes from Colorado. Scott set the pace with a score of seventy-four points. Panda Bear had an off day and although he spun in both directions, he was kind of slow.

Finally, the moment of truth was upon me. I eased down on #00 to an eruption of applause from the boisterous crowd. There was little doubt that a lot of the fans had come to the rodeo specifically to watch me compete. The rest were naturally pulling for the hometown guys because we were hosting the rodeo. My heart was beating so fast that I felt like it was going to pop right out of my shirt and cloth vest. We were required to wear a vest designating the college that we were representing and I was wearing a gold colored vest to represent the brown and gold colors of the University of Wyoming.

Double Ought Buckshot kicked hard out of the chute, made two jumps and turned back to the left and started to spin. I had a good seat on him and was making big sweeping motions with my left free arm. I knew that he was bucking hard. I was trying so hard that I could hear myself screaming during the entire eight seconds ride. It was pretty much a total blur to me. I was really hustling my right foot on every jump and it looked as if I was trying to spur the bull. My ride seemed to last for a long time and I could hear the deafening cheers. We were definitely raising the roof and rocking the house.

Finally, I heard the eight seconds whistle blow and I reached down and grabbed the tail of my bull rope with my free hand to untie myself and loosen my grip. As I dismounted #00 and was sailing through the air, I arched my back in exultation and threw both of my arms into the air. I looked like a gymnast dismounting the rings or pommel horse in an Olympic competition.

I landed on my feet and headed straight towards the grandstand and heaved my cowboy hat towards the screaming crowd. To say that I was ecstatic would be a major understatement.

The judges only scored me sixty-seven points. I took it very personally. It was one of the best rides that I ever made. Everyone knew that I should have been scored a lot higher. In comparison to today's scoring—which is much higher than when I was competing on a regular basis—I should have been about eighty-eight or eighty-nine points. I was very happy that I'd made a jam up ride in front of the hometown fans and equally disappointed that the judges would slight me by giving me such a low score. But I accepted it, knowing that there was nothing that I could do about it. I had done my part. I had lived up to all of the hype of the article in *The Branding Iron*.

Jerry LaValley competed during the slack after the rodeo performance was over. He rode a skinny black steer-looking bull that spun and did not have a lot of power. Jerry spurred his bull and was awarded seventy-one points. Again, I was disappointed by the judges because there was no comparison between the size and caliber of my bull and the small bull that Jerry rode. I didn't have any grudge toward Jerry, though. Even he told me that there was absolutely no way that his ride should have been scored higher than mine.

After the rodeo I went downtown to celebrate. I was feeling pretty good because I had handled the pressure well and ridden #00 this time around.

The next night I was slighted again by the judges. Britt Givens had bull #39 and clearly bucked off the bull before the eight seconds whistle. Number 39 was a really good bucking bull. "T.V." Tommy Jones, the rodeo announcer from Cheyenne, did not give the crowd the judges' decision right after the ride and so everyone assumed that Britt would receive a no score. Recalling my disappointment from the Spring of 1975 at this same college rodeo, I checked the judges' sheets before I left the rodeo to make sure that I was listed as placing 3rd following the first go-round (or long go-round). The finals or short go-round would start the following afternoon.

When I looked at the results from the first round, my name was not listed in third place. I was listed as fourth. In a panic I looked to see who was listed as placing ahead of me. The judges had scored Britt Givens seventy-one points and he had not even made the whistle. His older brother, Ronnie Givens, was one of the rodeo judges. I knew that I had been robbed again.

Britt Givens was a world-class bull rider who had already qualified for the College National Finals Rodeo on a couple of occasions. A few years later he would also become the World Champion Bull Rider at the Indian National Finals Rodeo. I knew that there was only one bull that he could not ride in this pen of bulls and that was #12, a high leaping white bull with horns who was known to jerk guys down and hurt them.

I said to someone, "That's okay, that's okay. Those judges cannot control the draw for tomorrow. God will intervene. Britt is going to draw #12 because he was not supposed to make the finals in the first place. I will draw just right and justice will be served."

There was one bull that I certainly did not want to draw and that was #14W. He bucked hard and intimidated bull riders with that huge rack of horns that curved right back into the bull rider's lap.

Sure enough, Britt drew #12 and was bucked off the next day. All of the other bull riders that competed before I did also bucked off. Finally, I was introduced to the roar of the home crowd again. I had drawn a black bull with big horns and a white face named Kingpin branded #49, also a past NFR bull originally from the Rolling Rock Rodeo Company owned by Dave Dancey from Pennsylvania.

Kingpin jumped and kicked pretty good. I was determined to let it all hang out and go for first place so I started spurring him at about the four seconds mark. I wore another one of my classic polyester shirts. This one was a pretty green one with various animals on it. After the whistle blew, Kingpin jerked me down and slammed me hard against the arena floor. The force knocked all of the air out of me. Even though I was hurting, self-preservation kicked in and I immediately jumped up and climbed over the panel fence. I was holding my stomach and I went back down again. A few people came over to see if I was okay but momentarily, I couldn't talk. I tried to say, "He knocked the wind out of me." But I could not speak.

I just sat there with my fingers crossed and watched the rest of the Bull Riding event. Only one other bull rider, Bobby Becker, made a qualified ride. Both of my scores were higher than his and as a result I was declared the 1978 University of Wyoming Laramie River Rendezvous College Rodeo Bull Riding Champion. The contestant with the highest total scores on two bulls would be the average (overall) winner.

I didn't stand up until the very last bull rider had bucked off and I knew that I had won the Bull Riding at our college rodeo. I kept thinking to myself, *I did it, I did it!* Even after the rodeo was over, I still knew that the judges could change their scores and so I told myself that I would not be satisfied until I was officially presented with the Bull Riding buckle. I had never won a trophy buckle and did not want to be so close and yet so far again.

A lot of people were coming up to me with their

congratulations. Although I was extremely happy, I refrained from getting too excited until I had that buckle in my hands.

Little did I know that I was going to have to deal with another big surprise. I remember the long, long wait following the rodeo to see if the judges were going to change the scores on me again. I told someone that if I didn't win the rodeo as announced that, "I will be the most disappointed person on Earth."

I was presented with the Bull Riding buckle. As I was handed my buckle by our rodeo team coach, Dr. Thomas Dunn, I thanked him and then I looked upward toward the heavens and also said, "Thank you God." Our rodeo also awarded a buckle to the UW male and female students who won the most points at our college rodeo.

Points were awarded as follows: forty points for First Place; thirty points for Second Place; twenty points for Third Place; and ten points for Fourth Place in the first and the second go-rounds and the "average winner"with the highest total accumulated points in that event.

I won ten points in the first go-round and forty points each for winning the second go-round as well as the average. My ninety point total also garnered me a second trophy buckle for the High Point UW Cowboy. As I was handed my second buckle, I again looked up and said, "Thanks." The big surprise—at least this time around—was a very pleasant one. I had come to the performance hoping to win one buckle and ended up winning two! I also ended up winning over three hundred fifty dollars for sixteen seconds worth of work.

Winning the Bull Riding after the big write up in the school newspaper was one of the highlights of my entire rodeo career. A good friend on my floor in Orr Hall, Ed Minnick from Hastings, Nebraska, made one of those little stars that are on the doors of Hollywood celebrities' dressing rooms and taped it to my dorm room door. I took it down but he insisted that I leave it alone so I reluctantly put it back up. I still have that little star.

All of my fellow students started to call me the "celebrity" for the rest of the semester. I was very happy and relieved that I'd finally won my own buckle. I could not wait to return Genie's and tell him the good news. There could not have been a better script written for this story. I had lived up to the billing of the article in *The Branding Iron* and had won the Bull Riding at my own hometown college rodeo. I would no longer be an unknown cowboy on the University of Wyoming campus.

After that rodeo I set my sights on a qualification to the College National Finals Rodeo in Bozeman, Montana, in June. I came up a little short and ended up in fifth place. (The top two finishers in each event qualified to compete at the CNFR.)

I was a little disappointed. Overall, it had been a good semester and one that I will not forget for the rest of my life.

After school was over I went to Grand Junction, Colorado, for a couple of weeks and stayed with bull riders Mike Clarke, Rocky Chadwick, and Craig Kemp. They were attending Mesa Jr. College. We had planned to go to Inglewood, California and Las Vegas, Nevada to a couple of rodeos. Wes Melvin, a bareback rider, came along with us.

We arrived in Las Vegas at night and acted just like a bunch of kids in a candy store, in awe of all of those bright lights. After spending a few hours in Vegas, we drove on to Inglewood to compete in the rodeo. I remember watching Mick Whitely, a good bull rider, compete. A couple of years later he was accidentally killed at that same rodeo when he was stepped on by a bull, #55 McClintock.

When I heard Mick had died, I remembered watching him in that rodeo in Inglewood. You feel like you know someone when you do the same crazy thing for money. There is an instant brotherhood among bull riders, sort of like being in the same branch of the military in a war.

Even though I never had the chance to meet Mick, I felt like I had lost a comrade.

We went back to the rodeo in Las Vegas and I competed in the midnight performance at the Convention Center. It was very strange riding a bull at about 2:30 in the morning. I was making a good ride on the spinning #52 EJ, of the Cervi Rodeo Co. and bucked off at about the seven seconds mark. *The Rodeo Sports News* put a picture of me on that bull in the June 28, 1978 issue. Jerome Robinson from Brandon, Nebraska, tied the Bull Riding on NFR bull #17 General Issamo with Vern Smith from Texas who also scored eighty points.

After this road trip I drove my Chevy Malibu back to New Jersey for the summer. I was very eager to show my family my two rodeo buckles and the newspaper articles from college. My parents, sisters, brothers, cousins and friends were all very proud of me. It made me feel really good. My sister Rosalyn asked if she could wear one of my buckles to school. I said, yes. I was delighted to let her sport one of my new shiny buckles. She was awfully proud of her big brother "Skaber."

Okay, I'll take the credit for starting the nicknames. I began putting an "Sk" in front of people's names. I called Cindy Harp *Skindy*, Jimmy Lee *Skimmy Lee*, and my name became *Skaber*. Only my nickname and Jimmy Lee's stuck. My closest friends called me "Aber Skaber." We called Jimmy Lee "Skimmer".

I remember attending my younger brother David's high school graduation. I was wearing one of my shiny "silk" shirts and one of my new shiny trophy belt buckles. I was feeling pretty good about myself. I had gone "out West" and now I had something to show off to all of the naysayers who didn't think I was ever going to amount to anything in the sport of rodeo.

My rodeo season at Cowtown was dismal. I was riding well but they would not let me get on any of the good bulls. As a consequence, I didn't win very much money.

I placed the first week that I competed and then was pretty much shut out for the rest of the season. The second week I rode #12W Bunny, but I slapped him and received a no score. As usual, Bunny had another good trip. I was not intimidated at all, even though he was a lot bigger and stronger than when I'd first gotten on him. I knew that I slapped him. I got upset because I felt that my little touch probably would have been overlooked if I'd been one of the selected favorites at the Cowtown Rodeo. I had seen other contestants slap bulls a lot harder than I did and still receive a score.

I saw Kaye Kirby successfully ride #2046 Brown Mule (Cowtown) in 1968 and slap him three times with his free hand. On his way back to the bucking chutes, he received a score of seventy-one points and Howard Harris asked, "Kaye, how many times did you slap him?" At this stage Kaye held up three fingers and said, "Three times Howard, three times." As a result the judges subtracted three points from his score and he still ended up winning first place in the Bull Riding at Cowtown that particular week.

Howard Harris started bucking all of his "A" string best bulls in the third section during the rodeo performances. The mediocre "B" and "C" string bulls were bucked in the first two sections. At the time, there were enough talented bull riders coming to Cowtown that if you didn't ride one of the good bulls, then you weren't going to place in the rodeo.

We figured out that the bull riders were put into sections according to when they called into the rodeo office to enter the Bull Riding. I got frustrated because I kept ending up in the first section of the Bull Riding. So I waited until the last minute to enter the rodeo, even though I was right there at Cowtown and working during the summer months again.

The rodeo secretary questioned why I always waited until the last minute to enter the rodeo even though I was on the property working all day on Fridays. I told her the reason why and the rest of the summer no matter when I entered the rodeo, I ended up in the first section of the Bull Riding.

I didn't take it well. I became pretty bitter as well as vocal about the whole affair. Even the timer showed her consternation at my attitude. One week I rode my bull for about twelve seconds before she finally blew the whistle. I walked back to the chutes talking trash and glaring up at the women in the crow's nest. Stanley Thomas said, "Ham, next week you are only going to have to ride your bull for four seconds in order to get a score." The rodeo judges didn't use a stop watch in those days. If you didn't make the whistle then you didn't get a score.

My parents, family, cousins, and friends all agreed that I was being treated unfairly. For a mild mannered person, I even started acting a little radical at times, as well. I would also show up to the rodeos and go behind the bucking chutes in short sleeve shirts and without a cowboy hat. I would later put on my cowboy hat and boots just in time to compete. I was not getting on any of the rank bulls so I didn't see any reason to mentally get psyched up. After I competed, I would take off my long sleeved shirt, boots and cowboy hat and go and sit in the grandstand and try to be incognito.

I made it very clear to all who would listen that because of this treatment, this would be my last season of competition at Cowtown Rodeo. I was going to rodeo out West in the future. I only drew two good bulls, Cowtown and Bunny, the rest of the season and both of these were at the road shows. I'm sure that the rodeo administration was tired of hearing me complain and I figured that it was just a good time for us to go our separate ways.

I bucked off of #W21 Cowtown, a black bull with little nub banana horns on a race track rodeo in Horseheads, New York. I landed on my head and momentarily was paralyzed. I could not move. I was very, very afraid. I couldn't even move my fingers. When my cousins and friends came to my rescue and asked if I was okay, I was going to say, "I can't feel anything. I'm paralyzed." But I was afraid to say the word "paralyzed" because I thought that I really was. So instead I said, "I'm, I'm dead." After a while I regained my physical senses and was able to walk out of the arena assisted but under my own power. I continued to feel a little tingling sensation for a spell. It was a very scary moment for me.

Howard Harris would tease me about this for the remainder of the season. Whenever I was getting on my bulls, he would crack a joke and say that I was the only man that he knew that returned from the dead to continue to ride bulls. Howard was like the old E.F. Hutton® commercials: Whenever he talked, people listened. And Howard loved it.

That was the first year that I entered the Cheyenne Frontier Days Rodeo ("the Daddy of 'em All"). I clearly remember watching Curt Gowdy call the action on ABC Wide World of Sports as I was growing up as a kid in New Jersey. I always envisioned myself competing at this prestigious rodeo someday. In my wildest dreams I never thought that I, myself, would be calling the action for the national TV broadcasts of that rodeo starting in 1989.

Several of the Northeast Circuit cowboys were also going to enter Cheyenne and we were going to drive out there together. At the last minute they all backed out. I decided to go by myself and ended up taking the Trailways bus.

I wore a very flashy, bright maroon shirt with mushrooms on it to compete in the rodeo on Tuesday July 25, 1978. My first bull, #6R, was black with horns. He jumped and kicked pretty good across the arena. I wanted to make a really good showing to the "toughs" so I started spurring him with both feet. Then Wick Peth, the bullfighter, turned him back and he started spinning to the left. I dropped my left foot, caught a good solid hold and continued spurring him with my right

Abe Morris

1978 Cheyenne, Wyoming
Wick Peth is the Bullfighter   *Photo: R.J. Satterfield*

foot. The gun went off and I stepped off on my feet and walked away as if to say, "Just another day at the office." I made it all look so easy.

On Wednesday, July 26th, I also successfully rode #F4, my second bull. Both of my scores were lower than I had expected. Again, I figured that one reason was because I was new and virtually unknown to the PRCA and major rodeos. The other reason, I am sure, was because I was black and from New Jersey. As a result, I didn't qualify for the finals but I had made a statement with my riding ability. The top fifteen cowboys in each event after the two rounds would compete again on Sunday afternoon.

I did not know very many of the top cowboys at this rodeo and I refused to go out of my way to bow down to them. I remember saying, "Hi Randy," to a well known Texas bull rider who qualified for the NFR several times. He looked right at me and just completely ignored me. I told myself right then and there that I would never say another word to that bull rider. And I never have. When I realized that I would not qualify for the finals, I hopped on the bus back to New Jersey.

I also started going to Lake Luzerne for their Friday evening rodeos. One evening I got on a black bull who was known to be particularly mean. He bucked okay but before the eight seconds whistle had sounded, the flank strap came off. We were out in the middle of a huge arena. I stepped off and started running for the side fence which seemed very far away. That bull ran me down from behind, mowed me over by stepping on me and then tripping and falling in the process. He was in between me and the fence. I jumped up and started running for the other fence in the opposite direction.

I made it safely, but since the flank strap had come off before the whistle, I had to get on him again for a re-ride. Willie Ed sure got a kick out of seeing me get caught from behind because he had constantly warned me about wearing chaps when I rode bulls. He was always telling me that one day my chaps would get me in trouble and slow me down and that a bull would run the length of my body. He sure did laugh pretty hard. He was even more amused because I was going to have to do it all over again.

Willie Ed was saying, "Boy, I done told you about wearing those chaps." Then he challenged me to wear them again during my re-ride. I had had enough of his harassment and did not want to give him any more excuses to keep on teasing me.

I didn't wear the chaps during my re-ride. This time after the whistle blew, I picked a better spot to get off but when I did, my spur got caught in my bull rope and jerked me to the ground. I didn't have a clue where the guys who called themselves bullfighters were during my first escapade. But this time I got safely away from that mean bull. To top it off, I placed in the rodeo on him.

But I still had to endure Willie Ed's teasing and bantering during the ride back to New Jersey and for the rest of the summer. He made sure that he told all of the guys back at Cowtown that I had gotten run over by my bull that night at Lake Luzerne.

I bucked off of #12W Bunny at the rodeo in North Washington, Pennsylvania. It was to be the last time I attempted to ride him. I guess if I wanted to brag, I could say that I successfully rode him three out of the four times that I got on him. I must admit that this was before he'd reached his prime. Bunny didn't receive the television or media coverage of the bucking bulls in the 1990s. Otherwise he would have been as famous or infamous as #J31 Bodacious, who was owned by Sammy Andrews from Texas. Any bull rider who ever saw him will tell you that Bunny in his prime was the "Bodacious" of the 1980s and was virtually unrideable.

After that rodeo I drove my Chevy Malibu back to college. That time I drove back alone because Cindy (Harp) Brandjord had fallen in love with the West and had chosen to stay in Wyoming for the summer.

I had met Gwen Mann, a fellow student in the fall of 1977. We hit if off pretty well but she had a big football player for a boyfriend. He didn't return to college that semester so we started dating in the fall of 1978.

I didn't exactly tear up the bull riding in the college rodeos but I did hold my own. At the Eastern Wyoming College rodeo in Torrington, I drew #49 Kingpin again. I had ridden him once and I figured that I could sure do it again.

He bucked a lot harder than he did when I won the UW college rodeo on him. He spun to the right after a few jumps and I had a good seat on him. I opened up and started spurring him with my left foot. He decided that he'd had enough of this action and then reversed the spin to the left. I had another good seat on him and I decided to spur him with my right foot while he was kicking and spinning to the left as well. All of a sudden he jerked the bull rope out of my hand. I was very, very disappointed. I was making the ride of my life and only bucked off because I lost my rope.

Patty, another student whom I didn't know, called in September and asked me to be a bouncer at the Holiday Inn during the National Finals Steer Roping. The Holiday Inn was going to be the official headquarters during that PRCA event. I told her I wasn't big enough to be a bouncer. She knew that I was on the rodeo team at UW and that I knew a lot of the cowboys. She just wanted someone on duty who could talk the cowboys out of acting up and dancing on the tables during the celebrations.

I accepted the job and was hired onto the banquet crew afterward. Larry Mahan and his rodeo band were the entertainers for the event. He gave me an autograph and one of his T-shirts with his name on it. I ended up working off and on at the Holiday Inn on the banquet crew until the summer of 1982. When I left, I had been promoted to Banquet Manager. During my tenure, I hired Gwen Mann, Brad Morris, Gerry Strom and Shaw Sullivan to work with me. But the call of the wild and the rodeo trail prompted me to hit the road once again.

17

Spring of 1979

I wasn't even able to purchase my PRCA card due to lack of funds. I went to the rodeo in Denver but I was relegated to spectator status and that did not sit very well with me. I also had a mediocre spring tour in the college rodeos and never did challenge for a qualification at the College National Finals Rodeo.

Gwen Mann had asked me to spend the summer in Laramie with her, so I did. She attended summer school at UW because she didn't want to go back to Lander, Wyoming for the summer. I had sworn not to rodeo in the Northeast (now First Frontier) Circuit anymore so this was my chance to live up to my statement. I was not financially able to enter a PRCA rodeo until the Laramie Jubilee Days rodeo which was held in July. I also changed my PRCA circuit affiliation to the Mountain States Circuit, which consisted of the states of Wyoming and Colorado.

I traveled to rodeos almost every weekend and then worked at the Holiday Inn during the weekdays. I traveled with Ronnie Christensen from Laramie. I didn't go to a lot of rodeos. I do remember winning second at Rock Springs, Wyoming and a nice paycheck for riding #U5 Clint. He went a few jumps before turning back and spinning to the right.

After summer school was over at UW, Gwen and I drove back to New Jersey and spent a couple of weeks visiting my family. Everyone thought for sure that we would eventually get married.

I entered the Bull Riding at Cowtown Rodeo when I was back there. I didn't mind entering rodeos on the East Coast but I was determined not to stay there for the rest of the summer and compete. On that particular evening I witnessed the best trip of any of Cowtown's bucking bulls in my entire life.

Charles Shorter, "Chan," the younger brother of Roland, had started riding bulls because of Junie's influence. They were distant cousins of Eddie Shorter. Charles had drawn #12W Bunny for the third or fourth time. It had rained pretty hard during the day and continued on and off during the rodeo performance. The rodeo arena was a deep sea of mud.

I was standing on the back of the bucking chutes with Stanley Thomas. Bunny jumped so high into the air that I had to look up. I was astounded at how high that bull could get in the air. Charles would have been better off if he'd had a pilot's license instead of a PRCA permit. I believe that he would have been safer holding onto the ripcord of a parachute rather than his bull rope for the air at that altitude must have been very thin. Bunny jerked Charles down extremely hard and they butted heads. Charles didn't get knocked out but walked away with a major headache.

I asked Stanley if Bunny had been bucking like that all year. Stanley's response was, "He has been bucking harder than that all year long." I could not believe that a bull could jump that high under such adverse arena conditions. I just shook my head in utter disbelief.

Later on I was told that Charles had gotten on Bunny at Herrington, Delaware. It was a racetrack rodeo and the ground was extremely hard and virtually served as a launch pad for that four-legged rocket ship. During that match Charles and Bunny had head butted each other again. They said Bunny had jerked Charles down so hard that on his way to the out gate and stripping chute, Bunny himself was shaking his head in surprise.

This prompted another sarcastic remark from Howard Harris, III, who said, "I am going to have to invest in some kind of a super helmet to protect the head of my prized bucking bull."

On our return trip to Wyoming, Gwen and I went to North Washington, Pennsylvania. I got on #131W Eveready, who would be selected to buck at the NFR in 1981.

When I was almost set to nod my head, Eveready was leaning against my leg and I couldn't slide up to my bull rope. I was about nine inches off of my rope and so I asked someone behind the bucking chutes to "push him over." I was looking down so I could slide up as soon as he released some of the pressure from my right leg. All of a sudden, the gate came open and I was immediately bucked off. I was very surprised because I didn't even see the gate swing open. Otherwise I could have at least reacted to that initial jump.

In disgust I took off my cowboy hat and threw it to the ground. I told the judge, Marty Stein, that I did not nod for the bull but he said that I'd attempted to ride him. All I really did was just get pulled along as Eveready left the bucking chute. I was denied a re-ride by the judges. There was a long heated argument right after the rodeo was over because I insisted that I did not call for my bull.

Willie Ed was ready to fight. He had pulled my rope for me and heard every word that I said prior to me getting bucked off. I was upset because Eveready was a very good bucking bull and I could win the Bull Riding event on him. I had won the Bull Riding at Cowtown on him in 1977 when he had gone unridden for a long time. He was now bigger and bucked a lot harder.

Marty Stein confronted me. He wanted to hear directly from me exactly what had happened. I looked Marty in the eye and told him that the last thing that I said was, "Push him over." The next thing I knew was that the gate came open. Any gate man that was paying attention would have seen that I was almost a foot off of my bull rope and would not have opened the gate.

Finally, in disgust I vowed never ever to come back to another Cowtown Rodeo production and headed off to put my equipment away in my rigging bag. Willie Ed was still throwing a fit. Marty threatened to fine him through the PRCA if he didn't back off and calm down. Someone came and told me that the judges had decided that I didn't have a fair shot in competing and decided to run my bull back into the bucking chutes.

Then Howard Harris got in on the act and wanted to know if he was going to have to load the chutes with all of the bulls that had bucked off their riders. He had to be sarcastic, as usual.

Eveready was again loaded into the bucking chutes. This time he bucked me off fair and square. It was a shame, though, that there had to be such an ugly incident and display of emotions in order for me to have a fair chance at riding him just like all of the other contestants.

After the rodeo, Gwen and I drove back out to Laramie. We were both previously selected and hired to be Resident Assistants in the dorms. We would be in charge of our floor in the residence halls and would have to work the front desk in the lobby. In exchange we'd be compensated with room and board. I still lived in Orr Hall and she would be residing in McIntyre Hall. McIntyre Hall, where the basketball players lived, had twelve stories and was the tallest building in the whole state of Wyoming.

By Fall of 1979 I had used up my four years of eligibility to compete at college rodeos. I did go to a couple of PRCA rodeos including Albuquerque, New Mexico. I bucked off of a pretty good bull at the New Mexico State Fair.

As usual, I spent a lot of time after classes either playing basketball in Corbett Gym or working out and lifting weights in the Fieldhouse. I'd figured out that the more that I exercised, the sharper my reflexes were. And the sharper my reflexes were, the better I rode bulls.

Gwen and I went to all the major sporting events including the football and basketball games. We continued to get along pretty well. In the spring of 1980 Gwen didn't return to school because she was enrolled in the Study Abroad program and going to Germany.

J.D. Hamaker, Britt Givens and I went to the Black Hills Stock Show and Rodeo in Rapid City, South Dakota. I remember Jerome Robinson putting his bull rope on a big Beefalo named Mount Rushmore. I didn't believe that this animal was in the Bull Riding but he was. It was the first and only time that I have seen a Beefalo used in the Bull Riding event. I had seen a few Scottish Highlanders used in the Bull Riding at some of our college rodeos. We didn't like them because they were extremely small with big horns. They were all slab sided without much of a back and they generally spun very fast.

I had #626 Erv, a small black bull that would spin in either direction. At the time I remember telling J.D., "I don't care which direction he spins. If I have a good seat when he turns back, I am going to spur him!" I was pretty confident of my riding as well as my spurring ability at that point. Number 626 turned back to the right and spun hard and fast. Sure enough, I spurred him and I ended up placing in the event. I guess one could say that I was pretty cocky at that time in my life. It was kind of like Babe Ruth pointing to the stands and then hitting a home run.

I was allowed to enter the UW Laramie River Rendezvous college rodeo on a permit which allowed a non-NIRA member to enter their hometown rodeo once during their college career. I bucked off of a bull named #13 Top Cat who was owned by Bill Milnes. (This was not the same bull as #C13 Top Cat from Cowtowbn.) That ride would officially end my college rodeo career. The UW Fieldhouse had given me memories that will last me for the rest of my life.

During this rodeo I ran into another young cowboy. For some reason we just did not hit it off and he kept giving me dirty looks. From a distance I saw him trying to read my trophy rodeo buckle. I zipped up my jacket in a very brazen gesture and he did not take it very well. Later on during the performance, he confronted me and tried to start a fight. I wasn't interested. The other cowboys asked me who he was. I told them that I didn't know and that I'd never seen him before. They were all saying, "Man you should have kicked his butt."

Later on I was just out to have a good time and was sitting on a pool table at the Cowboy Bar and Saloon downtown. I looked up and saw him. He noticed me look his way and then he started heading over in my direction. I thought, here he comes again just to start some more trouble. Instead he wanted to meet me and offered his hand. He said, "Hey man my name is Tony and I heard that you are a hell of a bull rider." That did not sit so well with me.

There were no apologies for wanting to fight me earlier. But now that he'd found out that I was a good bull rider, he wanted to meet me and be my friend. If he'd approached me differently, I would have been okay with him. But I didn't appreciate someone wanting to beat me up and now wanting to be my friend simply because he discovered that I was "somebody."

That has always been a pet peeve of mine. I've always been friendly enough to talk to anyone that is friendly to me. I've always despised people who act stuck up or refuse to speak until they find out that you're very talented and then go out of their way in order to try and get to know you.

I remember a bull rider from Oklahoma who qualified for the National Finals Rodeo in 1984. He always acted like he was too good to speak to me (although I will make a bold statement and say that there was no doubt in my mind that I was by far a more talented bull rider than he was!).

I was living with Gerry Strom in Laramie during the summer of 1985. I came home one morning and lo and behold, there was that Oklahoma bull rider, sitting in my living room. He'd spent the night and was on his way to another rodeo. I went out of my way to treat him just like he'd always treated me. I tried to make him as uncomfortable as possible because he never was friendly to me in the past.

I graduated in May from the college of Commerce and Industry with a Bachelor of Science degree in General Business Management. My mom, Christine Morris, flew out from New Jersey to watch me go through the graduation ceremonies. Graduating from college will always be one of the proudest personal accomplishments of my entire life.

18

1980-1981

When I graduated, I was flat broke. I really didn't have a place to live or to go. I knew one thing: I did not want to go back to New Jersey. So I opted to go to summer school. At least I would have a place to live and room and board in exchange for being a Resident Assistant. I was hoping that by the time summer school was over I would have won enough money rodeoing to find an apartment to live.

I did just that. I won first in Cañon City, Colorado in July. In August I moved out of Orr Hall to start from scratch and be completely on my own.

Pete Burns started a weekly open rodeo at the outdoor arena at the OK Corral. He was the announcer and Gerry Strom was flanking all of the livestock. One week Gerry was hurt and sore from riding bulls and couldn't flank. Pete said that he could flank the animals but he would need someone to announce the rodeo. By process of elimination they finally asked me if I would be willing to fill in as an announcer. I was not too thrilled. I was a bull rider and not an announcer but I finally consented to give it a try.

I said, "Good evening ladies and gentlemen. When I arrived here I did not know that I would be asked to announce this rodeo. Please bear with me and I will do the best I can." Afterward, the fans gave me a rousing round of applause. Pete Burns and the other cowboys were very impressed and I was asked to announce the remainder of the rodeos for the summer. My entry fees in the Bull Riding event would be paid in exchange for announcing. That's how my announcing career got started.

I had always been knowledgeable about the sport of rodeo and I had an excellent memory, so sharing my wealth of knowledge only seemed natural to me. I'm not a bit nervous to stand up and speak to an audience, especially if I know what I'm talking about. Since God gave me a good speaking voice, announcing and speaking was a natural fit for me. I eventually decided that I wanted to be a motivational speaker so announcing rodeos was a good start for me.

Gwen was in Bedford-Stuyvesant, New York, working as a nanny for most of the summer. She didn't return until right before school started again for the fall semester. I rodeoed with Ronnie Christensen again for the summer.

We went to a "Swanny" Kerby rodeo in Rifle, Colorado. My bull fouled me on the gate coming out of the chute and bucked me off. There was a big controversy afterward. One judge declared that I deserved a re-ride and the other refused to budge. I had to argue my case with the judge who refused to budge. Finally after the rodeo was over, there was a conference and I was awarded a re-ride.

I got on a black bull with horns who turned back to the right immediately out of the chutes and bucked hard. I opened up on him and spurred him every single jump. I should have won the Bull Riding event and yet did not even place in the rodeo. A friend, Jerry Dorenkamp, came up to me and said that he wanted to check my spurs because he was sure that they would be full of hair from that bull. Prejudice again; I was being judged by the color of my skin instead of my riding ability.

I would regularly practice and compete in jackpots at the OK Corral. Otherwise, I worked pretty steadily at the Holiday Inn in the banquet department.

I went to a rodeo in Phoenix in March of 1981. I bucked off of a pretty decent bull, #M23 Main Event of the Walt Alsbaugh (Alamosa, Colorado) bull herd. He went a good distance before turning back and spinning. He kicked me in the head when I bucked off and dazed me pretty good. I jumped up to run—my mind said to "go" but my body said, "no." I took about three steps and then I fell right back to the ground.

I was lying on my back and still trying to get up. Donnie Gay (the eight time PRCA World Champion Bull Rider) was the first cowboy to come to my rescue. He asked, "Are you alright Abe?" Then I knew for sure that I was still in a daze because Donnie Gay had never spoken to or said a word to me in my life. I had seen him many times but I didn't know he even knew my name until that moment.

That summer I rodeoed in the Mountain States Circuit with Ronnie Christensen again. We would go to a couple of circuit rodeos almost every weekend. Pete and Hal Burns' weekly rodeos were moved to the Albany County Fairgrounds in Laramie. They were held on Tuesday and Wednesday of each week so there wouldn't be a conflict of interest with other major rodeos. I was also paid thirty-five dollars for each performance where I handled the microphone.

At the Fourth of July rodeo in Greeley, Colorado, I drew up to compete in the morning slack. Slack is when there are too many contestants to compete in the designated performances and thus the overflow or extras must compete in the slack. The quality of the slack in the riding events usually is not near as good as the caliber of the stock in the regular performances where a stock contractor wants the paying audience to witness his best. This is the reason that a lot of the rough stock cowboys turn out in the slack by opting not to show up and compete. They really don't have a good chance of placing in the rodeo on the weaker bucking stock.

I had not been around a stock contractor by the name of Bennie Beutler very much. The bulls were in the process of being loaded. Usually in the slack there's no particular order. The cowboys compete as the stock comes into the bucking chutes. There were a few bulls already loaded. Finally, my bull was loaded and as soon as I put my rope on him Bennie yelled at me to get ready because I would be next. I didn't even have my glove tied on yet. There were at least three other guys who could have been bucked out before me. I always hated to be rushed by a stock contractor and I gave him a dirty look as if to say, *What about those other guys who have been standing here just waiting to get on their bulls?*

Bennie could sense my consternation and said, "Yeah, that's right, let's go here next. Come on cowboy up!" So I said to myself, *I'll "cowboy up" all right for you.* My bull just jumped and kicked and was weak so I started spurring him just like a bareback rider, every single jump with both feet. I made a qualified ride but I knew that I wouldn't place in the rodeo. After the whistle blew, I was walking back to the bucking chutes and Gene Oliver, a bull rider from Colorado yelled out to me, "Hey Abe, you get a no score because you missed him out."

In the Bareback Riding and the Saddle Bronc Riding events the cowboy must have his feet and spurs over the break of the horses' shoulders on the first jump out of the bucking chutes. This is designed to give the advantage to the animal. If a cowboy should have his feet and spurs out of position then it is considered "missing him out" and he will receive a no score. Bull riders are not required to spur. Gene was teasing me because I had spurred that bull like a bareback rider.

In August I went to the rodeo in Colorado Springs, Colorado. I had drawn a good black muley NFR bull, #2 Shadow, owned by Bruce Ford. Shadow was formerly owned by Sonny and Pat Linger from Montana. He jumped out and turned back in the gate to the left and spun. He had a good trip and I rode him very well. After the whistle, I was sitting on the fence and I was feeling very good because I just knew that I was going to win a lot of money at one of the major PRCA rodeos on the summer circuit. I was very, very disappointed when the judges only scored me seventy-four points.

Then, to add insult to injury, they moved me down to seventy-*three* points after the rodeo. Further insult occurred when Jeff Wahlert from Grover, Colorado, was scored eighty-one points on Shadow a few days later and won first place and over twenty-one hundred dollars. I was told by other cowboys that the bull had had a better trip with me and that information really only made matters worse. I didn't even place on the bull because it took seventy-*four* points to place in the Bull Riding.

I held no ill feelings for Jeff Wahlert because I always considered him to be a good friend. I would harbor some resentment though for the two judges that got to me. One judge's name was Jim. I never really liked him, and he never really liked me, either. He was determined that I was not going to place at any major PRCA rodeo where he was judging, though I'd never given him a reason to dislike me.

I got along with most of my peers and I was one of the most liked cowboys that was going down the road. I figured that the only reason he didn't like me was because I was black, and he showed it. He always had a surly look and never smiled whenever we crossed paths. I was bound and determined that if it took me to speak to him in order for him to start scoring me higher, then it was never going to happen. I had way too much pride and I was too stubborn so I refused to speak to him, especially since he screwed me over so many times during my rodeo career. I figured that sooner or later that he would get his due.

Ironically, I rode Shadow again in Longmont, Colorado about ten days later. When my score was announced, I immediately got an attitude and had some choice words for the judge as I was leaving the rodeo arena. I knew the judge, Jeff Chadwick personally, or otherwise I wouldn't have been so vocal. I admitted that it was wrong for me to throw a fit in the arena but I was being screwed again and I didn't like it.

My score had been incorrectly announced. After it was corrected I won first place in the Bull Riding event. I won about four hundred dollars. I would have preferred to have won the Bull Riding and the twenty-one hundred dollar check at Colorado Springs, but there was nothing that I could do about it except complain and just move on.

Gwen had graduated from college in May. She moved to Cheyenne and then to Denver in the fall. She broke up with me in the fall. I was really into riding bulls and I had a goal to qualify for the National Finals Rodeo. Gwen was leaning towards settling down and having a family. I was not going to quit riding bulls because I would have always wondered if I could have made it. She was looking for a career man with a good job and I didn't fit the bill.

In November, I competed in the American Royal Rodeo in Kansas City, Missouri at the Kemper Arena. I bucked off of my bull. I was featured in a half page article in the *Kansas City Times* on Thursday, November 12, 1981 titled, *Black Competitors Expected to Spur Rodeo*

Business in the Future. The article included two pictures of me, one a large headshot and the other one was of me competing during the rodeo performance.

19

1982

In February Bob Wren, a couple of other cowboys and I went to a rodeo in Minneapolis, Minnesota. It was extremely cold. My roommate, Shaw Sullivan, and I had drawn the same bull but he was scheduled to get on him earlier in the week. Shaw was traveling with another roommate, Hap Kellogg, who was California.

The bull had a very good trip with me and spun to the left. I made an excellent ride on him and even spurred him with my outside foot. The judges only scored me sixty-eight points. I didn't place in the event. After we returned to Laramie, I found out from Shaw that the same bull had an off day and did not even turn back with him and yet he was also scored sixty-eight points.

About a month later I saw Paul Chadwick from Fort Collins, Colorado, who was the rodeo secretary in Minneapolis at a party in

Laramie and he asked, "Abe, what place did you end up in Minneapolis?" I responded, "Man, I didn't even place." Paul thought that I was just pulling his leg, so he asked me a few more times. After telling him several more times that I didn't place, he was shocked. He couldn't believe I didn't win anything at that rodeo. Paul said, "In my opinion you should have won first place in the Bull Riding and yet you didn't even place. I really can't believe that. The judges must have deducted a point for every time that you spurred your bull. Man you sure got screwed!" My favorite rodeo judge, Jim, had made sure, once again, that I didn't place in a rodeo that he was judging.

This was the first year that I ventured south for the winter rodeos. At the time I was living with Shaw Sullivan, Brad Morris and Hap Kellogg in Laramie. I entered at Houston with Shaw, Dennis Humphrey and Chris Horton. Dennis would later qualify for the NFR in Bull Riding in 1985. It was pretty awesome competing in the Houston Astrodome.

I met a bull rider, Myrtis Dightman, from Crockett, Texas, for the first time. He, of course, was one of my heroes because he had been the first black man to qualify and compete in the NFR. I had always looked forward to meeting him. As a kid, when I rode junior bulls, people would call me "Myrtis" Morris and it had made me feel like a champion.

Myrtis invited us to come to his bar after the rodeo. We met up with B. Joe Coy from Torrington, Wyoming, and Charlie Needham from Riverton, Wyoming, and went to the Break Away Saloon. Charlie would later qualify for two trips to the NFR in the Bull Riding event. The guys that I was with were the only white people in the whole bar. Everyone was very friendly. Dennis was a little uneasy about being totally surrounded by black people in a bar setting so another one of the guys said, "Now you realize how Abe feels all of the time."

During the first performance at Houston, Charlie Needham got on #S7 Savage Seven, who was still owned by Tommy and Bobby Steiner. Savage Seven was the PRCA Bucking Bull of the Year in 1982. I saw #S7 buck on several occasions but I'm sure that this was the best trip I ever saw him have. I watched Donnie Gay ride him in Denver in 1986 and I saw Clint Green from Richton, Mississippi, ride him in Cheyenne in 1985. Clint fanned him with his cowboy hat to celebrate after he made the whistle. I don't believe that anyone could have ridden #S7 on that particular evening.

I rode my first bull and bucked off of my second. I didn't win any money. During Houston's rodeo we entered Monroe, Louisiana. After the performance several of the cowboys went to the Branding Iron bar to celebrate and dance. I went with Chris and Shaw. We had planned to stay overnight in a motel in Monroe and decided to take in the festivities, just like a lot of the other cowboys.

I did not know it was considered a "whites only" establishment but it wasn't long before I figured out that I was not welcome in that bar. At first, I thought that the animosity was generated because the locals didn't realize I was a cowboy. (I had left my cowboy hat in the car.) I told Chris that I was going outside to retrieve it and then hopefully the locals would ease their hostility after they discovered I was traveling with the other rodeo cowboys.

Chris went outside with me because I didn't dare go out alone. When we came back in, a guy who had been friendly to me came up to me and said, "Hey, if anything happens, man, you come and get me." Apparently there had been some arguments when we were outside. Then I really got cautious and became very, very aware of what was going on around me.

I was standing there, minding my own business, and all of a sudden some burly white guy came up from behind me and gave me a good forearm shiver right in the back. It knocked me off balance, especially since I'd never seen him coming. Then he hustled back and caught up with his lady friend and took her arm and sashayed onto the dance floor. That was a good enough hint for me. Chris was standing right next to me and saw the whole thing happen. I looked at Chris and said, "I think that it's time to go." He agreed.

As we were walking across the parking lot to the car, there were a few guys yelling after us. We had to run to the car in order to get out of harm's way. After this little incident I vowed that I would never go into another bar in the southern states again. I had been a little apprehensive about the Deep South before we even went to those rodeos. Now, I had first hand knowledge that racism was alive and well in the South. I don't mean to say that it doesn't exist anywhere else, it is just that in the South, it's pretty much in your face.

A few years later Chris Risoli told me that in October 1982 Charles Sampson was not allowed to go into a bar in Little Rock, Arkansas because of his race. Jimmy Lee Walker told me that in July 1980, a pickup full of white guys rolled down the street in Springdale, Arkansas firing racial slurs and telling them to, "be out of town by sundown."

We went back to Houston for the finals. Gary Toole, a regular NFR qualifier from Mangum, Oklahoma, won first and Charles Sampson from Inglewood, California, won third in the Bull Riding event. Charles Sampson, another African-American, would eventually be crowned the 1982 PRCA World Champion Bull Rider.

We hung out in Huntsville, Texas, for a few days with a friend of Charlie Needham's named Brady Williams, who was from South Dakota. Then we went on to Bay City, Texas for a rodeo. Charlie, Dennis and Shaw were all entered up in Phoenix, Arizona the next night, so we made an all night drive to Phoenix.

Chris Horton, "Hog," had obtained a doctor's release and caught a ride back home to New Raymer, Colorado. He'd suffered a major injury in his right hip pocket where his money was supposed to be. Hog gave us permission to keep his car and take it to Phoenix. Short of an accident, it seemed as if anything that could have gone wrong on that trip did.

We were on the road for less than two hours when we had a flat tire. All of the tires were already bald. Later on, the alternator started to go bad and we were stranded along the side of the highway. Luckily, someone was kind enough to stop and give us a jump so we could continue on our way. Then the car lights dimmed and eventually went out. Dennis continued to drive during the night without lights because otherwise we would not have made it to the rodeo in time.

Since the alternator was dead and we didn't have the time or much money to replace it, we had to leave the car running whenever we stopped. When we stopped for gas the next morning Charlie was pouring oil into the car and the engine caught on fire. Luckily we were able to quickly put it out with minimum damage.

The gas gauge on Hog's car didn't work so we had to constantly calculate our mileage between gas stations. Once we stopped for gas and asked the gas station attendant to fill it up. He asked us to shut off the car and we refused. He must have gotten afraid that a spark would set all of us on fire. He assured us that he had filled it up, but he hadn't.

Soon, we were flying down the road again and trying to make up for lost time when the low fuel warning light came on. We knew it couldn't be true since we'd recently filled the car up with gas. We decided to ignore it and keep on driving. Unfortunately, it was right and we were wrong. We were soon stranded on the side of the highway again. Fortunately we were close to a gas station.

Now, of course, we had to persuade someone to stop and give us another jump. After going to the gas station and making a few phone calls we decided to pool our money and purchase a re-built alternator for Hog's car.

It took some time for the mechanics to install it. We figured that we could still make it to Phoenix on time if we really hustled. Shaw got behind the wheel and was driving over ninety miles an hour. The front tires on Chris' car were out of alignment and the car would shimmy and vibrate as we flew down the highway. I was in the back seat and I packed the pillows around me because I just knew that we were going to crash and all be killed.

Somehow we made it to Phoenix but it was well after the rodeo had started. The guys still thought that they might luck out and be able to get on their bulls since the Bull Riding would be the last event. Dennis had #A7 Lollipop. Shaw had drawn Velvet Osgood. And Charlie had Liver Lips. These were all considered to be the better bulls in the Walt and Art Alsbaugh bucking bull herd. Each had a pretty good chance of placing in the rodeo.

I wouldn't have to compete for a few more days. After we arrived in Phoenix I became the designated driver so that the other guys could change into their riding pants and put on their spurs. Just about the time we all thought that they would make it, we were stopped by a very, very slow moving freight train. The guys could not believe that after all of the speeding and other misfortunes we'd endured, they would get shut out at the pay window by a freight train in downtown Phoenix.

After what seemed like forever we moved on. I dropped the three cowboys off at the top of the ramp and they ran because the bulls were already loaded into the bucking chutes. I parked the car and was able to watch each one buck off of their bulls. After this escapade they all headed back to Wyoming and left me in Phoenix. They gave me the option of keeping Chris' car and driving home alone in a few days. I told them, "No thanks" and that I would rather risk catching a ride with someone else later. I didn't want to drive that car another inch.

I bucked off #3 Goathead, of Bennie Beutler's bull herd from Elk City, Oklahoma. I was making really good ride when he jerked the bull rope right out of my hand. I placed on that same bull at Tucson in

1983. I caught a ride back to Wyoming with R.J. Satterfield, who lived in Cheyenne.

My cousins back in New Jersey told me about an all black rodeo that was going to be held in Washington, D.C. in early May. The Bull Riding entries were limited. I tried to enter but was told by the rodeo committee that I couldn't participate due to the number of entries. So, a little disheartened, I accepted the fact that I wasn't going to go to that rodeo. A little while later, I was invited to the rodeo over the telephone. I wanted verification that I would be entered in the Bull Riding and they assured that I would. I purchased my airline tickets and flew back East.

After we arrived in Washington, D.C. I was told that I wouldn't be allowed to compete because there were too many entries in the Bull Riding event. I got very upset and very vocal about the whole thing. I complained to the rodeo committee, the judges, my cousins and anyone else who would listen to me. I thought that it was inexcusable of them to invite me and after I forked out money for airline tickets, only to be told when I arrived that I was not entered. I was not concerned about "stepping on any toes" or making a scene because I knew I would never enter another rodeo produced by this organization. I didn't use any foul language but I did put on a good performance.

One bright spot was that I met Earl Campbell, a former Houston Oilers pro football player, who was then representing Copenhagen Skoal. He seemed like a really good guy. I had followed his football career when he was at Texas and loved to watch him play. He was a gifted and hard runner. I told him that I didn't want his autograph but I did want to shake his hand.

It was a two go-round rodeo. My younger cousin, Johnny Harp, made a good ride on a good spinning bull and won the first go-round. He ended up winning first in the average as well. After watching a couple of performances and wearing out my welcome, I decided to catch a ride back to Woodstown where my parents were now living on South Main Street.

I planned to go out to Cowtown Rodeo for spring practice on Sunday afternoon. I got on five bulls. Howard later loaded the chutes with his powerhouse bulls that included #O18 Brindle Velvet, #O30 Jersey Joe, #S8 Knocker, #C14 Elmer and #O27 Bucky. He told me to get on #O18 Brindle Velvet. Believe it or not I seriously considered getting on him. Then I changed my mind. Brindle Velvet had built up a reputation of being one "bad cat." There were cowboys who dreaded getting on him in rodeos and thus would turn him out. He was not worth getting on in practice and risking a serious injury.

Finally, I was convinced to get on #S8 Knocker. Howard named him Knocker because he had jerked Stanley Thomas down and knocked him in the head. He was a good size white bull and was well filled out. He would walk on his front end with a stutter step and then jerk cowboys down on his head. I didn't know anything about him before I got on him.

Knocker was kind of hard to get out on because he leaned against the back side of the chutes before I nodded my head. He blew out of the chute and bucked me off about the third jump. He was rank. I am sure that he only worked one or two seconds per week. Number S8 along with #O18 and #O30 would be selected to perform at the NFR later that year.

By the Summer of 1982 Pete Burns had obtained his PRCA Stock Contractor's card and planned to continue his summer rodeo series at the Albany County Fairgrounds. I applied for and was approved for my official PRCA announcer's card. This would allow me to continue announcing the weekly rodeos.

Initially, I would compete during the Bull Riding event. It was hard to go from announcing to competing right away. I could not adequately prepare myself physically and mentally to compete when I had been concentrating on announcing the rodeos. Non-competitors don't understand the psych job you have to do on yourself before you ride an eighteen hundred pound animal. Later, we started the rodeos with me competing on my bull. After I had a chance to catch my breath I would trade in my bull rope for the microphone and concentrate on my announcing for the duration of the rodeo.

I continued to travel throughout the Mountain States Circuit. That year I rodeoed with Bob Wren who was living in Laramie and attending UW. He was originally from Idaho. His close friends referred to him as "Spud" because Idaho was known for producing a lot of potatoes. Sometimes we would go over to Cheyenne to Rob Bunten's place and compete in small jackpot Bull Riding events. In a jackpot we would pay a small entry fee and a stock charge and compete. These sessions would usually only pay two places.

At Cheyenne Frontier Days Rodeo I drew #414 of the Pete Burns Rodeo Company. He was a huge white Chianina bull who weighed about twenty-one hundred pounds. I had been on him several times before at the OK Corral. He was a very thick and just seemed to get bigger every single year. And he was a strong bull. I remember him breaking the handhold on one of my grass bull ropes during one of his trips at the OK Corral. I had been one of the last holdouts for the grass ropes when most of the bull riders had already made the switch to poly.

Number 414 bucked me off pretty hard. I landed awkwardly on my head and I was knocked unconscious for the second time in my career. Later on, my friends told me that I did what was known as the "dead chicken." That's when you're out cold but an arm or a hand will quiver. It is very scary for the onlookers. Believe it or not, my friends teased me because I "took a dirt nap" and then quivered in the rodeo arena.

Later on that summer I was announcing a rodeo in Laramie and I made a comment to the audience about the bull's (#414's) bucking style. I said, "There is something about this bull that just knocks me out!" The crowd didn't pick up on the inside joke but all of the bull riders did and sure got a kick out of my comment.

During the Cheyenne Frontier Days Rodeo, many of the cowboys would go to the Hitching Post for the after hours celebrations and to take in "Ricky and the Redstreaks." They were an entertainment band who did a lot of zany stage skits. They had built up a pretty loyal following of rodeo groupies and fans. I'd never seen them in person and Bob Wren convinced me to go with him.

This was in the days when designer jeans were still popular. I decided to cast off my Wranglers, western long sleeved shirt, boots and cowboy hat. I wore a pair of designer jeans, casual short sleeved shirt and casual shoes. The only official thing that would connect me to the other cowboys was that I still wore my trophy UW rodeo belt buckle.

I was not the least bit concerned about fitting in with the other cowboys because I was still on what I considered to be home turf. Cheyenne was only forty-five miles from Laramie. I had been around rodeos long enough and I was pretty sure that most of the cowboys would know who I was. I soon found out that I could not have been more wrong.

Shaw Sullivan was in the bar and with a girl. I knew her because she had visited the house a few times in Laramie to see Shaw. I was just having a good old time, just like everyone else. I was minding my own business and she came over and started talking to me. She was having a little fun with Shaw. Well, for some reason, Shaw refused to come over and get her back. I was just chit-chatting with her and I had no intention of trying to take my roommate's girl away from him.

After a few minutes someone tapped me on the shoulder. I turned around and looked up to see four big cowboys. I recognized two of them. One was a PRCA World Champion Steer Wrestler from Texas and the other was an NFR qualifier in the Steer Wrestling event. They didn't have a clue who I was and really didn't care at that point in time.

The World Champion Steer Wrestler was the spokesman for the group. He said, "Hey, we saw you take that guy's girlfriend away from him and we don't like that stuff. So which one of us do you want first?" There had been people all around me in the bar until I turned around. They knew there was going to be a fight and they cleared out the tables and chairs and made a space like a boxing ring for the massacre.

Each one of these guys was bigger than me. I'm sure that any one of them could have beaten me up with no problem. Finally Shaw came to my rescue and explained to the big cowboys that I was his roommate. Their response was, "We don't care who he is. We saw him take your girl and we're going to kick his ass." Shaw continued to plead my case for me. I was speechless. I never said one single word during the whole confrontation. I knew that I was in for it and I was too afraid to talk.

They finally backed off and left me alone. But they continued to act very inappropriately for the rest of the evening. I stayed clear of them, but I never forgot that I was an innocent black man in a bar, just out to have a good time and they wanted to gang up on me because they didn't know that I was a rodeo cowboy, just like them.

The ironic thing was that the next day I saw them at the rodeo. I figured that they were still mad at me. I was decked out in my full rodeo cowboy clothes and none of them paid any attention to me, whatsoever.

In August 1989 I was competing in a rodeo in Dodge City, Kansas, and one of these cowboys offered to pull my rope for me in the Bull Riding event. I usually asked at least two guys to pull my bull rope. But he was big and stout enough that he didn't need any help and handled the job all by himself. By now he'd gotten to know me. I'm sure that he had no idea that he'd wanted to hurt me a few years earlier in Cheyenne. Now he was being nice to me.

In August, Bob and I were traveling to a rodeo in Colorado Springs. A major rainstorm had flooded the interstate in Denver and only one lane was passable. Traffic had slowed to a virtual crawl. We knew that this was going to make us late for the rodeo and we were not sure which exit to take to get to the arena. As we got close to Colorado Springs, I reached into the back of the Bob's car and retrieved my rigging bag. Remembering our trip to Phoenix earlier in the year, I changed into my riding pants, put on my spurs and taped the wrist on my riding arm.

Bob and I entered the arena from the time event side and could see that stock was already loaded in the bucking chutes. We flew down a narrow passageway between the rodeo arena and the grandstand. Bob claims that the fans saw us and cheered us on. I didn't hear them. Out of breath, I bailed over the fence and tripped on my rigging bag only to discover that we were just in time for the start of the Saddle Bronc Riding event.

I rode a big, brindle bull, #W2 of the Harry Vold string. He had a good trip and I spurred him the last three jumps and won fifth place on him. About a month later, Bob and I went to a rodeo in Imperial, Nebraska. I got on #111 of Harry Vold's and he stopped before the eight seconds whistle. Everyone hated this black bull with flat horns. He did not buck very well, was very mean and for sure he would hook you. The judges awarded me a re-ride.

Number W2 was going to be one of the re-ride bulls. He was hardly ever ridden and was considered to be a semi-eliminator. I was contemplating taking a re-ride and Shorty Garten from Sperry, Oklahoma, a NFR qualifier in the Bull Riding event, approached me and said, "If you draw #W2 for your re-ride don't get on him." I told him that if I drew #W2, I would have to get on him because I had placed on him a couple of weeks before at Colorado Springs.

Denny Flynn, a perennial NFR qualifier from Charleston, Arkansas, was winning the Bull Riding with an eighty-five point ride that evening on #3S9, a bull originally owned by the Sankey Rodeo Company out of Rose Hill, Kansas.

That night I made probably the best 7.9 seconds ride of my entire rodeo career. Number W2 blew out of the chute and kicked hard. But this time he turned back to the left and got it on. I knew that he was really bucking hard because I was screaming while I was trying to ride him. I could always tell how hard a bull was actually bucking because the harder they bucked, the louder I could hear myself screaming.

Jimmy Lee, being a bullfighter and always within hearing range of a lot of my bull rides, used to make fun of me because I would grunt and make some gosh awful sounds whenever I was really putting out a solid effort to make a qualified eight seconds ride.

I was trying so hard to ride the spinning #W2 that night that before the whistle, I over compensated and dropped into the well. I was hung up and I knew that he was going to beat the heck out of me, so as he swung his head and horns at me, I took my left, free arm and grabbed him around the neck. He was a tall brindle bull so my feet weren't touching the ground. Number W2 was still able to whack me right on my left eyebrow and split it open and leave me a permanent scar. I held on as best as I could until my hand came out of the bull rope.

I was stooped over on the platform on the back of the bucking chutes and I didn't know that my eyebrow was split until I saw a small pool of blood. The rodeo announcer called for the medical team but I turned down their request that I go to the hospital for stitches. Bob, Denny, Shorty and a few other bull riders gathered around me and I expressed my disappointment in bucking off right before the whistle. I said, "I was just hoping to place on him." Denny said, "Man you would have won the whole shooting match." I was told by Chris Horton, a pro rodeo judge, that I would have been scored ninety points for sure on that ride.

My eye was swollen shut for a few days after I took that hit. I wore my sunglasses whenever possible so that people couldn't see the damage.

Over the Labor Day weekend I won first at a rodeo in Greeley that was produced by the Bruce Ford Rodeo Co. from Kersey, Colorado. Bruce was a five time PRCA World Champion Bareback Rider and one of the greatest bareback riders of all time. I rode his best bull, #8 Clown's Velvet, for seventy-six points. I also won second place at the rodeo in Evanston, Wyoming, on bull #11 White of the Kerby Rodeo Company from Utah. I won over twelve hundred dollars for my sixteen seconds worth of fun.

A few weeks later Bob and I went to a rodeo and he drew Abdullah of the Dorenkamp Rodeo Company of Holly, Colorado. He was a weird bucking bull and no one liked to draw him. I laughed pretty hard because Bob drew him and that only served to make matters worse. He got pretty mad at me. Bob got bucked off.

The next Dorenkamp rodeo we entered was at Eads, Colorado. I knew that paybacks were going to get even with me and I told Bob even before we entered the rodeo that I was going to draw Abdullah at Eads. He did not believe me. When he called to ask me what bull I had drawn at Eads I said, "What did I tell you that I was going to draw?" Bob didn't believe me so he called PROCOM, to find out for himself that I really had drawn Abdullah. He still could not believe it.

When I nodded my head for the bull, he jumped into the air and twisted sideways as if to say, "This is where you can just get off." I bucked off and all I could do was to just smile. I wasn't even upset. I figured that if a bull could turn that much sideways in the air then I did not deserve to make a qualified ride on him.

Brad Morris had been going to get on bulls at the Bob West Arena in Arvada, Colorado, for quite a while. He finally convinced some of the other bull riders in Laramie to go because he claimed that the guy had some good bulls and a nice indoor arena in which to compete. He was right.

I finally went down to the West Arena for a Friday night jackpot. The bulls were loaded before they drew for the stock. The first bull to walk into the chutes was a colorful bull with a huge broad back. He was very well built and intimidating. My first thought was, *man I hope that I don't have to get on that broad backed son of a gun.* Well, I drew that bull named Blizzard.

Man did he buck. He is probably the first bull that I ever got on in my life that had actually turned back and was already spinning before I realized it. He first spun to the left. I usually knew and could feel it when a bull was initiating his move to turn back and start to spin. He was extremely quick for a big stout bull.

Then he reversed his spin and went back to the right. There was no such thing as spurring because this bull was bucking too hard. I had a good seat but I raised up my upper body and he bucked me off. Tommy Keith from Peyton, Colorado, was judging the jackpot and afterward he asked me if I had been going to any rodeos. When I told him, no, he said, "As well as you're riding, you need to get out of the house and start going to some rodeos." The comment sure made me feel a lot better even though I had bucked off of a rank bull that would easily have won first place in the jackpot.

In another jackpot I rode #111 Vic, a big tall slab sided white bull who jumped into the air. He would kick high and drop pretty good, just like a bareback bronc. He would have fit into the eliminator pen at the NFR. Back in those days I was very gung-ho and would spur almost everything that I got on if I had the opportunity. To spur a big bull like that would only be asking for trouble and risking getting jerked down on his head and possibly hit in the face, as well. But I did it anyway. It was a good trip for the both of us.

I should have won first place in the jackpot, but I didn't even place. I was just getting to know Bob, Steve and Scott West and I told them that I was not going to continue to come to their jackpots and be treated like this. I was pretty mad about it.

The very next week I drew #111 Vic again. Remembering the "screwing" that I had taken the previous week I started spurring sooner and harder on that particular trip. Vic even had a better trip with me as well. The scores were not announced during the jackpot and I was concerned that the judges were going to soak me again. Bob West kept saying, "I still have my money on you," meaning that he thought I should be winning first place on Vic.

After Randy Lopez and Dick turned in their score sheets they had me in a tie for second place with Mark Wade. Brad ended up winning first and his bull had only made one round and then cut a trail. (In other words he'd dinked off.)

I became very vocal and ballistic. Brad said to me, "Abe, at least my bull spun. Your bull never even turned back." I said, "Yea #37 made one round and then he ran off. My bull bucked three times harder than your bull did and I don't give a #@%*&^ what you have to say. You could not have ridden my bull with two hands!" I was hot!

I told the two judges (who were my peers) just what I thought of their judging skills and abilities. Later on we went to a bar because we were headed to a rodeo in Guymon, Oklahoma, the next day. Dick, one of the judges, confronted me in the bar and said that he didn't appreciate the way I'd carried on at the arena after the jackpot. He wanted to go outside so that we could fight it out. I told him, "No way." I wasn't afraid of him. I had better things to do than to get hurt fooling around with him. I had a whole bull riding career to look forward to and I was not interested in fighting him—or anyone else for that matter.

On another occasion I rode #3 Sam, a big strong white

bucking bull. At the time, he was the West's best bull and he didn't get ridden very often. He was called "Slamming Sam" because he always seemed to throw the power at his would-be riders and buck them off extremely hard. I won first in the jackpot on him. After the whistle, I stepped off right beside him and he kicked me with both feet in the back and knocked me down. I guess he was trying to make a statement that, one way or another, he was going to get me. Or maybe it was just his way of saying that he didn't appreciate anyone making a qualified ride on him.

Great bulls know when they've been ridden. I was told that after #7 Lizard of the Edker Wilson string from Alamosa, Colorado, was successfully ridden, he was so mad that he went back to the bull pen and started to fight all of the other bulls.

We went to jackpot bull riding sessions at the West arena for several years. Besides the Friday night jackpots they also held larger jackpots during the major holidays like Halloween, New Year's Eve, and St. Patrick's Day. The West family had a good pen of bucking bulls. The facility was first class and it even had a grandstand to allow spectators a safe place to watch the action. There was always a good crowd on hand for each jackpot and it became a very popular place to hang out. Bob, Joyce, Steve and Scott West were all extremely nice and congenial to all of their patrons. It was a very popular place for fans and riders to go to for many years.

There was an abundance of rodeo cowboys and good bull riders who lived in Colorado and Wyoming at this time because it was right after the "Urban Cowboy" fad had swept the country. Everyone wanted to be a cowboy and take their shot at riding either a mechanical or a real bull. We were fine with the urban cowboy fad. It brought a lot more interest and attention to the sport.

Over the years I won my share of the money at the –W/ Arena. Brad Morris, Gerry Strom, Hap Kellogg and I liked to go to Colorado because it always seemed to be warmer than Laramie. We always made it a point to stop at Verne's in Laporte to get a huge sweet roll. They were the best in the area. Sometimes we would buy two sweet rolls and save one for later. We always looked forward to making a pit stop there.

In the fall of 1982 I started working as a counselor at the Cathedral Home for Children in Laramie. It was a residential treatment facility for delinquent adolescents otherwise known as "at risk youths." It was a very challenging job and stressful at times. It sure made me thankful that I had been raised in a normal family setting. All of these kids came from dysfunctional homes and never had a fair chance in life. Even after being placed at this facility, many of them would return home only to resume the pattern of behavior that had gotten them into the social services system in the first place.

There were many times when I considered walking away from the job, but I always told myself that I was not a quitter and toughed it out. Later on, I would tell people that riding bulls was much easier than working with those types of kids. It turned out to be a good learning experience for me.

I flew home to Woodstown, New Jersey for Christmas. I was low on finances so my Aunt Vester Bowens (my mom's sister) had asked several family members for donations in order to help me purchase a round trip airline ticket. She sent me a check for one hundred dollars. I left a day before the "Blizzard of 1982" hit the metro Denver region. I didn't know about the storm until my mom saw it on TV. She called for me to come and watch but by the time I got into there, the newscast was over. I'd lucked out. God was looking out for me on that trip. If I'd tried to leave a day later, I wouldn't have made it because the airport was closed down for a couple of days.

I'd left my car out at the –W/ Arena in Arvada and Bob West

had given me a ride to Stapleton International Airport. There was going to be a big Bull Riding jackpot at the West Arena on New Year's Eve. I'd planned to fly back to Denver to compete. When I returned, half of my car was still buried in a huge snowdrift. I was told that for a few days it was completely covered. A friend and bullfighter, Roger Bennett, bet me that my car wouldn't start but I was sure that it would— it always did. Sure enough, it started up with no problems. However, I had to tow the car out of the snowdrift and there was still so much snow on it that it looked like a snow sculpture.

I didn't place in the jackpot because I drew a sorry bull that didn't buck very well. On the way back to Laramie, the highway still had a thick layer of ice on it in patches where there had been so much snow a week or so before. Denver and the areas to the north had definitely been caught off guard by that huge snowstorm.

20

1983

I resumed my duties at Cathedral Home and entered the Stock Show and Rodeo in Denver. I rode my first bull and then bucked off of my second. He was a good spinning brindle bull and I attempted to spur him. Afterward Leon Coffee, a very popular rodeo bullfighter and clown who was the first African-American to be selected to fight bulls at the NFR, warned me, "You need to learn to keep those feet down." (He meant for me not to always try to spur my bulls). I could have easily placed on this bull if I had ridden him, even without trying to spur him to garner some extra points from the rodeo judges. I agreed with him but it still didn't help. I enjoyed the challenge of trying to spur really good bucking bulls.

Later on Bob Wren, Keith Matteson, from Thornton, Colorado, and I went to the Black Hills Stock Show and Rodeo in Rapid City,

South Dakota. Gary Toole from Mangum, Oklahoma, and Ken Wilcox from Greenbrier, Arkansas, who were regular NFR qualifiers in the Bull Riding and also traveling partners, caught a ride with us back to Laramie. They were trying to get back to the Fort Worth, Texas rodeo on Sunday for the short go-round.

Going up to Rapid City we had not had to stop for gas. With the extra passengers and gear coming back we were going to cut it close on our gas supply. I was a little nervous being around those top bull riders. I guess it was probably because I wanted so bad to be totally accepted by my peers and especially the guys who were consistently in the Top Fifteen. I did not want to say or do anything out of line around these guys. I rode in the middle in the front seat of my car next to Gary. He could sense that I was nervous being around him. I was tired and wanting to fall asleep so he finally told me, "Man just relax."

I was asleep when we passed through Wheatland, Wyoming. Keith was driving and he made a decision not to stop for gas. When we were about twenty miles beyond Wheatland, Keith woke me up. I asked him why he hadn't stopped for gas. I looked at the gas gauge and told him that I didn't think that we were going to make it all the way to Laramie on one tank of gas. But the idea of driving all the way back to Wheatland was not very appealing.

Scott McClain was also living in Laramie and he had also been entered in Rapid City that evening. I knew that he was behind us because he was hauling horses and we had passed him. So we had a back up plan, just in case we didn't make it. We were not going to be stranded on that dark, cold highway all night.

There were a lot of jackrabbits on the road. Keith was being mean and whenever he saw one, he would speed up and hit the poor little creatures. Every time I would doze off, he would gun the car again and take out another jackrabbit. I told him to knock it off but he kept it up.

We were only about two miles outside of Laramie when we ran out of gas at the Diamond Horseshoe restaurant and dance hall. I told

Keith it was all his fault for killing all of those jackrabbits and that we deserved to run out of gas. It was too far to walk into town and besides it was in the dead of winter and very cold out. Ken, Bob, Gary and Keith wanted to sleep in my car so I decided to be the night watchman and keep an eye out for Scott.

I didn't want to miss him and stood out in the cold with a winter stocking hat on my head. We had pushed my car into the parking lot of the place so it wouldn't be right beside the road. I knew that Scott wouldn't recognize my car. Finally, it dawned on me that he probably wouldn't stop for a black man who was trying to flag him down at three o'clock in the morning, either. I decided I'd better go back to the car and put on my cowboy hat.

About thirty minutes later, Scott came blazing down the road and I was able to catch him. He gave a couple of us a ride into town to get some gas.

I told Scott about putting on my cowboy hat at the last minute and he told me that I was right; if I hadn't, he would have never stopped to help us out. After we returned to Laramie, Keith gave Gary and Ken a ride to Stapleton International Airport in Denver in order to fly to the rodeo in Fort Worth.

In March Bob and I decided to enter Tucson and Phoenix. There would be a about a week to ten days between the time we had to be in Tucson and then compete in Phoenix. The night we left, Bob informed me that we were going to go to Mexico in between the two rodeos. I had never been to Mexico and was excited. I'd had four years of Spanish in high school and that would be a perfect chance to put it to use.

It happened to be spring break for the UW students. We had a friend, Jess Driskill, whose grandparents had a winter home in Bahia Kino,Mexico, west of Hermosillo, right on the Gulf of California.

During the warm months they lived on their ranch near Devil's Tower in Wyoming and in the winter they lived in a beautiful home on the beach in Mexico.

In Tucson I rode #3 Goathead, of Bennie Beutler's bull herd. I ended up placing on him. This was the same bull that had bucked me off in Phoenix in 1982. We met up with Greg Leslie from Arvada, Colorado, at the rodeo in Tucson. He was traveling alone and was also entered in Phoenix. So Bob invited him to go along to Mexico with us. We left Bob's car at a motel in Tucson and loaded our stuff into Greg's van and drove to Nogales, Arizona to meet the other guys.

We crossed the border at Nogales and the locals didn't seem to care much for us Americans. They were a lot friendlier the farther south that we went. We kept missing our rendezvous with Jess Driskill and his two buddies from college, but somehow we met up on the highway before we got to Hermosillo.

Jess's grandparents treated us just like kings. They would cook breakfast for us each morning and then feed us a big lunch. Every night they treated us to dinner at a different restaurant. One day Bob, Jess, Greg and I attempted to take their little sailboat to an island about four miles offshore. We capsized and struggled in the water until a guy came along in a small motorboat to rescue us. Luckily I was wearing a life vest. I could swim but I couldn't possibly swim that far. I was afraid that floating was out of the question because I had such a low body to fat ratio and I knew I would just sink like a rock.

I grabbed hold of our rescuer's boat and noticed that he had a huge shark lying on the floor. I asked him in Spanish, "Did you catch that shark in these waters?" He replied, *"Si, si señor."* Without hesitation or permission I immediately jumped into his boat. The other guys in the water thought that I was crazy to be jumping into the boat of a complete stranger without his permission. After they swam over to his boat and saw the huge shark, they jumped into his boat, too.

He gave us a ride and we towed the little sailboat over to the island. There we met his two other partners. Later, we discovered that these three guys hunted sharks as a seasonal occupation. They invited us to go out with them the next morning. They could only take two of us at a time, so Greg and I would be the first. We spent a couple of hours on that small island and then they gave us a ride back to the mainland with our little boat in tow.

We obviously didn't even know these guys. For all we knew they might take us ten miles out and throw us overboard. The night before we left Greg said, "Are you afraid to go out with those strangers?" I said, "Of course I am, but I know that I'll never have this opportunity again, so I'm going for sure."

The next morning at 5:30 a.m. they picked us up on the beach and away we went. We had a blast! They took us to a deserted island that had a lot of big birds and seals on it. We also saw several pods of dolphin and a huge whale and its calf. Then to top it all off, we caught and landed two huge thresher sharks. One was about ten feet long and the other about twelve. I helped them pull the second one into the boat. Greg refused to help and thought that I was crazy. Many times, we were probably about twenty miles off shore and could see nothing but water in any direction. We were out for most of the day.

After that, they would come over to the house and take us to the village with them. One night, they took us out and we all got drunk on tequila. The next morning, instead of our usual breakfast, our hosts had set the aspirin bottle on the breakfast table. They knew we had gone out drinking the night before and that we were all sick. I was so sick that my bed felt like it was revolving and would not be still. I puked so much that I finally just laid on the rug in the bathroom because it did not make sense to continue to go back and forth from the bedroom to the bathroom. I was sick and still throwing up most of the next day, as well.

The last night that we were in Mexico, our new friends picked us up again and tried to set each one of us up with a woman from the local village. We drove around from house to house picking up our dates for the evening. Jess was the first eligible bachelor in line for the dating game. His nickname was "Tobie."

Tobie was the biggest of all of us guys from Wyoming. We crowded into Greg's van along with our new friends and stopped at the first home. The Mexicans took Tobie up to the front door to introduce him to his date. When she opened the door she blocked out all of the light coming from inside of the house. She was huge. I am sure that she was the biggest woman in the village. We laughed our heads off.

Tobie said, "No, gracias, no, gracias." I'd always served as the interpreter for our group because I was the only one that spoke Spanish but in the few days that we were in Mexico, the other guys had picked up on a little of the language. They hurried back to the van. We laughed all the way to the next house and could not wait to see what ladies our hosts had selected for the rest of us.

Eventually, we all ended up in the bar again. I was a light-weight and refused to drink any more tequila. Somehow we split up. We left the bar and Greg drove off somewhere out in the middle of nowhere. He told us to get out so that he could be alone with his girl. I told him, "No way. Here we are in a foreign country and you don't have any idea where we are. You're crazy if you think I'm leaving this van. I can assure you that wherever this van goes for the rest of the night, I will be in it."

The next morning I could not wake Greg up. I was rocking and rolling him from side to side and I still couldn't wake him. Bob poured some of Greg's cache of tequila down the drain. When we reached the border, the customs agents searched our van and confiscated the rest of it. He was not a happy camper.

We left Bahia Kino and said that we would return again but never did. Tobie's grandparents really liked me and invited all of us back. I still say that week comprised the most fun filled days I have ever experienced. I was sad when it was time for us to leave but we knew we had to get to Phoenix for the rodeo.

When Bob and I arrived in Phoenix, there was a message on the rodeo office board for me to call my parents at home. I knew that it must be serious. My parents had never attempted to track me down before when I was on the rodeo trail. There had been no way for them to reach me in Mexico and, in fact, I hadn't even told them I was going south of the border. I'd given my mom and dad the phone number to PROCOM, (the PRCA's central entry office) just in case they needed to track me down while I was on the road. (Keep in mind that cell phones didn't exist in those days.)

Rick Chatman, a friend and bullfighter, asked me if I had seen the note on the message board. Since I had to compete, I told him that I was going to wait until the rodeo was over before I called home because I knew that it was going to affect me emotionally. A couple of friends, Shaw Sullivan and Hap Kellogg, were at the Phoenix rodeo and wanted to catch a ride with Bob and me back to Laramie.

I bucked off of my bull. I guess that I can use the excuse that I had other things on my mind. I headed right for the pay phone so that I could call home.

My dad told me that a good friend and fellow black rodeo cowboy, Stanley Thomas, from Woodstown, had died in an automobile accident. Stanley was well-liked. They'd already had his funeral and he had been buried. Apparently, he'd had a brain aneurysm and ironically had crashed into one of the fences of the Cowtown ranch property right there on Route 40. Howard Harris, III, had come to the crash scene because he had seen all of the flashing emergency lights.

When I finally reached the car I was silent, trying to digest the loss of a good friend. Shaw misunderstood and told me that I didn't have to be so upset just because I had bucked off of my bull.

On the way out of Phoenix I reflected on the statement that Stanley had made during the Christmas Break of 1977-1978 when he said, "Y'all had better enjoy this moment because in ten years some of you guys are not going to be around." He was buried in Salem, New Jersey, right next to Kaye Kirby who was one of his best friends. The "Cowtown Rodeo Gang" had now lost two of its more popular members.

In May, right after Hap got out of college for the summer, we hit the rodeo trail again. First we went to Farmington, New Mexico. I placed on #101 of the Dorenkamp Rodeo Co. He was a big, arm jerking muley who bucked pretty hard. Hap had to get on Hesston Headhunter. I pulled his rope for him and he bucked off. Later, he told me that he could sense that I was nervous as he was getting on his bull. None of us liked that bull because he was very mean and Headhunter was a name that fit that him very well.

Then we went to Palos Verdes Estates, California, to visit his parents for a few days. Hiram Clay and Janice Kellogg were very nice and rolled out the red carpet for us. They took us to see the Queen Mary and the Spruce Goose in Long Beach. I also got to see Gene Walker, who was now married and living with his family in California. He had married Carol Johnson who had also graduated from Woodstown High School. He drove over to Hap's parents home for a short visit. Hap's mom told me that she was so glad that Hap and I were now traveling partners. Apparently she was not very happy with Hap traveling with Shaw and felt that Shaw was leading him down the wrong trail.

Shaw was known to be a womanizer and did not mind slamming down a few beers from time to time. Everyone knew that I was a lot more mature than Shaw and I would serve as a role model for Hap during his rookie season on the PRCA circuit.

Next, we headed out to Fort Worth, Texas. We stayed with my sister Rosalyn who was stationed at Carswell Air Force Base and went to a few rodeos including Mesquite and Grand Prairie. In Grand Prairie I got on a good young black bull named Poltergeist that turned back to the left and bucked. During the ride, he swung his tail and slapped me right across my face with it. I can only remember this happening twice in my career. This caused me to sit up and as a result I bucked off. It was a freak deal. I probably would have placed in the rodeo on him. I had tiny scratch marks on my face for a few days afterward. We also went to a Pointer Sisters concert at Billy Bob's of Texas, a huge dance hall and saloon in Fort Worth.

Then we headed over to Springfield, Missouri. I had drawn #71 of the Harry Vold bull string. He was a little black muley who was a good spinner. I was excited to have drawn him because I knew that I could place on him for sure.

As Hap and I walked into the building with our gear bags we ran into Harry Vold. He looked at me and asked, "Are you in the rodeo tonight?" I said, "Yes." Then Harry asked, "What event are you in?" I told him Bull Riding. I had known Harry Vold for several years but it was pretty obvious that he didn't have a clue who I was. He had seen me compete many times over the years. Here I was, carrying my rigging bag and he was asking me if I was in the Bull Riding. I didn't know the reason why, but I soon found out. After the rodeo started Harry approached me and told me that he had picked me to be in the Dodge Challenge.

The Dodge Challenge was a series sponsored by Dodge Trucks. At certain rodeos, Dodge put up a two hundred dollar bonus for each performance. A bull rider was selected. If the bull rider made a successful ride he would get the bonus money. (Two brand spanking new hundred dollar bills). If he bucked off, then the rodeo stock contractor would be awarded the bonus money. The stock contractor always had the advantage because he would look at the match-ups on the rodeo program and then pick a combination of bull rider versus bull that he thought would give him the edge. It was a cool deal for everybody concerned.

I was told that I would be spotlighted and introduced at the beginning of the Bull Riding event. I was supposed to walk out into the middle of the rodeo arena and shake hands with the stock contractor. I got pretty nervous and remembering my day at the UW Fieldhouse back in March 1978, I went and sat in the grandstand to be all alone.

Before the Bull Riding the rodeo announcer said, "And the challenger from Laramie, Wyoming, is Abe Morris." Number 71 had a really good trip. He jumped out, was pretty spunky and turned back to the right and started spinning. I was feeling pretty good and I opened up on him and started spurring with my left foot. He didn't like that and the next thing I knew he reversed the spin and started going back to the left. Again I was feeling a little cocky so I started spurring him with my right foot until the whistle blew to signal the end of my eight seconds ride. The crowd was cheering very loudly.

Immediately, I was asked to come to the center of the arena and was handed two nice crisp and brand new one hundred dollar bills by a corporate representative from Dodge Trucks. I was ecstatic. I remember having a huge smile as the rodeo photographer ran up and snapped a picture as I was handed the bonus money. But I'd only received a score of seventy-two points from the judges. I ended up placing fifth in the Bull Riding but should have placed a lot higher.

Hap and I then went to a few more rodeos including Cherokee, Iowa. Then we spent a few days with Kathy Fisher's (Hap's fiancée) parents, Frank and Mary Fisher, in Albia, Iowa. From there, we headed off to Fort Smith, Arkansas, which was another Harry Vold rodeo. I had drawn #W2 again and this time I was a little nervous. But I was primed and ready and looking forward to the challenge. And that is exactly what it turned out to be—another challenge.

After arriving at the rodeo I was told by Jack Lowry, the same Dodge representative who was at Springfield, that I had again been chosen by Harry Vold to be in the Dodge Challenge. The other Dodge Truck representatives were very, very nice to me and wished me good luck.

Apparently Harry Vold didn't recognize me or remember my name. The representatives from Dodge Trucks did, though. Harry knew that #W2 was a very good bucking bull and was seldom ridden. So, figuring that this would be easy pickings for a two hundred dollar bonus, he had selected #W2 and this unknown bull rider from Laramie.

Because there was an abundance of entries in the Bull Riding event there would be two sections. One would be at the beginning of the rodeo and one would be at the end. I was scheduled to compete in the first section. I was also told that my bull would be loaded in the bucking chutes and that I would be the very first bull rider.

Harry Vold was to be introduced first and walk out into the middle of the rodeo arena. Then I would be introduced again and would go out and shake hands with Harry Vold and go immediately to the bucking chute and get on #W2. I was nervously waiting for my introduction from Phil Gardenhire, the rodeo announcer, "... and in this corner the challenger weighing in at one hundred and fifty-five pounds. from Laramie, Wyoming, is Abe Morris."

As I approached Harry Vold, he got a very puzzled look on his face. He said, "Aren't you the same guy that rode that bull in the Dodge Challenge in Springfield last week?" I said, "Yes." He gave me a very sad and bewildered gesture. Then he put his head down as if he had already been defeated and said in a slightly disgusted voice, "Go get on him." Number W2 bucked hard again but nothing like the trip that he'd had with me previously in Imperial, Nebraska when he whacked me in the head. I had also successfully ridden him in Billings, Montana in October 1981.

I rode him again. I had successfully ridden #W2 three out of the four times I competed on him. I guess you could say that I had his number. The same Dodge representative handed me a new batch of fresh bills. After this second Dodge Challenge win, Harry Vold remembered me for the rest of my Bull Riding career. So much so that he never selected me again to participate in the Dodge Challenge at any of his future rodeos.

Hap and I were on the trail for about three weeks before

returning to Laramie. I'd had a very lucrative and successful run. But most of all we had a lot of fun and neither one of us got hurt.

We went to a few Circuit rodeos before venturing out on the rodeo trail again over the Fourth of July. The Fourth of July is called the "Cowboy Christmas" because there are more PRCA rodeos going on than at any other time during the rodeo season. A lot of cowboys will charter an airplane in order to get to as many of these rodeos as possible. The theory is that this gives them the opportunity to compete in as many of these lucrative rodeos as possible and enhances their chances of winning a world championship.

Over the Fourth, Hap and I entered Prescott, Arizona, and eventually we ended up in Cody, Wyoming. In Prescott I rode #3S9 of the Harry Vold Rodeo Company. He turned back to the left and spun. At first I made too big of a move with my upper body and was tilted inside the spin. Then I just kicked loose with both of my feet and was sitting just where I wanted to be. After this move, I really gapped open with my right foot and spurred him for the duration of the eight seconds ride. The rodeo judges scored me seventy-eight points and I ended up winning third and over fifteen hundred dollars. Charles Sampson won first place on bull #33 McVelvet.

Next, we went to West Jordan, Utah and then to Greeley, Colorado. We competed in the afternoon performance at Greeley. I made the whistle but only won some day money. Bobby DelVecchio and Lane Frost, who were traveling together, were scheduled to compete in the night performance. Bobby had drawn HR of Cervi's, one of the biggest bucking bulls ever in the PRCA. It was Lane's rookie season in the PRCA.

Hap didn't want to stay and watch the night performance so he went back to Laramie. We had to go to Red Lodge, Montana and Cody, Wyoming the next day to ride. I wanted to stay and watch Bobby and Lane compete. Bobby won the Bull Riding event on HR.

During the performance I was engaging in small talk with a

Abe Morris

NFR Bull #A7 Lollipop. Alsbaugh Rodeo Company
Pro Rodeo Judge Chris Horton in the background
Photo: Tim Brown

security guard who was posted near the entrance to the bucking chute area. He asked me if I was competing in the rodeo performance. I told him that I'd already ridden that afternoon and I was only sixty-eight points. Then, I left the area behind the bucking chutes. I didn't think anything of it until I returned to go behind the bucking chutes again. The same guard stopped me and said, "I can't let you go back behind the bucking chutes unless you're going to compete in this performance."

I thought for sure that he must be joking. His statement was totally absurd. I soon found out that he was serious. I explained to him that I was entered in the rodeo and I showed him my back number to prove it. I had paid a two hundred and fifty dollar entry fee in order to compete and I was allowed to be behind the bucking chutes during any performance of the rodeo.

I said, "You can't stop me from going behind the bucking chutes." He said, "No I can't, but if you go behind the chutes then I'll call the sheriff and not only will they throw you out from behind the bucking chutes, but they'll throw you out of Island Grove Park, as well." I told him he might as well go ahead and call the sheriff because I was going back there.

I went back behind the chutes and was sitting on a bench by myself. I was stewing. Sure enough, about ten minutes later there came the security guard and two deputy sheriffs. Being the only black man behind the chutes, it wasn't a difficult task to spot me. When they were standing over me reading me my rights, a few of the other cowboys got very curious and came over to see what was going on. I refused to even look up at them. Billy Schmidt, a bull rider from Greeley, asked me what was going on. I said, "These guys are trying to tell me that because I am not competing during this performance, I can't be behind the bucking chutes."

Billy Schmidt exploded, "What the hell?" He started throwing his arms and waving them like a little fighting rooster preparing for a battle. "Half of these guys behind these bucking chutes are not even entered in this rodeo and yet you are going to throw this man out who is?"

Finally convinced that they had grossly overreacted, they left me alone. Afterward, several cowboys kept coming over to me to ask me what the confrontation with the sheriff all about. Then several members of the Greeley Independence Stampede Rodeo committee came over to personally apologize for the misunderstanding. The committee men said that the security guard was from New York and that they had told him to be strict but they had not expected him to be that strict. They said they hoped that I would come back to their rodeo the following year.

After the rodeo in Cody, Wyoming, Hap and I eventually ended up in Cassie's Dance Hall and Saloon. Hap had given someone a ride out to the airport to meet up with Charlie Sampson and Ted Nuce. Ted Nuce from Manteca, California, would eventually be crowned the 1986 PRCA World Champion Bull Rider. Cassie's was a regular stopover for me during my rodeo years. I always had a good time there. I would always enter Cody for the last performance every single year.

Later on Hap and I entered a rodeo in Alamosa, Colorado. We stayed afterward for the rodeo dance. Instead of getting a motel room, we decided to tough it out and drive all the way back to Laramie. Hap assured me that he was okay to drive. I was sound asleep on I-25 when all of a sudden we were bouncing along because Hap had fallen asleep at the wheel and we were in the grassy median strip. I lunged at the steering wheel as I yelled, "Hap!" That really scared me. Hap kept saying, "I'm sorry, I'm sorry." Any job that takes you on the road puts you in harm's way. We all think we can take care of ourselves and can push ourselves a little farther. Sometimes we're lucky like we were that night. Others are not.

We were pretty close to Pueblo and we soon found a rest area to sleep. Hap fell back to sleep right away. I was wide awake and I couldn't fall back to sleep after this so I got behind the steering wheel and drove the rest of the way back to Laramie. I was dog tired when we arrived home the next morning.

In August, Rob Bunten, Billy Vossler, Ronnie Christensen, Hap Kellogg, Chris Horton and I went to a rodeo in Sterling, Colorado. We were all riding in Rob Bunten's van. I was on a roll with my "smart alec" comments, as usual. Chris Horton had all of his clothes for the weekend road trip in a paper grocery bag. I complimented him by saying, "That sure is a very nice garment bag that you have Chris, I wonder which store you bought it at?" Everyone in the van burst out laughing.

Ronnie had written a hot check for his entry fees at Cheyenne and was not able to cover it in time and so the check bounced. This put him in jeopardy of losing his "C." A C status with the PRCA allowed a member the privilege of being able to write checks for their entry fees at all rodeos. It was a major inconvenience to have to pay cash for your fees and therefore cowboys guarded their C status as if it were gold.

Ronnie complained all the way to the rodeo about the possibility of losing his C. We were all tired of hearing about it. He blamed the Cheyenne Frontier Days Rodeo committee and we didn't buy into it because Ronnie had known he had insufficient funds when he wrote the check.

After the rodeo was over, we all piled back into the van for the ride home. To our consternation, Ronnie started whining about his C again. We all moaned aloud but he refused to stop. He said, "Tomorrow I am going to get in my pickup truck and drive down to the PRCA National Headquarters in Colorado Springs and demand to see Ken Stemler." At the time Ken Stemler was one of the PRCA's top executives.

So I said, "Yeah and I know exactly what Ken Stemler is going to tell you when you walk into the great halls of the PRCA office." At this Ronnie, already irritated because he was not getting any sympathy from the other cowboys, said, "What, what, what is Ken Stemler going to say to me?"

I said—imitating the Wizard of Oz's booming voice—"Come forward." Everyone in the van erupted in a hysterical laughter. Ronnie immediately got upset. Ronnie said something to me but I continued in the same voice: "How dare you come to me and ask to get your C back." Again, everyone in the van burst out laughing.

Then Ronnie got really mad and started to curse me and flip me off. So I said, "Silence whippersnapper." This brought even more laughter from the guys and the more they laughed, the madder poor Ronnie got.

Then I said, "The great and powerful PRCA knows why you have come." Ronnie continued to get flustered and more upset and he said something else to me so, doing my best cowardly lion, I said, "I do believe in C's, I do believe in C's, I do, I do, I do, I do believe in C's."

Ronnie blasted me with another response. So I fired back at him with, "The great and powerful PRCA has spoken." There was more laughter from the cowboys in Rob's van. Then I said, "Now go." Ronnie came back with another response but I interrupted him by saying, "I said go!"

We continued to laugh about this all the way to Cheyenne and when we arrived at Billy Vossler's home we were laughing so loud that his wife, Melanie, came to the door to see what all the noise was about. Rob Bunten was driving and laughing so hard that we bounced around in the van from hitting the holes in the dirt driveway too fast. He stopped the van, threw the gearshift into park, bailed out of the van and fell to the ground laughing and holding his stomach. As he exited the van Rob exclaimed, "I've got to get some air!"

Other cowboys asked me to repeat this story several times during the summer. Sometimes I refused because I knew that Ronnie was already mad at me for using lines on him from *The Wizard of Oz*. I didn't want him to continue to be upset with me for the rest of the summer for making fun of him.

During the week I played softball in the summer city recreation league. After the summer was over, I didn't want to go back out to Cathedral Home so I got a manual labor job working at the Bighorn Lumber Company. We would start at six in the morning and get off at 3:30 p.m. so sometimes I would go up to the University to play either racquetball or basketball.

In November I was laid off and I returned to the Cathedral Home for Children. I always made it very clear with them that as soon as the rodeo season was in full swing I would be taking off again.

Brad Morris and Shaw Sullivan had moved out, so only Hap and I lived together in the little yellow house at 410 Russell. I knew quite a few of the guys and girls who competed on the UW Rodeo team and I was a regular at their parties. The rodeo team parties were some of the most entertaining experiences of my whole life. I have always loved to laugh and my laugh is contagious. Whenever my cousin Johnny Harp and I talked we would laugh our heads off and we drove anyone within earshot of us crazy with our silly laughter. That's why I would always tell people that when I stop laughing, it's time for me to check out of this world.

In the fall Kenny Behling, a PRCA bull rider from Idaho, moved into the house with Hap and me. I qualified for the Mountain States Circuit Finals but I don't remember what I did there.

I could not go back to New Jersey for Christmas and I always hated to spend the Christmas Holidays alone, away from my family. On New Year's Eve, I went to the big Jackpot at the –W/ Arena in Arvada. I was seventy-one points on #18 Yellow Jacket owned by Bill Milnes. Number 18 was bucked at a lot of Harry Vold's rodeos including Cheyenne. I won sixth place in the jackpot. Yellow Jacket was well known in the PRCA because he would back up as he was bucking and spinning and jerk guys down onto his head. It felt good to make a qualified ride on him.

Abe Morris

National Western
Stock Show & Rodeo,
Denver, Colorado
January 1984
J 26 Dynamite
from the
Mike Cervi
Rodeo Company

Mike Cervi
and
Steve Mowry
(Bullfighter)
in the background

Photo:
Jerry Gustafson

At the party that night, I met a guy who had been at the jackpot that day who said, "Just judging from the way that you walked and carried yourself when you came into the arena, I knew that you were a good bull rider and that you were going to do well." He also told me that he didn't know anything about rodeos. It felt good to know that even new fans to the sport of rodeo could see me for who I am.

21

1984

Without any notice, Kenny Behling moved out of the house because he wanted to be closer to the UW campus. Financially it did not put Hap and me in much of a bind but we had to do without a television and a couch for awhile. I was a little upset that he'd moved out without telling us.

I rode my first bull, #7, at the National Western Stock Show and Rodeo in Denver. He did not buck very well and I spurred him and only received sixty-two points. Denver was a major rodeo on the PRCA circuit but it was never one of my favorites. The performances at Denver were always long because of the horse show events held during the rodeo. Today they are held separately in a new Events Center on the other side of Interstate 70.

At a party at the UW Rodeo Cowboy's Animal House I talked

to Steve Mowry, a PRCA bullfighter from South Dakota. He said, "In a year or so you will be right at the top with the big boys. Someday you will make it to the Finals, I know you will. I've seen you ride. I've talked to Miles Hare and he's the one that would like to see that happen. All you have to do is to go and get on 'em."

Steve is the one who brought up the conversation. As wonderful as it was to be complimented by someone who didn't know anything about rodeos, this, coming from two great bullfighters lifted me up. I felt like people I admired and competed with recognized me and my ability.

I went south again to Fort Worth and stayed with my sister Rosalyn. On the way down I stopped in Umbarger, Texas, near Canyon, and spent the night with Junie and Vera Shorter.

In Fort Worth I rode #140, of Harry Vold's, for sixty-eight points. He was always "hard to get out on" because he would lean up against the backside of the bucking chute in anticipation of the chute gate opening up. As soon as he felt the bull rope tightening around his middle he would lean hard against the back of the chute. When it was time for the bull rider to slide up to his rope he couldn't because his leg was being squeezed pretty solidly against the chute. The bull would be trying to get the advantage on the rider and bracing himself for the initial first jump out of the chute. This is very similar to how a sprinter braces himself to spring out of the starting blocks during a race.

In later years, the stock contractor would use a post to place against #140's front shoulder to prevent him from squeezing the rider's leg before he left the chute. This same method was also used against his bucking mate, #150, of the Vold string, because he would do the exact same thing. These two bulls both qualified to compete at the NFR and they looked very similar. Both bulls were black with white faces. Number 140 was smaller and stockier and #150 was tall and slab sided. In their prime, they were both good money bulls that the cowboys liked to draw.

Ronnie Christensen and Jamie Davis, a black bull rider from Arkansas, also stayed a couple of days with me at my sister Rosalyn's place. I was traveling alone and catching rides from one rodeo to the next. It's always easy to catch rides when you're traveling alone. Most of the time cowboys are glad to have someone else jump in with them in order to help them drive and also pay for some of the other traveling expenses.

Also it helped break up the monotony of traveling with the same guys all year long. It is especially easy during the winter rodeos because most of the cowboys seem to be headed in the same direction. The rodeos—Denver, Rapid City, Fort Worth, El Paso, Jackson, San Antonio, Houston and San Angelo—were the indoor or building rodeos.

I bucked off of my second bull at Fort Worth, #40 Typhoon, owned by Neal Gay. He jumped and kicked pretty well. I didn't think that he was going to turn back and so I started spurring him. He started spinning and caught me with my inside foot out. Then, to add insult to injury, he stepped on me and one of my contact lenses popped right out of my eye. I have been nearsighted for most of my life. Sometimes I wore glasses but I never competed in them. The bulls were big enough that I had no problems seeing them without my glasses.

At El Paso I scored seventy-two points on a high leaping, crowd pleasing bull, #165, of the Vold Rodeo Company. Afterward, I had several fans tell me how much that they'd enjoyed my ride. I loved it whenever fans complimented me. I just could not wait to get on my next bull. But that would not be for at least another week. After the rodeo I met Kerry Bonner, another black bull rider from California. He was a short and stocky cowboy who went by the nickname of "Pooch."

I bucked off of a good bull, #17, of Del Hall's in San Antonio, Texas. He was spinning and as he bucked me off, he hit me with his hip and really launched me for another ride. I tightened up before I hit the ground. The ground right in front of the bucking chutes had become compacted and it was extremely hard.

I sustained a very serious injury to my lower back when I hit the ground. I knew that I was hurt because I could feel a tingling sensation in my nerve endings. I somehow managed to get up and drag myself to safety. I immediately went to see Jackie Romer who was working on the Justin Sports Medicine Team. I told her that I was headed back to Fort Worth to my sister's place. I was entered in a few more rodeos but I already knew that I was hurt pretty bad.

She gave me the phone number to make an appointment with Don Andrews, another Justin Sports Medicine Team member who had his office in Fort Worth. Jackie gave me a velcro back brace to wear and made me promise her that I would consult with Don. For some reason she figured I would do the usual cowboy thing and play "tough guy" and refuse to go and see a doctor. There was no doubt in my mind that I was going to a doctor. I was in excruciating pain and could barely walk. At times it felt as if someone had stuck a knife in my back. The guys that I was catching a ride with back to Fort Worth had to carry my rigging bag and my clothes to their car.

When I went in to see Don Andrews he told me, "Come on back." A minute later he peeked around the corner and said, "Today, today." I said, "I'm trying, I'm trying." I was still holding on and trying to raise myself out of the chair that I was sitting in. I would get into certain positions and then freeze. It hurt me to be in that position and yet it would also hurt me to try and move out of it. Every movement that I made was at a snail's pace and I could not even put my own shoes on. It hurt me the most whenever I was trying to get in or out of a car. Roy Hairston (Rosalyn's fiancé) was just super in helping me whenever I needed it, and I needed it. At times I felt like an invalid.

I had some pelvic X-rays taken and although nothing was broken, I discovered that my right leg is shorter than my left leg. This probably explains why I have an unusual gait to my walk. I tend to sway my shoulders from side to side.

I went to physical therapy for two weeks and I felt better each day. I was given a series of back exercises that helped a lot. Also, I was hooked up to a machine to get electric shock stem therapy for my back. Roy was great. He would take me and pick me up for each of my therapy sessions.

During all of my therapy, I didn't get depressed because I realized that my situation was just a temporary setback. I saw people in therapy who were confined to wheelchairs and I knew that although they would show some improvements, they would never be the same again. The risk of paralysis or a career ending injury was always there so I was happy that this one was only temporary.

I was also seeing another doctor during my regular therapy sessions. On my last visit, I asked him how much longer he wanted me to continue doing the back exercises. I figured that he would say two to three more weeks. To my surprise he said, "I want you to do those back exercises every single day for the rest of your life." I just laughed at him.

The first week in March I flew back to Denver and then caught the bus to Laramie. In less than two weeks I would practice again at the OK Corral but because my back bothered me afterward, I decided to remain on the sideline for awhile.

In April, I went to a college rodeo with Hap and his fiancée, Kathy Fisher, in Fort Collins and pulled Hap's bull rope for him. Hap won the Bull Riding and I was very happy to have been there to share the moment.

On May 2nd and 3rd, I announced the UW College Rodeo out at the Albany County Fairgrounds. The college rodeos were no longer held indoors at the Fieldhouse because they had put astro turf down for the football team. As a result, the crowds were almost non-existent and nothing compared to the rodeo crowds that regularly attended the college rodeos in the Fieldhouse.

Afterward, we went to a big rodeo party at the OK Corral. I

was paid four hundred dollars to announce the rodeo. I did a good job and received a lot of compliments. I had a lot of fun as well. It was great to still be a part of the rodeo performance even when I couldn't compete.

Brad Morris, Randy Kinsey, Shaw Sullivan and I drove to Albia, Iowa, to go to Hap's and Kathy's wedding. We surprised him because he didn't think that we were going to show up. I was asked to be one of the groomsmen in the wedding. We all had a blast! A cowboy wedding is about as much fun as anyone can have legally.

On June 16th, Jed McKinlay, a bareback rider, Hap, Chris Horton and I went to Grand Junction, Colorado for a rodeo. It would be my first PRCA rodeo in exactly four months to the day, so I was excited and raring to go. I took along my walkman so I could listen to music in order to psyche myself up.

I had drawn #-D Dusty, a new bull in the Alsbaugh pen who had gone unridden so far for his career. He jumped and kicked pretty good and then reared up and blew into the air. He threw his head back trying to hook me. It made me sit up and kind of rocked me back. Then he turned back very quickly to the left and started spinning. I started sliding into the deep, dark and lonely well. I desperately reached across to the right side of the bull with my free hand and had every intention of double grabbing, if necessary, in order to save myself. As it turned out, I didn't have to. I got out of the well.

And with precision timing, I made a big move and *bam!* everything fell right into place. I knew exactly where everything was and there was no way that he was going to throw me off. After a round, I knew that I was tapped off and I started spurring him with my right foot.

After the ride, my friends were telling me to throw my cowboy hat. Since it was rare for me to show a lot of emotion, I decided to wait until my score was announced. When the announcer said seventy-two points I was very, very disappointed. In fact, I was more disappointed than mad. The crowd also agreed and rang out loud and clear with a chorus of boos for the two judges. That made me feel a little better. So I faced the crowd, took off my hat and raised both arms as if to salute them. This made me even more determined to ride my butt off in the future.

Everyone came up to me to tell me just how bad the rodeo judges had "screwed" me. I agreed. I should have been scored about eighty-three to eighty-five points very easily. One cowboy asked me how long I had been a PRCA card carrying member. I had been a member since 1977. Then he said, "Those judges deducted a point from your score for each year that you've been a member." Usually they tended to be a little stingy with their points for the rookies and unknown cowboys in the association.

When the judges posted their scores I was moved up to seventy-six points and I ended up winning second in the Bull Riding and over twelve hundred and sixty dollars. I should have won first. I figured that seventy-six points were better than seventy-two points so I didn't complain too much.

After we got back into the car, the first song that we heard was *Don't You Get So Mad About It* by Jeffrey Osbourne. I had to turn up the volume because I was already feeling great and my riding was speaking volumes, as well. After a four month hiatus, I had returned to the bull riding arena with a vengeance and a mission.

I bucked off of a sorry fighting bull at Grover, Colorado. At first I was upset and then I got over it pretty quickly. He was not bucking very well and got me into bad shape and I just quit trying. All he wanted to do was to hurt me. The name of the game is to stay healthy and it was not worth it to risk getting injured on a sorry bull that I had no chance of placing on.

I flew home to New Jersey on June 19th for Rosalyn and Roy Hairston's wedding. They were married in the Morning Star Baptist

Church in Woodstown on June 23rd. My brother Reuben and Chris Pope, our cousin, wanted to talk trash on Roy and I since we were older than they were. So we had to go to the basketball court and school them. It was the two older family members against the two younger guys. Chris is so competitive and he hates to lose at anything.

I always hated to lose but I would not allow losses to get to me. I thought that it was funny because Chris kept yelling at Reuben as I continued to drain twenty foot rainbow shots. I have always been proud of my sharpshooting basketball skills. I consider myself to be a great outside shooter.

The wedding and the reception were great. It was a total family effort. Janice made all of the dresses for the women. It always amazed me how our family would pitch in whenever we had a major function. All of the food was cooked by different family members.

The reception was also fun. Reuben and I showed off to onlookers by doing the moonwalk. Everyone was surprised because my brother David had always been known as the dancer in the family but the kids at Cathedral Home had taught me the moves.

After the reception, I went home and got out of my tuxedo and headed for Cowtown to the rodeo. I had drawn bull #13 Palmetto. I was so tired from all of the activities that I sat down behind the bucking chutes and fell asleep. Now that's what I call really relaxing before competition!

Palmetto blew out of the bucking chute pretty hard and rocked me back. I had to scramble to get a good seat. He was solid and bucking pretty hard but I had some good holds with both of my spurs. I could feel him trying to jerk me down. I felt good so I started styling. Then the last few jumps I cut loose on him and started firing on him with my left foot.

When the whistle blew I stepped off, landed on my feet and just stood there looking at him. Palmetto came after me so I threw my cowboy hat at him and coolly high-stepped it to the chutes. Jimmy Lee,

Abe Morris

Cowtown Rodeo, Woodstown, New Jersey
June 23, 1984   # 13 Palmetto, Cowtown Rodeo, Inc. Stock

who was fighting bulls, yelled something at me about being a "big ol' clown."

I was only scored sixty-nine points. I thought I should have been scored higher but I still won second place. Buck Howard won first place. I was happy that I'd come home to the place where I'd started riding and had made a good showing for myself. I hung out with Skimmer after the rodeo and I must have laughed all night long. It was getting to be light when I finally drove home the next morning.

That day, June 24th, was my birthday. Although I'd turned twenty-eight years old, I felt like I was in as good shape physically as I'd ever been. My family surprised me with a birthday cake with candles and a bunch of cards with money in them. Needless to say, they made me feel pretty good.

On Friday, June 29th, Jimmy Lee, Kerry Nelson and I went to Lake Luzerne, New York to the rodeo. Before the rodeo started I called PROCOM to get all of my stock for my Fourth of July Run out West. I had a weird feeling that I was going to draw an old Cowtown bull at the rodeo in Greeley. Bennie Beutler had purchased #O18 Brindle Velvet, #O30 Jersey Joe and #S8 Knocker from Howard Harris. Sure enough, I drew #S8 Knocker. In 1983 he was voted the second best bucking bull at the NFR.

At Lake Luzerne, I rode #7X of the All American Rodeo Company for a split of third and fourth place. I bucked off a little bull named Bimbo the following night at Cowtown. I was hoping I would draw #H1 Wedgehead. He was a cool bucking little dude that would get it on to the left. He was later sold to Bennie Beutler and his name was changed to Mr. C. He was nominated and bucked at the NFR in 1985 and 1986. I didn't see #H1 again until the Stock Show in Denver in 1985 and I could not believe how much bigger he was. It looked like someone had stuck an air hose in him and pumped him up!

When it was time to say all of my goodbyes Willie Ed said, "What I want to know is when are you going to make it to the Finals?"

I told him I was still working on it.

Sunday, July 1st, I flew from Philadelphia to Denver. Hap, Gerry, Brad and Kathy picked me up at the airport. I was feeling pretty good about myself. I had a feeling that I was going to ride Knocker and possibly even win first place in the rodeo. I was also entered in West Jordan, Utah, for the following night and had made an airline reservation just in case I couldn't catch a ride with some other cowboys.

Donnie Gay, Charles Sampson, Ted Nuce, Ricky Bolin, and Joe Gaskin were all scheduled to compete in the same performance and this didn't bother me at all. I wanted to do well for myself. I didn't have to prove anything to those guys. They all knew that I could ride well. I found out later that Knocker had not been ridden successfully in 1984 and I hoped to be the first bull rider to get him covered.

When they were trying to load the bulls, #S8 kept jumping out and running down the alley. Bennie Beutler said that the bull had been squatting pretty bad in the box (chute) and that I might have to call for him like that. Then he said, "You've already been on him, haven't you?" I said, "Yes, believe it or not I got on him at Cowtown two years ago for practice."

There would be no excuses. I was determined not to let a fantastic ride be ruined by the bull jerking my rope out of my hand. If that were to happen, then I knew I would be extremely mad at myself. I noticed that my bull rope and glove were very, very sticky. I was sure that it was probably due to the humidity on the East coast.

Number S8 Knocker was smaller than he was the first time that I got on him. He had lost at least a couple of hundred pounds. I warmed up my bull rope before I even sat on him because I figured that he would start squatting in the chute. I made sure that I stuck my hand in the bull rope just a small fraction more that I usually did. Just like the first time I got on him at Cowtown, he refused to stand up straight and was squatting in order to get a good spring on his initial first jump out of the chute. I finally called for the gate even though he was still squatting.

The bull hopped and skipped and had a miserable trip. My left foot came out but I was not trying to spur this bull. I knew better. Everything was happening too fast and I really was not aware of what was going on. I could tell that he was really bucking and all I could think about was to TRY. The last thing that I knew was that I had a good seat.

Before I realized what was happening, I was whipped down, hit in the chin, and was dazed. I was hung up and my riding arm was in a very awkward position. I was like this for a few moments and all I wanted was out. I opened my hand and pulled like crazy but nothing gave. He was jumping over my head and jerking me off of my feet on every jump. At one point I was hoping that one of the bullfighters, Rick Chatman or Leon Coffee, would arrive on the scene and help to untie me. For as long as I was hung up, I just knew that one of them would get there soon.

Then #S8 jerked me forward and whacked me right in the face with his horn. That blow stunned me and knocked me off of my feet. Up until that point I had somehow managed to stay on my feet. Then my hand turned over and my thumb was against the bull's back. It was virtually impossible to open my hand because my thumb was locked down over the rest of my fingers. The next jump he blew into the air and came down on my right leg which was then fully extended. When the bull made contact, I let out a big "aaahhh" and at the same time my hand was ripped free from my bull rope. I felt something give and thought he'd hyper-extended my knee.

I could not get up and run. I knew that I was hurt. Instantly I had people out in the arena helping me to safety. I held my leg up all the way to the chutes and didn't put any weight on it. I felt even worse when I looked down and saw the blood on my shirt. After they got the bull out of the arena, they helped me out and had me sit down. Shelly Burmeister, a very attractive television and rodeo commentator, asked me if I could stand on my right leg. I tried to but I collapsed and said a curse word as I winced in pain.

At about the same time, the ambulance backed up in preparation to haul me off to the hospital. I said, "I ain't hurt that bad." Don Andrews, the Justin Heeler, told the emergency crew that their services wouldn't be needed. At that point, Hap and someone else helped me over to the Justin Sports Medicine trailer. I was hurt bad but I didn't yet know the extent. I was in a lot of pain.

The first thing that Jackie Romer did was to put some ice on my knee. After awhile Don held up my right leg and told me to relax. He moved it to the side. I jumped like a fish out of water but did not let out even the slightest whimper. This exact same procedure was repeated again a while later. I jumped just like a fish, again.

Don said that he didn't think it was broken. He thought that I had sustained some ligament damage and that I would be out of action for about three weeks. One of my first thoughts was *three whole weeks and just when I thought I was riding so well.* I had already made a decision to "go hard" for the rest of the season and then take my shot at an NFR qualification in 1985.

Jackie wrapped up my knee with Ace bandages and I put on a pair of gym shorts. I had been so involved with my leg that I hadn't paid much attention to the cut on my lip and my sore arm. My arm was rock hard and hurt like crazy from being jerked on when I was hung up.

I borrowed Brad's crutches because he had injured his leg at Grover and had to have surgery. When I came out of the trailer, the whole area was virtually deserted. I kept my distance from Hap's car while it was being packed. I asked myself, why this had to happen, especially when I was having what was shaping out to be a super summer. I hung my head down and started to get all fogged up. I would have cried right then and there if Gerry had not yelled at me to come on! That brought me back to the real world. I did a lot of blinking as I hobbled toward the car so no one would see any tears in my eyes.

It was a long ride back to Laramie, but the painkillers made it tolerable. When we got back, Hap asked if I wanted to go to the hospital and I said no. Instead, we went next door to a barbecue. I called my parents in New Jersey to tell them that I had been injured. I made out as best as I could until bedtime and, although I tossed and turned worrying about my injury as I tried to find a comfortable position, somehow I managed to finally fall asleep.

The next morning when I woke up, my leg was very swollen from my knee to my foot. It looked like a balloon. When I moved my leg I felt something loose and I knew that there was something wrong. My first thought was, let's go and get this thing fixed.

Hap took me to the emergency room at Ivinson Memorial Hospital. All morning, I had a positive mental attitude, telling myself that it was just a minor injury and that I would be able to compete again soon. At the same time, I had a feeling that I would not be going back to the house with Hap. I kept up my positive thinking until the doctor read my X-rays and said, "Believe it or not you broke your leg." Needless to say I was sick.

I asked for Dr. David Kieffer to handle my case because I had grown to trust him over the years. The doctor called him and he showed up within thirty minutes. He walked in and gave me his prognosis.

Dr. Kieffer asked, "Well, Abe, how are you feeling?"

"Not too bad, it hurts a little," I said.

"You broke it pretty bad. You're out for the rest of the season."

"Did I break it that bad?"

"You broke it pretty bad," he said. "Let me get your X-rays and I'll show you." He put the film up where I could see it. "See, you broke it in three places—here, here, and here."

"How long will I be out and when will I be able to ride again?"

"Six to eight months at the earliest. It will be at least six months before you can even jump up and down on it."

"What about Denver?"

"When is Denver?"

"The middle of January. How long will I have to wear a cast?"

"I'm not going to put you in a cast. We're going to have to operate on you."

"You mean surgery?"

"Yes."

"A little operation?"

"No, major surgery. We're going to have to put some screws in your leg. We may even have to take some bone grafts from your hip."

We had a long conversation concerning that season and my hopes and aspirations for my future in bull riding. I had just sustained a very serious and possibly career-ending injury. I assured Dr. Kieffer that I was currently riding as well as I ever had and that I would be back!

As my words echoed off the walls, Dr. Kieffer shook his head. He did not sound very positive about me being physically able to compete again at the same level and he glumly said, "Maybe."

You can just imagine how I felt. Things were far worse than I had ever imagined. I was really devastated.

After I was admitted to the hospital, I called my family with an update. I was scheduled for surgery the following morning. I had never had an operation before, so I was pretty nervous. When the anesthesiologist stopped by for a visit, I related the story of my injury in April of 1973, when I was taken to the Intensive Care Unit after breaking my leg.

I told him that I was scared and he assured me that he personally would be there and would watch over me very carefully.

The only food that I'd had all day long was a glass of orange juice. As I lay in bed, I wondered if I would wake up at all this time around. I wanted to go to sleep but at the same time I didn't want to miss out on any hours that I might have left in my journey through life.

I was awakened before seven a.m. because my surgery was scheduled for 7:30. I was still scared and didn't have a whole lot to say. Dr. Kieffer came by and just the minute or so that he spent in my room made me feel a hundred percent better.

It wasn't long before I was off to the operating room. They put a small oxygen mask over my nose and I remember the strong smell of rubber. My anesthesiologist said that they would knock me out through the IV tube in my hand. He told me to think pleasant thoughts. So I said, "In that case I'll think of going to the National Finals Rodeo." After that I was out like a light.

When I came to, the first thing that I saw was the clock on the wall. It was 11:30 a.m.. I was not awake very long before they were wheeling me back to my room. I was a little disappointed to discover that I had a full cast on my leg. From what the doctor had said, I wasn't expecting a cast. After I was back in bed, the nurse asked me if I needed anything and all I could manage to say was, "pain." She immediately came back with a long needle and stuck it in my butt. In no time at all I was out like a light. Later on that afternoon I woke up and asked for another shot for pain.

When I was served dinner that night, I fell asleep during my meal. It was the first food I'd had in two days. A nurse came in and changed a bag full of blood that had drained from my knee. I was so out of it that I hadn't even noticed it was there. No one had told me about it before my surgery. I also remember checking my hips to see if there had been any bone grafts taken from them. I was relieved to find them intact. I slept most of that day.

Phone calls and visitors helped to brighten my day on the Fourth of July. During the night I'd started having severe chest pains. The hospital staff got very concerned and ran some tests on me. They also hooked me up to an EKG. You would have thought that I was in the intensive care unit. I had intravenous tubes in my hand, tubes in my leg for drainage and tubes in my nose. I hated it. I took the tubes out of my nose because they were bugging me.

When they carted me off to do the radiology tests on my chest, a staff member showed me the new X-rays of my leg. I was totally amazed at the size of the screws in my leg. Dr. Kieffer said "screws" but he should have said bolts. They were very long. He had stopped by earlier in the day to tell me that the operation was a total success and that they'd put six screws into my leg.

They couldn't find a reason for those chest pains I was experiencing. I didn't ask for any painkillers that day. I was still in pain but I decided to just tough it out.

Bob Wren stopped to visit and told me "Just wait until your doctor pulls those drain tubes out of your leg. They have little anchors on them and they are going to hurt like crazy," he said. One of the hardest things for me was to see the looks on my visitors' faces as they watched me lying in my hospital bed in pain. This really got to me. They looked at me like I was dying.

On Thursday morning, July 5th, Dr. Kieffer stopped by and said, "How about we get rid of this drain?" I responded, "Wait a minute, I had a friend come by yesterday who said this was going to hurt like crazy."

"Nah, a tough bull rider like you—this won't hurt a bit." He unhooked the blood bag and then grabbed the plastic tubing. He took a couple of wraps around his hand and said, "Okay, here we go."

I held my breath and grabbed hold of my bed with both hands and held on tightly. He jerked on the tubes and I let out a huge "Wheeewww."

"See that did not hurt a bit, did it?"

"Noooooo," and sounding as if I was laughing I said, "that did not hurt at all." The reality was that it hurt like crazy, just like Bob Wren told me it would.

I had been experiencing hot and cold spells at night. One minute I would be burning up and the next I would be freezing cold. I was given several extra blankets and I would wrap up in them just like a mummy.

Not much later, I was cruising down the hallways on my

crutches and I ran into Dr. Kieffer. He wanted to show me the X-rays of my leg so we went down to the X-ray lab. He said, "We got it put back together real well." He was like an artist who had spent several months working on a painting—very, very proud of his masterpiece and you could see it on his face. I told him that since he felt so good about it, it made me feel even better.

I think that this was part of the reason we'd had a heart to heart conversation before my surgery about my aspirations for the future. I had told him that I would be back in the arena. Otherwise he probably would not have spent as much time trying to get my shattered leg put back together. That injury could have just become a good excuse for me to walk or limp away from my career. But I wanted to continue to ride bulls for several more years.

On Friday, July 6th, Dr. Kieffer gave me the okay to go home. I was delighted because I didn't like being cooped up in the hospital. As my nurse was getting my things ready so I could go home, she showed another nurse a picture of me competing in a rodeo. The other nurse had hardly spoken to me all week but when she found out why I was in the hospital, she became friendly and wanted to talk my head off.

By Sunday, July 8th, I just wanted to have a good crying session and get it out of my system. The personal forecast was for a torrential downpour with several inches of solid facial rain. Before I could even get started with the sprinkling, Hap showed up and wanted me to go fishing with his sister and some other friends. I didn't want to go and I knew if I could just be left alone, that the dam was going to burst. But somehow they talked me into going fishing with them.

I managed to stay very active by going out to the bars, the movies and to a few softball games. In times like those you really appreciate your family and friends. And since all of my family was seventeen hundred miles away, I had to depend on my friends to get me through my recuperation.

Hap's sister Kathy and her friend Doreen were kind enough to take me to the Gem City Bone and Joint Clinic on Tuesday July 10th for physical therapy. A doctor looked at my X-rays on the screen and said to someone else, "So there's the guy who blew his knee all to smithereens." I didn't appreciate the comment, especially since I would rather be out on the circuit competing and so I ignored him. He could sense my resentment and did not say another word to me.

My big heavy cast was cut off. Man was that a relief! It was very uncomfortable lugging that thing around. Due to inactivity, my leg muscle had shrunk in only a week. I was amazed. At first I was a little leery about looking at the scar. It wasn't nearly as bad as I thought it would be and I was relieved to see that it was just a small straight line.

I went down to the therapy room and I was given a few exercises to do. Then Dr. Kieffer had me put on a removable splint with velcro straps. That was a blessing compared to the big old bulky plaster cast. My attitude improved a hundred percent. Whenever I'd stand up with that cast on, it felt as if it was going to pull my leg right off. I knew wearing the splint would be a cinch. Like all things, you need to experience the bad with the good so that you know how lucky you are.

My knee was still pretty swollen and looked just like a balloon. I was told to put ice on it every day. I still could not completely straighten my right arm and it hurt like crazy. I had a small afro then and couldn't seem to comb it with my left hand, and I had to use my left hand to lift and work my right, just so I could comb my hair.

On Friday, July 13th, I went to watch the first performance of the Laramie Jubilee Days Rodeo. It was good to be in a rodeo atmosphere again although I did not enjoy being on injured reserve and relegated to spectator status. For some reason, I kind of felt ashamed being on the injured reserve list.

After only two weeks, I was told to start putting a little weight on my leg but not to try to walk on it. I was too afraid to walk on my leg. I was afraid that even with the big old screws in it, that it might fall apart. I was also given additional exercises to help with the mobility and the healing process.

At the Cheyenne Frontier Days Rodeo I saw Charles Sampson and Ted Nuce. They wanted to know what had happened to me and where I got hurt. They had both been in Greeley on the day that I was injured and neither one of them realized that I had broken my leg.

On July 26th, during another appointment, my doctor and therapist were both very pleased with my progress. I was told to start walking on my leg using my crutches. The act of walking would make my leg stronger as well as help the healing process. I could also start to use a weight bench and lift weights with my leg.

Dr. Kieffer confirmed my feelings that I would not have to wear the splint any more on August 1st. During one of my previous visits my therapist told me that Dr. Kieffer had told him that my tibial plateau break was the worst one that he'd ever had to set. This was something that Dr. Kieffer never mentioned to me.

In August, Kenny Behling and Scott Kesl stopped at the house on 410 Russell Street on their way to Loveland, Colorado, for the rodeo. We asked them what bulls that they had drawn and they told us that they had not called PROCOM for stock. Kenny said, "I know one thing for sure, I did not draw #O18 Cowtown because he's dead."

This had been the rumor that was floating around the PRCA. And it could not have been farther from the truth. Not only was #O18 still alive and kicking but Kenny would get on him the very next night.

Kenny bucked off of #O18 and was hung up and knocked out cold. He took a severe beating from the horns of that bad bull. After that trip, Bryan McDonald, the PRCA Bull Riding director, said that #O18 could be classified as a "human egg beater." Many cowboys who witnessed this barrage said they would never get on that infamous Bucking Bull of the Year.

Kenny was in Laramie again the following day, after his mishap with #O18. He was going to compete in a small PRCA rodeo at the fairgrounds. His face was swollen and he had to have several stitches to close up the wounds #O18 had inflicted on him. He also had to make a visit to the dentist.

Hap injured his leg at that small rodeo in Laramie and had to spend the night in the hospital. Gerry and I went to visit him and I went to say hello to the nurses who had taken care of me during my stay in Ivinson Memorial Hospital. These ladies were extremely nice and, without a doubt, the best staff of nurses I had ever been around.

I'd also become good friends with an intern from Cathedral Home named Bridget. We had gone out a couple of times and probably would have gotten to know each other a lot better if I hadn't been injured. I had played racquetball with her before I was hurt. She was pretty cool.

During my doctor appointment on August 15th, I was given permission to put the crutches away for good and to start riding my bike. I was elated. It was hard to believe that seven weeks after I had suffered a severely broken leg, I could walk on it again. When I was sixteen years old I'd worn that cast for twenty consecutive weeks.

During the entire time I was injured, I had not broken down and cried—although there were several times when I wanted to. Normally, I would dream about riding bulls on a regular basis. While I was hurt, my subconscious mind must have known that I was physically unable to ride and I never once dreamed about it. But soon my dreams were once again filled with bucking bulls.

At times when I would contemplate my dilemma, I thought about people who had lost a leg or were confined to a wheelchair for the rest of their lives. My setback had been temporary but theirs was permanent. I had plenty to be thankful for.

On Sunday, September 2nd, I met a very attractive woman by the name of Carol Gross at the Cathedral Home for Children. We seemed to have an instant attraction and so we started to date.

On September 24th, I rode my bike up to Gem City Bone and Joint for my appointment. I could walk with only a slight limp then. My therapist said, "Look at you, you probably just can't wait to go and get on a bull. You probably already have, haven't you?" Just for kicks I said, "Yes," even though it wasn't true. His reply was, "You had better be careful." Then I told him the truth.

I did some strength tests and I was at about seventy-three percent on one and a hundred percent on the other. I simply took it in stride but I was amazed and also proud of the results.

Dr. Kieffer asked, "Have you been playing any basketball?"

"Yes," I said.

"That's fine," he said, "You can also play racquetball." I didn't tell him that I had already been playing racquetball for over a month. Judging from my results, I was probably about three months ahead of schedule. After my appointment, I stopped at the UW Fieldhouse and played racquetball with Joe Dowler and Kevin McKinney.

I got into a regular routine of playing racquetball, riding my bike and working out at the Player's West Health Club. I was determined to get back into good shape as soon as possible.

On Saturday, October 6th, and Sunday, October 7th, Carol and I went out to the fairgrounds to watch the UW College Rodeo. It was always good to be around the rodeo atmosphere and contestants again.

I had another appointment at Gem City Bone and Joint on October 25th. I had been working a lot at Cathedral Home and was not doing my exercises on a regular basis as I should have.

Dr. Kieffer said that I looked real good almost four months after my accident. He said, "I really want you to pound on your leg and get it ready. I suggest that you run stairs and play more basketball. You can start getting on again sometime after Thanksgiving."

On Saturday, November 3rd, Carol and I went down to the

-W/ Arena in Arvada for the annual Halloween rough stock jackpots. The Bareback Riding and the Saddle Bronc Riding were in progress when we arrived. I was asked to announce the Bull Riding. The weather was nice and sunny and we both had a good time.

The annual UW Rodeo Club Buckfest that was to be held out at the OK Corral was cancelled due to liability problems on Saturday November 10th. It had been a very popular Bull Riding event which many of the rowdy Wyoming students would attend and drink beer.

Later in November, I flew back East for my Ten Year High School Class Reunion. Carol gave me a ride to the airport in Denver. It was nice to see some of my old classmates and friends from years gone by. I hit the dance floor and stayed on it for most of the evening. I danced up a storm and thoroughly enjoyed myself as well as the affair. Gone was the shyness of my high school years. I probably even did a little showing off. I was the only one at the reunion who could do the moonwalk. Some of my classmates did not even recognize me. I was taller and bigger than when I had graduated in 1974.

On the night before Thanksgiving I got on #14 Snuffy at the OK Corral High Plains Arena. He dinked off but it felt good just to get on a bull again and to walk away afterward.

During my appointment on Tuesday, November 27th, Dr. Kieffer gave me the green light to start riding again. I didn't tell him that I had already ridden my first practice bull. I still was lagging behind on my leg exercises because I was working a lot at the Cathedral Home. I felt guilty about not doing the exercises that were expected of me.

On Tuesday, December 11th, I went with Gerry Strom and Billy Vossler from Cheyenne to Arvada to practice. I got on Blizzard for the second time. He had another good trip but was not rank like he was two years earlier, the first time that I'd gotten on him. He turned back to the left and spun and then he jumped out of it and bucked straight off. After the whistle, he was really slinging his head and I made a decision to get off away from my riding hand.

He slung me way up into the air and I landed right on my right knee. It did not hurt me one bit and that kind of took me by surprise. Several people complimented me for making a good ride. Considering that it was only my second bull in over four months, I knew they were right. I realized that I had a lot to be thankful for. So I took it in stride and kept right on stepping.

On Thursday, December 20th, I watched some VHS rodeo tapes from the Mountain States Circuit Finals in 1982. That was the first time I'd seen them. I watched them over and over again. It was pretty cool watching myself ride. I was impressed at how solid I looked riding bulls.

The following Wednesday, Gerry and I went out to the OK Corral and got on a couple of bulls for practice. I got on #15 Super Trooper. He turned back and spun to the left and had a decent trip with me. I felt solid during the entire ride. Again, I was complimented after my ride. Next I got on Baby Knothead and he spun to the right. Afterward, I was so out of breath that I just stood by the fence for a while. I was surprised at how well I was riding considering the layoff. I also knew that I definitely needed to work on building up my wind and get into better shape because both of those bulls had worn me out.

For the annual New Year's Eve jackpot at the -W/ Arena, I rode #10 RTD. He didn't buck very well so I spurred him but I didn't place in the jackpot. It was the first bull that I had spurred since my return to the arena. He lunged and did not kick very well and as a result he jerked on my riding arm pretty good. Bulls that lunge forward tend to rock the rider back to the end of their riding arm. Bulls that kick are actually easier to ride because they keep you up on your bull rope and you don't have to work as hard.

This was also the first of many times that Carol was able to watch me compete.

22

1985

Rob Bunten, Billy Vossler, Gerry Strom, Greg Leslie, Darrell Hoss, Steve Cooper and I drove to Odessa, Texas, in Rob's van. It was to be my first PRCA rodeo in six months. It was also very cold in Odessa and I was glad that I had my down vest along for the ride.

At the rodeo I saw two of my favorite bull riders, Kenny Wilcox and Gary Toole. I had not seen them since Cheyenne Frontier Days, when I was still on crutches. They were traveling partners who had both also been injured in 1984 and were cracking out together again. Gary had been seriously injured when he was stepped on by a bull at Sidney, Iowa and had lost a little weight. This prompted him to start wearing his trademark suspenders which he kept for the rest of his rodeo career.

Before the Bull Riding I didn't feel quite "in the groove" so I went back into the locker room to be alone and pump up. I am sure that part of the reason was because I had not competed in a rodeo in six months. I was not real nervous because I was not getting on a "bad one." I just needed to be alone for a spell. I assured myself that after I got a few bulls under my belt, I would be back to my old self again.

It was interesting to watch all of the behind the scenes preparations of the cowboys putting on tape, wraps, and braces, etc. before entering the arena to get abused. I guess this is what athletes call "the love of the sport."

My bull, #69, was young and a little hooky. He hesitated and then bucked in the chute when the gate was opened. I was hoping that he would not come out backwards. He didn't. He just jumped and kicked and then he hit and pushed the clown's barrel for a distance. For a second it got a little spooky and I was glad that he didn't trip over it.

When the whistle blew, I jumped off and landed on my feet but I fell backwards onto my butt. As usual I showed no emotion and probably even had a little frown on my face. But don't get me wrong, every time that I could walk away after a ride, win or lose, I considered it a great accomplishment. Believe me, I always count my blessings.

On the way back to Wyoming we stopped at the PRCA National Headquarters in Colorado Springs. Billy Vossler and I picked up our membership cards for the 1985 season.

I entered the winter rodeos and was on the rodeo trail for five weeks. I spent quite a bit of time at Roz and Roy's place in Fort Worth, Texas. Gerry Strom drove down alone from Laramie and picked me up at Rosalyn's apartment. Gerry and I were driving down the interstate in broad daylight to Lake Charles, Louisiana. I was asleep and I was awakened by Gerry talking out of the window to some people in another vehicle.

I looked at the driver and realized that it was Andy Harris who now was married to Mary Ann Rogers and living in Tyler, Texas. Apparently he had passed us once and had noticed the Wyoming license plates and the PRCA window sticker on Gerry's truck. He had slowed down when he noticed a black guy sleeping against the window on the passenger side of the truck. Putting two and two together he figured it couldn't be anyone but Abe Morris.

It had sort of alarmed Gerry that this guy would pass him on the four-lane highway and then purposely slow down and let us pass him. After he figured out I was in the truck, he pulled up beside us and motioned for Gerry to wind his window down. Andy asked, "Is that Abe Morris riding with you?"

Andy wanted to know where we going and asked us to stop at his house since we were going to drive right through Tyler. We had time to kill and so we followed him home. We visited and caught up on old times and then went on to Lake Charles.

The ironic part of that story is that a few weeks before that chance encounter I had seen Beau Bridges, another cowboy who also had gotten his start at Cowtown, at the rodeo in Fort Worth, Texas. Beau was then living in Texas, as well. I'd told Beau I hadn't seen Andy Harris in about five years. And then I see Andy on the highway about two weeks later.

I had a really good bucking bull of Bradford Ivy's at San Antonio in the morning slack. He got it on away from my hand to the left. I was making one of the best rides of my career and he bucked me off because I started seeing dollar signs.

Afterward, I was complimented by Jamie Davis who was traveling with Denny Flynn at the time. Jamie said, "Man you were making one of the prettiest bull rides that I have ever seen in my life." Lyle Sankey also talked to me because I was very disappointed in bucking off at the 7.9 seconds mark. I told him that my goal was to get to as many rodeos as possible. He made an offer that I could start traveling with him. I didn't take him up on it and that's something I've always regretted. I honestly believe that if I had traveled with Lyle Sankey, I would have qualified for the National

Finals Rodeo. Lyle, from Rose Hill, Kansas, qualified several times for the NFR in all three riding events.

After San Antonio, Gerry left and went back to Laramie. I jumped in with Mark Wade, a two event cowboy from Bailey, Colorado. We went to Jackson, Mississippi and then we were going to go to Baton Rouge, Louisiana. All the way there, he kept talking about his girlfriend back in Colorado. He was boasting about sending her roses for Valentine's Day. I got tired of hearing about her. He was giving me a hard time because I hadn't sent anything to Carol.

In the motel room the first night in Jackson, he called his girlfriend several times and couldn't reach her. Being a smart alec, I said, "Just face it Mark, she's probably out with some other guy and that's why you can't get in touch with her."

We both competed in the rodeo the next night. Randy Hoffman from Utah and another bronc rider jumped in the motel room with us for the night. Mark got on the telephone from the room again and this time was successful in reaching his girlfriend. It was obvious that the conversation was not going well. We heard Mark say, "I already told you that this is the last year that I'm going to the winter rodeos."

I got a little worried and figured that I'd better check in with Carol back in Laramie since I hadn't talked to her for a few days. I went outside and was using a pay phone because I knew that Mark was going to be on the telephone in the room for awhile. I reached Carol and everything seemed to be going well with us.

All of a sudden, I saw Mark drive up to the motel manager's office and then go inside for about ten minutes. When he came out I yelled across the parking lot, "Mark, where are you going?"

He replied, "I'm going home."

I'd left my rodeo equipment bag in his car and I asked, "Where's my rigging bag?"

"In the motel room."

So I asked, "How am I going to get to Baton Rouge?"

"With those bronc riders." Then he jumped back into his car for a late night drive alone back to Colorado to try and salvage his relationship. It was already almost midnight when he left. I thought it was a very foolish thing to do, but he was in love.

After I went back to the motel room, Randy told me that Mark's girlfriend *had* been seeing someone else while he was on the rodeo trail. Then I really felt bad for teasing him about it.

Mark called PROCOM the next day and turned out his bull in Baton Rouge. A couple of weeks later we saw him at the rodeo in Houston. He had broken up with his girlfriend and was happy to be on the trail again. Mark should have stayed with us on the road and never gone back to Colorado in the first place.

That summer I spent my time either with Carol, working at Cathedral Home, or going to rodeos. I traveled alone for the most part and ended up catching rides to a lot of circuit rodeos.

In early July at the Greeley, Colorado, rodeo I drew one of the bucking mates to #S8 Knocker from Cowtown. Number 030 Jersey Joe, another NFR bull, bucked me off and just like in the previous year, I hung up again and my hand was still stuck in the bull rope. This time I didn't panic and kept a cool head. I remained calm, stayed on my feet and I reached up with my free hand and untied myself. To add insult to injury, he kicked me right in the stomach and knocked the wind out of me. After a few minutes I was okay, though.

Carol and I traveled together to a few rodeos. At the end of the summer, since we were getting along so well, we decided to move in together. My dad and mom did not approve of Carol and I living together because of their religious upbringing, but they were very accepting of our relationship. I told my mom that we had decided to move in together before we actually did. I didn't want them to call me and be totally shocked if Carol answered the phone at some odd hour of the day or night .

I had another good year in the circuit and again qualified for the Circuit Finals rodeo. I do not remember what I accomplished at the Circuit Finals that were held in Cheyenne, Wyoming.

That fall, Carol and I decided to take a vacation together completely away from the rodeo scene. We went to Yellowstone Park in Wyoming and then we drove across Idaho and up to Puget Sound. From there we drove down the coast of Washington, Oregon and California. When we were in Washington, her dog, Sydney, broke her leg and we had to take her to the veterinarian.

We stopped and camped in some beautiful places on our trip including the Redwood Forest and the giant Sequoias. In California we spent one night with my cousin Gene Walker and his family and another night with Hap Kellogg and his family. It was a nice break from the hustle and bustle of the rodeo trail and always being under a time crunch in order to get to the next one.

For Thanksgiving, Carol and I drove down to Fort Worth, Texas, and spent the holiday with Roz and Roy. We stopped in Umbarger and spent the night with Junie and Vera (Harp) Shorter.

23

1986

I ventured south again for the winter rodeos but I didn't win very much money. After the run, I opted to return to Laramie and work until the summer run was in full swing again.

In the spring, Shaw Sullivan, Brad Morris, Mike Ostoff and I went out to Gary Leffew's place in California for an impromptu bull riding session. Gary Leffew, the 1970 PRCA World Champion Bull Rider was considered to be the guru of modern day bull riders. He stressed a positive mental attitude and visualization. It was not one of his regularly scheduled sessions. We already had earned our PRCA cards and had decided to ask Gary to conduct a school exclusively for us so we could get tuned up, primed and ready for the summer.

In June, we took the Cathedral Home kids to Estes Park again for a week's vacation. Afterward, since Carol was also from New Jersey, we went to visit our families.

In New Jersey I was not paying as much attention to my rodeo business and as a result I neglected to enter the Cheyenne Frontier Days Rodeo. I called PROCOM about an hour after the entries had closed and I was devastated. Cheyenne Frontier Days had always been my favorite rodeo.

Carol told me many times that she did not want to get married. It had nothing to do with me because we both felt like I was a good candidate. She had just decided several years before we met that she wasn't interested in marriage.

My family all really liked Carol Gross. Thay had also really liked Gwen Mann. Gwen and I had gone to New Jersey in the summer of 1979. Carol Gross and I went to New Jersey in the summer of 1986. When we said all of our goodbyes and drove down the road to head back to Wyoming, Carol looked over at me and said, "I see now that we are going to have to come back here when we get married." I asked her if she was serious and her reply was, "Yes." Of course I was shocked because of what she had said in the past.

When Carol and I returned to Wyoming we decided to take the entire summer off work and go rodeoing together. We traveled in her little car and she was great about doing most of the driving. We went all over the western United States. Most of the rodeos that we went to were in the Mountain States Circuit. We had two dogs then, Kato and Sydney, and we took them everywhere with us.

In July, at West Jordan, Utah, I was pretty proud of myself for successfully riding #OA, Circle A of the Bruce Ford Rodeo Company. He had previously been owned by Elmer Anderson and then Dell Hall, stock contractors from Oklahoma. I was dreading getting on him because he had gone to the NFR on a few occasions and was known to jerk guys down onto his head. Granted, he had slowed down a little and was not as rank as he used to be but he still bucked hard.

Bobby DelVecchio and Lee Newman split first and second place on him. I also rode him at the same rodeo and didn't even place. Kenny Behling said that #OA had the exact same trip with me as he did with those other two guys. I rode him well. Kenny also said that, he didn't see any reason why those two guys could split the Bull Riding on him while I didn't even place. Once again, the judges saw it differently. One might say that once again they were looking through colored glasses.

In August, I got on #109 Break Dancer, a Don Hight bull at Deadwood, South Dakota. The bull riders dreaded these Hight bulls because they had the longest horns in the PRCA. Whenever these bulls were loaded into the bucking chutes, they had to turn their heads sideways in order to navigate the passageway because their horns were so long. There was always a loud clang-a-clang-a-clang when these bulls were being loaded. This cacophony served as a wake up call for the bull riders to prepare for battle.

My bull, Break Dancer, spun to the right and dropped me into the well right before the whistle. At first he was spinning and kicking and then he flattened out. He continued to spin but the change made it more difficult to stay on my bull rope and he whacked me in the rib cage with one of those horns. I do believe that he cracked one of my ribs. I didn't go the doctor in order to get it checked out but I was in a lot of pain. I was entered in several rodeos following that one and had drawn some good bulls. So I opted to wrap a wide ace bandage around my rib cage and keep on trucking.

In the span of a week, I placed in Rapid City, South Dakota; won second in Wheatland, Wyoming; won first in Springfield, Colorado on Dorenkamp's Toy Tiger; and topped off my run by winning first at Loveland, Colorado on #132 a NFR bull from Bennie Beutler. I placed at four rodeos in a row and won over $2,700 despite being in a fair amount of pain during each of those rides.

In the fall, Carol and I started working almost exclusively at the Satellite House which was a smaller annex of the Cathedral Home system. Satellite House was located in Laramie whereas Cathedral Home was located about four miles outside of the city limits.

In October, I entered the rodeo in Billings, Montana with Brad Morris. I rode #11, a blue roan bull that was owned by Harry Vold. He had a good trip and spun to the right. At about the five seconds mark he jerked the bull rope right out of my hand hold but somehow I was able to still hold on to the tail. I kept lifting on my bull rope for leverage and I was able to bend the tail of the bull rope over my right leg. He kept spinning to the right and I had a good spur hold with my inside right foot.

I still made an excellent ride on this good spinning bull and when the whistle blew all I had to do was open my hand. The sad thing was that, although I had made an excellent ride on a good bull, I was again slighted by the judges and did not even place in the Bull Riding event. We spent the night at Brad's parents home in Harden and his father, Bill Morris, a former RCA bull rider said, "Abe, you should be winning the Bull Riding."

Later on I received a proof in the mail from a rodeo photographer named Jerry Gustafson from Byers, Colorado. He also enclosed this note. "Abe, I should have been judging! You'd have won the Bull Riding if I was. I thought your ride was one of the best I've seen in a while. You were in total control and were classic in your style."

I had another good season and again qualified for the Mountain States Circuit Finals in the Bull Riding. Paul Gallegos from Colorado Springs and I went to Kansas City, Missouri in early November for the PRCA rodeo. We had planned to drive to Cheyenne together to compete in the Circuit Finals rodeo. At Kansas City, Paul was injured and decided that he could not compete at the Circuit Finals. He said that he knew a timed event cowboy who lived near his home who had also qualified. He would get in touch with him so that I could catch a ride to Cheyenne.

Thanks to Paul I hooked up with this cowboy and then I met Carol in Cheyenne. Again, I don't remember what I did at the Circuit Finals. A week or so later I spoke with Paul and he told me that the timed event cowboy had said to him, "Well Paul, you didn't tell me beforehand that Abe was black." Paul's response to that remark was, "Well I didn't tell Abe beforehand that you were white, either."

24

1987

Again, I took some time off work to go to the winter rodeos. I met Paul Gallegos and Mark Longoria in Colorado Springs and we headed to Fort Worth. We stopped in Umbarger on our way down and spent the night with the Shorters. We stayed with Rosalyn and Roy again in their new home in the Fort Worth suburb of Forest Hill.

In March, I qualified to compete in the first ever Dodge National Circuit Finals Rodeo in Pocatello, Idaho. It was a thrill and an honor to represent the Mountain States Circuit in this very prestigious event. I caught a ride with Joe and Tom Farrelly and Vern Edwards who were contestants from the First Frontier Circuit (Northeast) since they would be driving right through Laramie on their way to Pocatello.

A photo-journalist from New Jersey was also in Pocatello to assist with an article about the eastern cowboys who had gone west to do battle with the cowboys from the western United States. Bob Hill from Salem, New Jersey, took pictures that were featured in an issue of the *Philadelphia Inquirer's* daily newspaper a few weeks later. Since I was originally from New Jersey, I was included in the article.

My grandfather, Roosevelt Pope, who also lived in Woodstown, New Jersey, read the newspaper on a daily basis. He was sure proud and excited when he picked up a copy on Monday, March 23rd, to see an article entitled, *East Meets Wild West* and a picture of his grandson, the professional rodeo cowboy.

The rodeo was not only considered an individual competition but points were also tallied from each circuit. There were twelve geographical circuits in the United States and two contestants from each event, including the Barrel Racing. A team trophy was awarded at the end of the Dodge National Circuit Finals Rodeo to the circuit cowboys and cowgirls who had garnered the most points at the Finals.

It was a neat deal. All of the contestants were awarded jackets for qualifying for that rodeo. I was cool and proud to be able to sport my PRCA National Circuit Finals jacket around for the rest of my life. I did not win any money at the rodeo but I had a great time.

I also got to know a lot of other people, some of them timed event cowboys including Dee Pickett, an All Around World Champion, and Jake Barnes, seven time World Champion Team Roper. Dee Pickett played quarterback in college but chose to rodeo instead. His son, Cody, currently plays quarterback for the San Francisco Forty-Niners in the NFL.

Several of us, including Steve Fleming, the PRCA Director of Media Relations, played some pick up games of basketball. During one game I blocked a shot attempt by Dee Pickett underneath the boards. He curiously looked around to see who had blocked his shot and said, "I forgot that you were out here, I thought that we were playing with all white boys." I just laughed because I really got a kick out of his comment.

All of the contestants stayed at the Holiday Inn, which was the official headquarters for the event. Because of the setting, it was ideal for socializing with other cowboys who usually were on the go, rushing up and down the highways and byways of the rodeo trail. It was a nice opportunity to get to know people I would not have met otherwise.

I bucked off of my first bull. My second bull reared up and flipped in the bucking chute and pinned me to the back of it. It was kind of a scary thing. After I was rescued by some of my fellow bull riders, we decided to tie a rope horizontally above his neck so that he could not rear up again. I was able to get out of the bucking chute okay and make a successful and qualified ride.

At Pocatello I met Kendra K. Santos, a writer for the *Prorodeo Sports News*. The newspaper was the official publication of the PRCA. She asked me to do an interview for a feature article in the bi-monthly newspaper. The article was titled, *Wyoming bulls lured Abe to West* and was printed in the April 29, 1987 issue of the *Prorodeo Sports News*.

This rodeo served as a major step in my professional Bull Riding career. Combined with the two newspaper articles and other interviews, I was starting to get some attention and make a name for myself in the professional rodeo ranks.

That summer, during the Fourth of July Rodeo in Greeley, Colorado, Marty Staneart from Sanger, California, rode Mr. T of the Burns Rodeo Company for 7.8 seconds. It was a great ride and I thought that he was going to become the first man to successfully make a qualified ride on that rank bull.

I'd had another good year in the Mountain States Circuit rodeos. I won first in the Bull Riding and over eleven hundred dollars at my hometown rodeo during the Laramie Jubilee Days. I also was eighty points and placed in the first go-round at the Cheyenne Frontier Days Rodeo.

The day prior to my ride at Cheyenne, I pulled the groin

muscle in my left leg at Gunnison, Colorado, on a tall, slab sided bull, #T22 Mongrel, of the Alsbaugh Rodeo Company. I competed in the second section of the first performance at Cheyenne on Saturday, July 18th and took the lead in the Bull Riding with my eighty point score. I rode #2 of the Harry Vold bull herd. He was a black and white horned bull that turned back to the left right there in the gate and spun. He had an excellent trip.

After the gun sounded at Cheyenne I was so happy that I dismounted and threw my cowboy hat into the air. Then I raised both arms in exultation and proceeded to limp back to the bucking chutes. The crowd went wild because I was considered to be a hometown hero, even though I lived in Laramie.

After the section was over, I was mauled by the media people. They were sticking microphones in my face and asking me questions about my ride. It really felt good to be attracting all of that positive attention and I was on cloud nine. I also did a couple of short radio and television interviews. Film clips of my ride and a subsequent interview were aired that evening on television during the "Rodeo Roundup" on CBS Channel 5, which did a daily update of the rodeo results.

Lane Frost took the lead in the Bull Riding with a score of eighty-eight points in the third section of the Bull Riding and was leading it after the first day. I ended up sitting in second place after the first performance was completed. The next day the *Laramie Daily Boomerang* printed an article about Cheyenne Frontier Days and reported my good fortune from the previous day. The lead was, "Despite stumbling bull, Frost takes early lead at Frontier Days Laramie's Abe Morris, Jr. in second place."

That same day, which was Sunday, July 19th, I flew out to the California Rodeo in Salinas. I was complimented by several cowboys at Salinas who had seen my ride at Cheyenne. It made me feel pretty good. By this time my pulled groin muscle was killing me though I had iced it during the flight out to California, and I bucked off at Salinas. I could not run at all.

During the week I returned to Cheyenne on a couple of different days to the Justin Heeler medical trailer in order to get my groin muscle some electric shock and stem treatments. Jackie Romer was great about trying to keep me in top form for my second bull at Cheyenne. I also did another television interview with Lacy Reeves, a former Miss America candidate, who represented the state of Wyoming. She was doing a segment for the Cheyenne news station on the modern day rodeo cowboy and the theme was based on *Mommas Don't Let Your Babies Grow Up to be Cowboys*.

During the week Carol and I drove to Salt Lake City so I could compete in the Days of '47 Rodeo at the Salt Palace. I had drawn a good bull, otherwise, I was in so much pain that I would have turned him out and not risked further injury to my groin.

I bucked off. Rick Foster, a Justin Heeler from Longmont, Colorado, scolded me because I didn't consult them before I competed. I didn't know they were on the premises at Salt Lake City unil after I'd ridden.

As the week progressed my groin hurt me more and more. The swelling increased.

I ended up in a tie for fourth place in the first go-round and I won $1,101. By the time I competed on my second bull in Cheyenne on Saturday, August 1st, I was in a lot of pain. I did not place on my second bull, #3T of the Rudy Vela bull pen, but I did make the eight seconds whistle and was scored seventy-one points. I ended up qualifying for the finals to be held on Sunday afternoon. The top fifteen cowboys in each event after two go-rounds of competition would qualify for the finals and I ended up in eighth place going in.

I went over to Cheyenne about two hours before the rodeo started so that I could again get some electric stem treatments for my ailing groin muscle. By this time I had completely torn the muscle from the bone and it had rolled up and had knotted itself on my inner thigh.

Jackie Romer asked me before the rodeo where I would be going after I competed in Cheyenne. I told her that I was planning to go to several more rodeos because I was on a roll. My thigh was swollen from my groin area all the way to my knee. It looked just like a big old piece of bologna. She advised me to take a few weeks off to let my groin muscle try to heal.

I was very nervous to be competing in the Finals of the Cheyenne Frontier Days Rodeo. I got on a good spinning black bull of Sammy Andrews that turned back right in the gate and was quick about it. He bucked me off and I was very dismayed. I remember looking at a picture that was taken immediately after my ride and I had my head down in a posture of disappointment.

Carol and I returned to Laramie to put my Bull Riding career and my torn groin muscle on ice for a few weeks. Meanwhile, I purchased a neoprene girdle through a mail order service to help support my groin. I would wear it during every single ride for the rest of my rodeo career.

I returned to competition a few weeks later in Rapid City, South Dakota. It was too soon. I could not take hold of a bull with my left spur. Massive pain would shoot up my leg. Even during the ride, I could feel the pain in my leg. I had to dismount before the eight seconds whistle and running was a chore. After that attempt, I did not compete again for about another month.

Near the end of the Mountain States Circuit rodeos Carol and I again went camping. In September I competed in Pueblo and got seventy-six points on NFR bull #21 Voodoo of the Dorenkamp Rodeo Company. I won fifth place and over five hundred dollars at the Colorado State Fair and Rodeo. Then we drove to a state park in Nevada and stayed in the wilderness for a few days.

In October, Carol, Sydney, Kato and I left Laramie, Wyoming and moved to Fort Collins, Colorado. I got another job working with at risk youths. I also worked part time for Wyatt Construction Company.

My supervisor was Bruce (B.A.) Anderson. We got along very well.

In October I got on #171 Mr. T of the Burns Rodeo Company in Casper, Wyoming. Mr. T had not been successfully ridden at a PRCA rodeo since he had started to really buck. I simply became another notch on his long record of bruised and abused cowboys.

I qualified for the Circuit Finals Rodeo again in the Bull Riding event which was held in Cheyenne in November. I do not remember what I did at the Circuit Finals.

25

1988

In January I started entering rodeos with Zane Garstad who was originally from Canada. His father was Gid Garstad, a Canadian Bull Riding Champion. Zane had also attended the University of Wyoming and was then living in Sheridan, Wyoming. I worked with the at risk kids until the summer rodeos and then I took off and went on the rodeo trail again. Zane and I both had good years.

In early June I won first place at Elizabeth, Colorado, on #3 Sam of the Bob West (-W/ Rodeo Company) string. I competed in the morning slack at eight a.m. Then we drove to Cortez, Colorado. That evening I bucked off of #F13 Friday (Alsbaugh) at 7.9 seconds or I would have ended up winning first at two rodeos in the same day. Carlos Washington from Denver, a black bull rider, good friend and well-known country and western singer, pulled my rope for me at Cortez.

In July, at the Cheyenne Frontier Days Rodeo, I appeared on a televised show for the United Cable Company that was based out of Denver. A production crew was behind the chutes at Cheyenne and interviewing various cowboys. I was also interviewed and afterward was invited to be a guest on one of their live shows on the following Tuesday.

I sat down with Drew Goodman who was a well-known sports commentator from Denver. Drew does the commentary for the Colorado Rockies Major League baseball games. (The Rockies franchise did not exist in 1989). Drew asked me several questions concerning my rodeo career. During the interview he discovered that I was also a rodeo announcer. After the show, I wanted to know why I had been asked to appear. Drew said that when they were conducting their interviews, I seemed very comfortable on camera and had spoken very well.

The Rocky Mountain News did an interview with me and printed a story in their newspaper on July 24th entitled, *He's Different But the Bulls Don't Care.* The story talked about my rodeo career. The ironic thing was that the same newspaper printed the exact same article on the same date and also titled it *Counselor Sheds T-shirt for Chaps, Spurs* in other issues of the same paper. I purchased a few copies in Fort Collins and someone later sent my mom a copy they had seen in the newspaper purchased in Denver.

In August, a highlight of that summer was riding bull #193 Muhammad Ali, of the Burns Rodeo Company, who had bucked me off earlier that year in Laramie. I was scored eighty points on him in the morning slack and won over five hundred dollars and first place in the Bull Riding at Wheatland, Wyoming.

That same day I rode #1 Wau of the Bob West Rodeo Company in Golden, Colorado. He was a Watusi cross bull and he had the biggest horns of any bull that I ever got on during my bull riding career. They would definitely get your attention. When I was sitting on him and

August 1998, Golden, Colorado
#1 Wau, Bob West -W/ Rodeo Company   Bob Donaldson is the bullfighter on the left

getting my rope pulled tight, I refused to glance at those majestic horns.

Wau had a good trip and I made a successful ride on him. Afterward Kendra Santos commented, "You made a great ride and you got off and acted like it was nothing." I told her that I always expect to make the whistle so when I do, it is not that big of a deal.

It was whenever I bucked off that I was really hard on myself. I took my qualified rides in stride. I had a lot of talent and equally high expectations.

In September, Carol and I went to Albuquerque, New Mexico. I had drawn #1RC, a NFR Hereford-cross bull that really bucked hard with a lot of belly rolls. He was originally owned by Roy Carter from Crockett, Texas. Roy now provides bucking bulls for the PBR and is the proud owner of Kid Rock. Number 1RC was then owned by Mike Cervi from Sterling, Colorado. I knew that if I could ride this bull, there was a good chance I could win a lot of money on him. I was riding him just fine and then he jerked the bull rope to the fingertips of my riding hand. I was trying my best to just hold on. I could feel that I was going to have the bull rope jerked out of my hand at any moment but I had a good solid hold of him with both of my feet.

All of a sudden he whipped me down and I smacked my chin onto the top of his head. My hand was still barely in the bull rope and at this juncture I simply opened it. It had happened so fast that I didn't even have time to react by getting my free arm up to protect my face. As I was bucking off and still in the air he decided to wave goodbye with both feet. Luckily, he missed me.

When I hit the ground I kept thinking to myself, "He broke my jaw, he broke my jaw." I ran over to the side of the arena and stooped down in pain. The paramedics and other arena personnel came over to check on me and there were several people all huddled around. I left the arena under my own power but thinking that I might have also suffered some kind of very serious neck injury. Someone held their hands on each side of my face as I walked out so that I couldn't turn my head.

I had grabbed my chin with my gloved hand right after the knockout blow and held on to it. I was escorted to a folding chair behind the bucking chutes and I sat down. There was no doubt in my mind that I had suffered a broken jaw. I could picture having my jaw wired and having to consume my meals through a straw.

John Hester, the Justin Heeler, asked me to take my hand away from my chin so that he could look at it. My glove was soaked with blood. I didn't realize how bad I was bleeding because of the direct pressure I was applying to the wound. Blood was running like it was coming out of a faucet. There was a small puddle of my blood on the concrete floor.

I took the mouthpiece out and it was covered with blood. Later, I discovered that I'd chipped three teeth when they were smashed together by the force of the hit. Two of those were upper teeth that were inside my mouthpiece. I also had teeth marks in my tongue. They lasted for several weeks.

John said, "It was a good thing that you were wearing a mouthpiece or you probably would have lost a few teeth." He also said, "That mouthpiece also served as a shock absorber and probably kept you from being knocked unconscious." I probably would have bitten off part of my tongue if I hadn't used that mouthpiece. The ironic thing was that I had never worn a mouthpiece during my bull riding career and had only started wearing one about a month before that mishap.

John told me right away that I was split open pretty badly and that I was going to have to go the hospital in order to get some stitches. A message was relayed to Hadley Barrett the rodeo announcer to ask Carol Gross to report immediately behind the bucking chutes in order to transport me to the hospital.

After we arrived at the hospital, I was relieved to find out that I hadn't broken my jaw. The hospital staff ran several tests including X-rays and a CAT scan on my head. They were able to stop the bleeding and I was cleaned up and prepared for stitches. Just as I was heading into a room for stitches Carol said, "I want to see what it looks like before they stitch you up." I removed the gauze from my chin and she gasped and shuddered in disgust.

After seeing her reaction, I asked for a mirror because I wanted to see it for myself as well. When I saw it, I understood. My chin was completely filleted open. It was a very deep gash. It was not something you would want to see on someone else, let alone yourself. It was very gross to look at. The doctor used two different kinds of stitches for my chin. The first set was deep inside of the gash and they would dissolve in a few days. The second set was on the outside and would have to be removed later by another doctor in Fort Collins. It was a long sore drive back home. Carol and I gave a bronc rider a ride back to Fort Collins, so I didn't have to drive on the return trip.

Soon after that I started a new job with a highway construction company that was working on I-25 in Fort Collins. Zane and I both qualified for the Mountain States Circuit Finals in the Bull Riding event. I do not remember how I did at the Circuit Finals.

I caught a ride home for Christmas with another guy who also lived in New Jersey. The two of us drove non-stop to New Jersey and then back again after the holidays. My family really appreciated that Carol allowed me to spend the time there and it was great to see all of them. My mom noticed my new scar right away but I laughed it off as a shaving scar and then told them all the story of my spill fated trip in Albuquerque.

26

1989-1990

I didn't win any money at the National Western Stock Show and Rodeo in Denver. A round trip ticket through Continental Airlines was given away in each performance to the "hard luck" cowboy and I was selected!

I'd made a successful ride but did not dismount very well after the whistle sounded. I knew the bull was close by and that I was in the danger zone from the reaction and noise of the crowd. He got close to me but did not touch me. I guess it looked pretty scary and as a result I was given the "hard luck" award for that performance. Afterward, some of the other cowboys gave me a hard time because that bull had never even touched me and yet I still won the airline tickets.

At Fort Worth, I made a super ride on a bull that blew into the air and dropped just like a bareback horse. He never even turned back and the crowd went absolutely wild. I was disqualified for slapping the bull with my free hand. I was very disappointed as were Roy and Roz. They were very impressed with my riding ability though. I had no complaints because I was well aware that I *had* accidentally touched the bull.

We turned right around and drove back to Colorado and didn't even spend the night in Fort Worth because I had to go to Rapid City, South Dakota. Roy and Rosalyn Hairston were a little disappointed that I didn't return and had turned out my second bull at Fort Worth.

I entered Rapid City and drew a NFR bull called Crow's I-90. I was debating on whether or not I was willing to drive five hours alone to get on him. At the last minute I decided to go because Carol got on me for complaining about not drawing very well at a lot of rodeos. Crow's I-90 was supposed to be a good bull. So I got in my little Nissan pickup truck and drove.

The bull had a good trip and spun to the right. I ended up being scored seventy-eight points and winning third place and $678.00 in the first go-round behind Marty Staneart and Glen Keeley. The top ten would qualify for the finals or the short go-round the following week-end. Before I could return to Rapid City, we were hit by a huge arctic air front. It got to be very, very cold and it had snowed. The finals would be held on Saturday night.

I called PROCOM on Saturday morning to find out that I had drawn #13 Ajax, a former NFR bull. The operator at PROCOM tried to talk me out of going out in those treacherous and adverse conditions just to compete in a rodeo. When I started up my pickup to leave it was eight below zero. It was so cold that I wore a ski hat, a scarf, a down vest, insulated long underwear and placed a blanket between myself and the door of my pickup truck. I had an ice scraper and I had to constantly scrape the ice off of the inside of my windshield in order to see.

When I stopped for gas in Lusk, Wyoming, I refused to turn off the engine. I also stopped at a rest area to run to the bathroom and I left the truck running. A person could freeze to death if they happened to slide off of the road in those bitter conditions. It was so cold that you could see the exhaust fumes pouring out of the vehicles on the interstate and highways.

The cold had caused water pipes in several businesses in Rapid City to burst. Also one of the bucking bulls, a Brahma, had frozen to death. The severe cold was hard on some of the warm blooded breeds. Some of the spectators were constantly leaving the performance in order to go outside and warm up their vehicles for a spell.

Ajax had a good trip and I was scored seventy-six points in the short go-round, or finals. I also ended up winning first in the average. My check was for $2,498.00. Marty Staneart bucked off of Skoal's Wipeout. The bull had not been successfully ridden at that time. Glen Keeley won fourth in the average. (Glen died in February 2000 in Albuquerque after he was stepped on by the bull Promiseland at a PBR event.)

I stayed overnight in Rapid City with Dwayne Hargo, an African-American bullfighter from Placerville, California. Dwayne was the 1989 PRCA World Champion Bullfighter. I took the battery out of my pickup truck and took it into the motel room to keep it warm so that my truck would start the next morning.

The next day, Sunday February 4th, the top contestants from the regular rodeo competed for a chance to win a pickup truck. There was no prize money involved. There were two pickup trucks. One would be awarded to the top rough stock rider and the other would go to the top timed event contestant. I was bucked off of my first bull and did not advance to the second round. Glen Keeley from Canada won the truck for the rough stock events.

On Monday morning, I flew to El Paso. I bucked off when my bull jerked the rope out of my hand so I caught a ride back to Fort Collins with Jeff Cathcart from Cheyenne.

The Prorodeo Sports News did a nice write up about me for

winning the Bull Riding in Rapid City. The story, along with a picture, appeared in the February 15, 1989 issue and was titled, *Abe Morris is Best on Black Hills Bulls.*

A few weeks later I caught another ride south with Jeff to a few more of the winter rodeos. We got caught in a blizzard outside of Raton, New Mexico. Highway 287 was closed and we had to spend a very bitter and miserable night on the highway, stuck in his pickup truck. We froze.

I did okay at the winter rodeos but I didn't win much money down South.

In the Spring I won first place at a small rodeo in Newcastle, Wyoming, that was produced by Harlan Gunville from South Dakota. I continued to work for the highway construction company until May. After completing a job in east Denver on I-70, I was ready to hit the rodeo trail again.

In May I competed at the rodeo in Fort Smith, Arkansas. My bull did not buck very well and I was only scored fifty-nine points on him. During the rodeo, I was interviewed for an article that was later printed in the *Southwest Times Record* on Friday, June 2, 1989. The title of the newspaper article was, *Bull Rider Stands Out in a Crowd.*

Also in May, I was contacted by Dave DeLozier from 9 News KUSA in Denver about doing a television story about my life and rodeo career. I was curious as to how he had gotten my name and my telephone number. The station had contacted the PRCA office in Colorado Springs and I had been recommended for the story.

We started the story with an interview and then I got on a few practice bulls at the -W/ Arena in Arvada. Dave met me in Elizabeth, Colorado, in early June where I bucked off of a bull, #6 Tippy. He was named Tippy because he had a tendency to tip and fall over on his would-be riders. Before I got on him he had injured a couple of bull riders by actually falling down on them.He pulled a cheap shot on me by trying to fall over and then he stood back up and bucked me off. He was soon banned by the PRCA Bull Riding director Bryan McDonald.

In June, I won first place on #11 Aces of the Burns Rodeo Company in Grover, Colorado. Aces was an NFR bull that was bucked in the eliminator pen at the National Finals Rodeo. He had a swoop move when he turned back to the right that was extremely difficult for left-handed bull riders to master. Winning first at the Earl Anderson Memorial Rodeo also earned me my first PRCA trophy belt buckle.

Then Dave DeLozier came up to Fort Collins to get some footage of me spending time with some of the at risk kids at the Larico treatment facility where I had worked. We played some volleyball in the backyard.

The fourth weekend in June I won first place and a check for $757.80 in Moab, Utah. I rode a little red bull that spun to the right and was owned by Mickey Young. I spurred him and made a good solid ride. It turned out to be a nice birthday present because the rodeo ended on June 24th. I was traveling solo at the time though I never enjoyed traveling alone.

Next, I competed in the Fourth of July rodeo at Greeley. The kids from Larico Youth Services facility were special guests at the rodeo and came to watch me compete. I chatted with some of them in the grandstand on camera before competing. I made a qualified ride but my bull did not buck very well.

After the rodeo I chatted with the kids again on camera and then Todd Steinbock, my new traveling partner, and I headed down the road. We were scheduled to compete in Prescott, Arizona the following night. I was informed that the KUSA story would be edited and aired on television sometime in the next few weeks.

In Prescott I ran afoul of my least favorite PRCA pro judge again. I rode #JW (Harry Vold's) and he had a really good trip. He was extremely hard to ride and I was very proud of myself for an all out effort and getting him ridden. Todd rode #U2 and was seventy-nine points. I was scored seventy-four points and was extremely disappointed. I knew that I should have been scored at least eighty points on my bull.

When I checked the score sheet of my least favorite judge, Jim, had scored me a nineteen points ride on a nineteen points bull. Then he had taken his pencil and very clearly erased my scores and changed them to an eighteen points ride on an eighteen points bull. This was another reason why I'll repeat that I came to resent this PRCA judge and dreaded showing up at a major rodeo to discover that he was judging it.

After the rodeo Scott Dawson, the flank man for Harry Vold, said to me, "I cannot believe that Todd was scored higher than you were. To me there was no comparison between the trip that JW had and the trip that his bull had. In my opinion you should be winning the Bull Riding without a doubt." I could not have agreed more.

Todd ended up splitting first and second place with Lane Frost and he won a very nice trophy belt buckle. Because he was my traveling partner, I saw that buckle on a regular basis and could not help but think that I should have been wearing it instead of Todd. I held no animosity towards my traveling partner, but my resentment towards that PRCA pro judge continued to grow.

I still placed in the Bull Riding at Prescott. I also placed in the Fourth of July rodeo in Steamboat Springs, Colorado. Steamboat Springs was a weekly rodeo during the summer months on Friday and Saturday nights. The committee increased their purse for a special rodeo to coincide with the Fourth of July. I had a good run during the "Cowboy Christmas."

Soon after the Fourth of July run I purchased a VHS camera. The first rodeo that we took it to was in Pretty Prairie, Kansas. I wish that I could have found someone to run my camera on me that time because I won first place in the Bull Riding and over twelve hundred dollars.

The next morning, Todd dropped me off at the airport in

Denver and I flew to Houston on my way to a Morris Family Reunion in Jacksonville, Florida. I met Rosalyn and her son Randall at the airport in Houston. I had previously told everyone in my immediate family that I was not going to make it to the reunion. Then I contacted Roz and found out that we could hook up in Houston and fly together to Jacksonville. She would be flying in from Fort Worth. My family was driving a van from New Jersey to Florida and they were picking up Roz from the airport in Jacksonville so finding me there as well would be a big surprise. Several times over the years, I surprised my family by dropping in unannounced.

As we were descending for the landing at Jacksonville, the plane suddenly dropped and it startled everyone. People that were holding drinks tossed them into the air. The pilot came on the loudspeaker and apologized but said it really was not his fault. I think that we had hit some kind of an air pocket. He said, "I was just checking to see that everyone was still awake on this flight."

I made sure that I waited until all of the passengers had gone before I deplaned. I got off and stopped right by the entrance door to the airport. Everyone was standing around getting their hugs and saying hello to Roz and Randall Hairston. Christine, Patricia, Janice and David Morris from my immediate family and my Grandmom Minnie Pope from Woodstown had all come down for the reunion.

At the time, Randall was only three years old so we had to make sure that he didn't mention that Uncle Abe was on the airplane. When my sister Patricia saw me standing there, she let out a blood curdling scream. You would have thought that someone was either having a heart attack or getting robbed. After attracting all that attention, she was very apologetic and explaining to strangers around her, "That's my brother, we didn't know he was coming."

I wish that I had caught that on my camera but I got a lot of good footage of the folks at the reunion and saw a lot of familiar faces as well as new family members. I was very glad I had it along.

After the reunion we took a trip to Disney World. Then we stopped in New Smyrna to see some of the family members who didn't make it to the reunion and to see the house where we'd lived when we were kids. I was born in Florida in New Smyrna Beach. My siblings, Patricia Medina, Janice Ellen and David Wayne Morris had all been born in New Smyrna Beach. Rosalyn Rashel and Reuben Darryl Morris had been born in Salem, New Jersey.

The next morning I flew back to Denver and Todd picked me up at the airport. I stopped at the house only for a few minutes and then we were back on the road again. We drove to Salt Lake City to compete in a rodeo that night and we spent the night there. Todd had not entered the rodeo in Nampa, Idaho, so he caught a ride home and another cowboy, Brian Hawk, jumped in with me and we drove my pickup truck to Nampa.

I was fouled at the gate on my first bull and was awarded a re-ride by the judges. I rode my second bull after the rodeo performance but I only won some day money on him. I could not find any cowboys at Nampa who were going back to the Denver area. Todd and I had a red eye flight out of Denver to Monterey, California the next night, so I had to drive all night by myself in order to make it on time. We were entered in Salinas and Monterey was the closest airport.

I stopped for gas at a convenience store at about one a.m. and saw a front page newspaper article about a United Airlines flight crashing in an Iowa cornfield. This unnerved me because I was driving like crazy just to get to Denver on time to strap myself into an airplane. By the time that I arrived in Fort Collins the next evening I was totally exhausted. I had just enough time to take a shower, get rid of my dirty clothes and pack some clean ones, grab a quick bite to eat and then head off to the airport to catch our flight.

We left at about ten p.m. and landed in Las Vegas with a two hour layover. When we went to our gate, there was only one person sitting in a chair in the entire area and he was sound asleep. Todd and I decided to kill some time by playing a few slot machines.

The guy sleeping in the waiting area was tossing and turning and kept talking in his sleep. As a result, no one would sit down next to him. Finally, an elderly Hispanic man showed up with his grandson and reluctantly sat down next to the stranger. The guy continued to toss and turn in his chair as well as mumble and talk in his sleep.

After awhile, he shifted again and said something and then he took in a huge long hawk as if he was preparing to spit. Upon hearing this, all of the people near him got up to run. But the elderly gentleman was too slow in reacting and, as he was in mid-stride making his escape, the sleeping man spit a nasty gob of phlegm into the air.

Fearing the worst, the elderly man stopped and was trying to twist his shirt around and the same time look over his shoulder to see if it was a direct hit. A lady seeing his anguish and sitting near him pointed to the back of his shirt and said, "Heeee got you."

The elderly gentleman retreated to the restroom in order to get cleaned up from the splat. When he came back, he was carrying his soiled shirt and was only wearing his undershirt. He was very upset and went and stood over the sleeping man and started to curse him in Spanish. Some of the other travelers were telling the man, "Hit 'im, hit 'im." The gentleman was hot and rightfully so. He even stomped on the floor a few times and gestured like he was going to pop that man with a fist.

Soon, a travel agent came over the loudspeaker and we started to board our flight. The man was still sound asleep and we knew that no one was going to wake him up for fear that they would be seated next to him on the flight. As a result, he missed the flight and was left in Las Vegas.

Todd and I told this story for the rest of that rodeo season. I could not believe that a man could hawk and then spit in his sleep and never even wake up. How gross can you get?

Todd and I competed in Salinas, California and stayed overnight. The next morning we flew back to Denver and drove up to Cheyenne to compete in the first go-round. I had a really good money bull of Mac Altizer out of Texas. He really blew into the air and had a good day. I could have ridden him a little better but I was scored seventy-six points and that ended up being good enough to place fifth in the first go.

Afterward, Rob Bunten said that I had ridden a little stiff and he had been yelling at me to, "Move, move." All of the running up and down the road had taken a toll on me. I was tired and not as aggressive as I should have been.

After the rodeo I was leaving the area behind the bucking chutes and Gary Leffew yelled my name. He gestured for me to come over because he wanted to talk to me. I walked in his direction asking myself, "Now what does Gary want to talk to me about?" I was tired and wanted to go home.

He started out by saying, "I have been watching you ride for the last couple of years and you have ridden better each year. Right now you ride as well as the middle of the top fifteen guys who go to the Finals each year."

I said, "Well thanks, Gary. My cousins have been telling me for years that I rode well enough to qualify for the National Finals Rodeo but I figured that they were just telling me that because I was family and they wanted to see me accomplish that feat. I would love to qualify for the Finals."

Gary said, "The only reason that you haven't qualified for the Finals is because you don't go to enough rodeos. I can guarantee you that if you will get out there and start going hard and get to some rodeos, you *will* qualify for the Finals."

We chatted a little more and then I thanked him for the compliments and encouragement. I was dog tired at this point but that little chat had pumped me up and I was feeling pretty good about myself by the time I drove back to Fort Collins for some badly needed rest.

My 9 News story on KUSA was aired on a Saturday evening show called *Tonight in Colorado*. I knew that I would be on the rodeo trail so I had set the VCR in order to tape it. I was very impressed with the producer, Dave DeLozier, and how the story turned out.

Carol was home at the time and said that there was a pouring rainstorm right after it aired. She heard someone pounding on the door and asked herself who in the world could be knocking on our door in that weather? It turned out to be the boy from just down the street. No one in his family had a clue that I was a rodeo cowboy and he came over to tell Carol that he had just seen me on the television. He had two young sisters and we saw them weekly because we were always walking our dogs down to the river. Those kids were always out back in the pastures or down at the river. I never wore my cowboy hat or boots when I was walking the dogs so none of them had a clue that I was a cowboy or rode bulls. He was pretty excited that he had just seen his friend Abe on television.

I did not draw very well in the second go-round at Cheyenne. I was only sixty-seven points on my second bull and as a result did not qualify for the (Top 15) Finals.

About ten days before the rodeo in Cheyenne I received a phone call from Prime Sports Network (now Fox Sports Network). They had plans to film the Finals of the Cheyenne Frontier Days Rodeo and they were in need of a broadcast commentator for the show. My response was that I had never done any television work. Because of my interview with them the previous year at Cheyenne, they were aware that I had my PRCA announcer's card. I was told, "Well we know that you have your PRCA announcer's card and we would be delighted to have you be one of the broadcast commentators for our show."

I agreed saying, I couldn't promise them anything. But if they wanted to give me a shot at it then I was more than happy to do it. This was to be the launch of my career as a television commentator. Little did I know at the time but it would last for nine years at Cheyenne Frontier Days.

I would be working with Drew Goodman who had done quite a bit of work with Prime Sports Network. Drew is now the broadcast commentator for Fox Sports. I showed up at the rodeo a couple of hours early in order to do our stand-up interview before the show started. This would be the first year of the telecasts for Prime Sports. I didn't have any coaching, Drew and I simply discussed what we would talk about and then it was "lights, camera, action."

Sunday, July 30th, was a rainy, cool and dreary day. I had no idea at the time that it would turn out to be one of the saddest days of my rodeo career. We talked about the various events and the match-ups in the Bull Riding. I talked about Marty Staneart getting on Mr. T of the Burns Rodeo Company and Lane Frost getting on #SO of the Mac Altizer Rodeo Company. Mr. T still carried an unblemished record in the PRCA since he had really started to buck. I had seen the 7.8 seconds attempt when Marty almost rode him in Greeley in 1987. I made a prediction on camera that Marty would be successful on this day and become the first man to ever ride that famous bull.

The Bull Riding was gearing up to be a thrilling event because Lane Frost from Quanah, Texas, the 1987 PRCA World Champion Bull Rider, had drawn #SO, and he had not been successfully ridden in 1989. Clint Branger had drawn #W7 Stinger of the Bob West -W/ Rodeo Company and he had never been successfully ridden, either.

Before the rodeo started, I interviewed a lot of the cowboys on camera who had done well and who had a good chance to win it all at the "Daddy of 'em All." I interviewed Marty and Lane and shook their hands and wished them both good luck. Thinking back now, I did not realize when I shook Lane's hand and said, "good luck" that in reality I was really saying goodbye to a dear friend.

At the time Tuff Hedeman, Lane Frost, Jim Sharp and Clint Branger were all traveling together and they all had qualified for the Finals at Cheyenne in Bull Riding.

In the first section of Bull Riding Tuff, the 1986 World Champion, rode #57 Ambush of the Rudy Vela bull herd. David Berry rode #104 Top Gun from the Hank Franzen (Powder River Rodeo Company) from Gillette, Wyoming. He was scored eighty-four points. After the whistle sounded he was hit in the face by the bull's horn and suffered a fractured jaw. In the second section, Clint Branger bucked off of #W7 Stinger.

Then there was a big build-up because Marty was settling down on Mr. T. Marty wowed the rodeo world and the Frontier Days crowd by successfully riding Mr. T for the full eight seconds and a Cheyenne Frontier Days record of ninety-three points. The crowd was still buzzing when Lane Frost nodded his head about two rides later on #SO Taking Care of Business. Lane made a fantastic ride on #SO and was scored eighty-five points. But when the gun sounded either he jerked his hand out of the bull rope or it popped out. He did not make a good dismount and as the bull continued to spin Lane landed right in harm's way.

At first Lane made an attempt to crawl away and then, realizing that he was in trouble, he stopped and kind of braced himself for the hit. Number SO was still kicking and put a horn on Lane's side and then pushed him about a foot or so in the slightly muddy arena. Lane got up but you could tell right away that he had been very seriously injured because he was staggering and he was waving for someone to come and help him out of the arena. Then he collapsed.

A throng of people rushed to his aid, including his traveling partner and best friend, Tuff Hedeman. It was pretty obvious that he was seriously injured. At one point, someone ran out into the arena with a stethoscope. Then someone else ran out there with an oxygen tank. A stretcher was called for and after he was placed on the stretcher, the helpers ran out of the arena. I had been around rodeos for most of my life and I had never seen paramedics run out of the arena with an injured cowboy.

I was standing on the back of the bucking chutes. I was only two chutes away from the chute that Lane had come out of. I could have gone out there to see what was going on but I didn't want to.

Doug Vold came back to the bucking chutes. I said, "Doug, what was going on out there?" Doug shook and then lowered his head saying, "He wasn't breathing when they carried him out of here."

I watched the rest of the rodeo in a daze. All I could think about was Lane. After the rodeo I did several interviews with the winners in each event.

Marty Staneart had ended up in a tie for first place with Jim Sharp, the 1988 PRCA World Champion from Kermit, Texas. Jim had successfully ridden #V3 Bandito of the Rudy Vela Rodeo Company. A lot of the media people wanted to interview Marty because he had successfully ridden Mr. T, who had already been named the 1986 PRCA Bucking Bull of the Year.

Even though I had a job to do, all I could think about was Lane Frost.

I was just about ready to conduct the television interview with Marty Staneart when Pete Burns said to me, "I just heard that Lane did not make it. But that hasn't been confirmed yet." Drew Goodman was standing right next to me, out of the camera's view, and Marty was just about ready to start talking. I was holding the microphone and I kind of threw it at Drew and in an emotional voice said, "Here you do it." Then I walked away and sat down because I was devastated. Marty gave me a look of bewilderment as if to say, "What is wrong with you?" He had been caught off guard by my sudden change of mind to interview him.

Drew and I were scheduled to go back over to the other side of the rodeo arena to do a wrap-up for the TV show. When I arrived at the television trailer, some of the station employees were reviewing the tape of Lane's ride. Someone put their hand on my chest as I was about to enter the trailer and refused to let me in saying, "We don't want you to see this."

The TV crew said we could skip the close and that they would think of something else to do in its place. They were trying to be considerate because they knew I was pretty upset. Drew kept telling me, "Don't count him out. Don't count him out."

I told them to at least let me attempt to talk and, if I didn't make it through the whole segment without falling apart, they could decide not to air it. Drew and I decided to talk about the rodeo events and results and not to mention anything about Lane riding #SO because I told him that if we did, I would fall apart and not be able to continue the taping.

We got through the close okay but my voice was cracked and my eyes were bloodshot because it was very apparent that I had been crying. This was probably about an hour or so after the conclusion of the rodeo and there still was no official word on Lane's status.

When I trudged back across the muddy arena and got to the other side, I saw Rick Chatman, the bullfighter, standing all alone by the fence near the bucking chutes with his head down. I asked if he had heard anything about Lane. Rick said to me in a very, very sad voice, "He passed away." Up until that point I'd held onto the hope that he was going to survive and be okay. But then I knew.

I stayed around because I needed to get the official final results for our television production. I remember just walking over to the bull pen and breaking down. Russell "Pinky" Walter came up behind me and put his hand on my shoulder to try to console me. I saw a lot of other people who I could tell had also been crying including Butch Kirby and George Michael (Sports Machine host).

After awhile, I just wanted to go home and be alone. I broke down and cried pretty much all the way back to Fort Collins. When I arrived, I called Charles Sampson in Casa Grande, Arizona to tell him. When I did, he kept asking what exactly had happened. I repeated two or three times just what I had seen. Charlie kept saying, "No, no, no." Finally I lost my composure again and burst out crying saying, "I don't know how, I don't know how."

Later on Jeff Hart, an NFR bareback rider from Laporte, Colorado, came over to get his pickup truck. I had driven it back from the rodeo in Rock Springs, Wyoming, and he had caught a ride to another rodeo in Salinas. I was trying to explain to Jeff what had happened at Cheyenne and I broke down and cried again. After Jeff left, I took my dogs for a walk down to the Poudre River and just sat down and cried my head off.

I watched and taped the ten p.m. news from Cheyenne on CBS Channel 5. When Carol got home from work that evening, she said that she knew something terrible had happened. I didn't know how she sensed it because I was quietly sitting on the couch in the dark with the TV on and she asked me what was wrong. Instantly I burst into tears and I could not even tell her what had happened. She came over and gave me a big hug. I still could not tell her what had happened and so I played the VCR tape instead.

I was in a daze, a virtual fog for the next few days. I had to get out of the house and I went to the Healthworks club to work out. When I was there, a friend Mike, said to me, "You lost one of the guys in your fraternity." I almost lost it again and was just about to run into the locker room so that people wouldn't see my grief.

We were entered in Hill City, Kansas, on Wednesday and then Dodge City, Kansas, on Thursday. I was more afraid to get on a bull than at any other time during my career. I was absolutely terrified. I really had not drawn a particularly bad bull, I was just plain scared to death. I simply wanted to survive and be able to be behind the chutes and put my stuff back in my rigging bag again. I didn't tell anyone that I was afraid.

At Dodge City, the committee had a memorial service for Lane at the rodeo arena on Thursday morning. Many cowboys spoke including Harry Vold who said, "Lane always showed up to the rodeo with a smile on his face." Todd and I attended that service.

Lane Frost and I had hit it off right from the beginning of his PRCA career. He would always go out of his way to come over and say hello whenever he saw me at a rodeo. Without a doubt, he was one of the most popular guys, by far, on the circuit. He was well loved by his peers and the rodeo fans alike.

I remember talking to him in Kansas City, Missouri, in November 1983 when he ended up in sixteenth place in the World Standings and barely missed qualifying for the NFR in his rookie season. He had also ended up second for the Rookie of the Year in the Bull Riding event behind Jackie Gibbs from Ivanhoe, Texas.

I was okay and kept my composure throughout most of the memorial service until they started playing that sad piano music. That's when I had to get up and go and I never came back. I headed straight for the bathroom and reeled off a batch of toilet paper so I could dam up the floodgates.

Butch Kirby, the 1978 World Champion Bull rider who was also originally from Woodstown, New Jersey, tried to console me and get me to stop crying but it didn't help at all. The raindrops continued to fall from my eyes. It was like a monsoon. I was not one who was known to cry in public—I kept saying to Butch, "I just can't help it, I just can't help it."

Ironically, some of Mac Altizer's bulls were also in the draw at Dodge City and I saw #SO in the pen. I just kept staring at the bull thinking that he'd killed my friend. I didn't hate the bull. I knew that it was a freak accident and death was something that bull riders knew they were facing every time that they nodded their heads.

Next, Todd and I went to Casper, Wyoming. We caught a ride

the next day to Deadwood, South Dakota with Marty Staneart. We talked a lot about what had happened six days earlier at Cheyenne. I explained to Marty why I had given the microphone to Drew Goodman and walked away right before our interview. Marty said that if he had known, he wouldn't have been able to go through with it.

Todd and I would continue to rodeo together for the rest of the season. Lane Frost's death would stick with me and continue to bother me for a long time. During the rodeo in Douglas, Wyoming, in August, I was chatting with some women who were also in Cheyenne on that same day. They told me that when the ambulance left the area behind the bucking chutes, the emergency lights weren't turned on. I had not realized that Lane had died within minutes of the accident. Later on, I was told that he had broken four ribs and one of them had cut his aorta. He'd died from internal bleeding.

I remember talking to outsiders about his death and they all had different versions of what exactly had happened. It bothered me that they were saying that Lane had turned his back on that bull after a successful ride and was hit from behind. A lot of these "experts" were not even at the rodeo that day.

On television, I saw some footage of Lane Frost in the music video of *The Dance* by Garth Brooks. The song and the video became very popular. From that moment forward, every time that I saw the video or heard the song, my eyes would fog up with tears and I would get very quiet. It didn't matter if I was in a bar or driving down the road to another rodeo. I would have to blink back tears. The song has always reminded me of that tragic day in Cheyenne.

In August 1999, the Prorodeo Sports News ran a story because it was the tenth anniversary of Lane's death. While reading the article my eyes welled up with tears when it talked about Tuff Hedeman kissing his best friend goodbye as soon as he realized that Lane had passed away. When I read the part about Tuff riding his bull in Casper a week later and then going back behind the chute area and breaking down and crying, I had to put the newspaper down because I started crying again. I could not finish reading the article until the following day.

On Wednesday, August 2nd, the *Fort Collins Coloradoan* daily newspaper ran a full page story about me and my rodeo career entitled, *Cowboy Knows What It Takes*. The story was written by Yvonne Barth. It included a picture of me decked out in full rodeo attire, including my chaps and spurs. I lived in Fort Collins, very close to the boundary line of the town of Laporte. The caption under my picture incorrectly stated that I lived in Laporte.

A few weeks later, I met a lady from Laporte down at the Poudre River when I was walking my dogs. At the time there were not any black men residing in the town of Laporte. She started asking questions. When she said, "So what do you do?" my response was, "If I told you then you wouldn't believe me."

Then she said, "Don't tell me that you're the guy who rides those big bulls."

I said, "Indeed I am."

She had read all about me in the newspaper article and knew that she had never seen me in the local grocery store. Rose Brinks was her name and she was so excited to meet a "celebrity," as she called me. She told me that I had to come home with her so that she could introduce me to her family. So I followed her home. Rose invited me over for dinner a few times and we stayed in touch until I moved to Denver in September 1998.

During the Labor Day weekend, Todd and I went to Ellensburg and Walla Walla, Washington, and then headed back to Evanston, Wyoming for a circuit rodeo. We were both in contention for the Wrangler Circuit Series in the Bull Riding event. Wrangler jeans would award a thousand dollar bonus to the champion at the conclusion of the Mountain States Circuit Finals. The Wrangler Circuit Series was based on points at a few pre-designated rodeos. In the regular circuit standings, which were based on money, Johnny Shea from Delta, Colorado, was in first place and Todd Steinbock in second. I was in third. I kept on telling Todd that I was going to catch and pass him in the regular circuit standings and his response was always, "Come on!"

Evanston was the final rodeo before the circuit finals that counted in the point standings for the Wrangler series. When we arrived in Evanston on Monday morning, we went to the arena to check out our bulls because those Kerby bulls only had numbers and no names. As we approached the bull pen, there was a huge red bull lying down. My first thought was, *man look at the size of that monster, I sure hope that is not my bull #419.* He easily weighed over a ton. In looking at the brands I could not locate my bull and finally I got around the pen and saw #419 on that huge red bull.

My bull had a really good trip and spun to the right. I rode him well and when the whistle blew I made sure that I made a good dismount. I wanted to land on my feet and as far away from that big bull as possible. I knew if I didn't and he stepped on me, that he would break me in half. I had a good dismount and was scored seventy-nine points and I won the Bull Riding event and over eleven hundred dollars. I would rarely throw my hat but I tossed it frisbee-style, low across the arena. I had not only won the Bull Riding but I also took over the lead in the Wrangler Circuit Series.

The first time that I saw Tuff Hedeman again was at Pendleton, Oregon in September. I wanted to say something to him about Lane but the words just didn't come. I rode my bull but I was only about sixty-eight points. Johnny Chavez from Bosque, New Mexico, won both go-rounds and the average in the Bull Riding and a very nice saddle. I had seen the Pendleton Round Up rodeo on television when I was growing up in New Jersey. I had always wanted to compete there.

I knew that it had a small race track and then a large grass infield. During the Bull Riding, the committee would put up a PVC plastic pipe fence to try and keep the bulls in an enclosed area.

Sometimes the bulls would knock over the fence and then things would get very interesting. A lot of the committee men and cowboys would hang out on the other side of the fence and they would look like a bunch of mice scattering whenever a bull busted through the fence.

During the rodeo we stayed at the Severe Brothers ranch. They were well-known leather craftsmen and saddle makers. They had a bunkhouse with several beds and they would put up any of the PRCA cowboys who were in town for the rodeo. It was a very cool place. I had heard a lot about it and it was neat to finally see it for myself.

We hauled Johnny's saddle to Albuquerque for him in my pickup truck because he didn't have a way to get it back to New Mexico. Later in Omaha, Nebraska, I witnessed one of the best bull rides of my rodeo career. Ervin Williams, another black bull rider from Tulsa, Oklahoma, rode #S27 Wrangler Brush Popper of Cervi's for eighty-eight points and first place in the Bull Riding. This big bull jumped and kicked and then turned back to the right which was into Ervin's riding hand. Ervin made a jam up ride and really spurred this NFR bull. It was a great ride. By today's standards he would have been over ninety points, easily. Ervin was a regular qualifier for the National Finals Rodeo in the Bull Riding and had a very successful rodeo career.

In October, when the rodeo season came to a grinding halt in our area, I went out and got a job at a pipe coating facility in Fort Collins. It would be something to tide me over and get me through the winter until the big rodeos kicked off in January.

Carol and I went up to the Circuit Finals rodeo. It was held November 3rd—5th in Cheyenne, Wyoming. In the first round I rode #OH Thain & Johnson of Harry Vold's for seventy-six points and third place. It was the third time that I'd gotten on him. He had previously bucked me off in Pueblo in 1988 and also in Casper at the season finale rodeo in October that same year. Charlie Needham pulled my rope and warned me to, "Just stay down on him and you won't have any trouble getting him covered." It worked. He spun to the left and then jumped out of it.

In the second go-round I didn't place but I made a good ride on Terminator of the Darrell Geyer bull pen out of Cedaredge, Colorado. Everything was going to be decided in the last go-round. I was still hoping to return to the Dodge National Circuit Finals rodeo in Pocatello. Johnny Shea had drawn #W7 Copenhagen Stinger of the Bob West -W/ Rodeo Company. He had never been ridden. Todd drew #171 Mr. T, (Burns Rodeo Company) and he had only been ridden once. I had drawn #5- Sankey of Jerome Robinson's Western Trails Rodeo Company.

Johnny and Todd competed before I did and they both bucked off. My bull had a good trip. He jumped and kicked and then turned back to the left. As he was spinning, he kept fading farther and farther away from the bucking chutes. It was weird. I had been on many spinning bulls before in my career, but never one that faded at the same time that he was spinning. Most bulls that spin pretty much stay in one spot while they're spinning. When the whistle blew, I jumped off and landed on my feet and instantly grabbed my cowboy hat with both hands and lofted it to the heavens. I raised both of my hands in a celebratory gesture. I was ecstatic.

In that moment I knew that I had won the Wrangler Circuit Series and the thousand dollar bonus, as well. The rodeo judges scored me eighty-four points. As I was walking across the arena to retrieve my hat, my score was announced and I raised my hands to show my approval and salute the cheering crowd again.

Because I was winning the third go-round, I was already mounted on a horse to take a victory lap around the rodeo arena. Jeff Cathcart from Cheyenne was the final bull rider and he didn't beat my score. We were the only two to make a qualified ride on all three bulls. I was crowned the Average (over all due to the highest aggregate scores or the most total points) Winner at the 1989 Mountain

Abe Morris

Mountain States Circuit Finals, November 1989, Cheyenne Wyoming
Bull Riding Trophy Buckle (won a trip to the Dodge National Circuit Finals Rodeo)
Photo: Carol Steinbock

States Circuit Finals in the Bull Riding event.

I was very happy to be winning the third go-round and the thought of winning the average had not even occurred to me. Along with winning the average would come another invitation and qualification to the Dodge National Circuit Finals Rodeo in Pocatello. It was awhile before I finally realized that I would be making a return trip to the DNCFR. I also won a beautiful trophy belt buckle from Award Design Medals. At the awards ceremony I would receive yet another surprise in the form of another $250.00 bonus for winning the Circuit Finals average. Altogether I won almost twenty-five hundred dollars.

Carol and I spent the night in Cheyenne and there was a great write up in the newspaper the next day about the rodeo. It was a nice drive back to Fort Collins.

The next week Todd and I went to Kansas City, and I did not even wear my new trophy belt buckle. I wanted to let my newest achievement really sink in before I started to sport it.

I fell off of my first bull at Denver in January 1990 and I was not very pleased with myself. A couple of days later I would be competing in the Mid-Winter Open to the World Bull Riding jackpot in Cheyenne. It would be held in conjunction with the National Western Stock Show and Rodeo in Denver. The competition was held on January 12-14th at the Laramie County Community College indoor arena and would also draw a lot of the top bull riders because of the big rodeo being held in Denver.

I was determined to redeem myself for such a poor showing in Denver. Steve Bulke traveled up to Cheyenne with me. I knew that Pete and Hal Burns' bulls were going to be in the draw for that Saturday night performance. I had a feeling that I was going to draw #11 Aces. I paid my fees and drew out a poker chip that had *Burns #11* marked on it. I knew that I was going to draw him again.

Aces had another one of his miserable, hard-to-ride trips but I rode him and was scored seventy-nine points by the rodeo judges. I threw my cowboy hat and then raised my arms again just like I had done two months earlier at the Mountain States Circuit Finals. I ended up winning the Bull Riding again. I received a check for twenty-five hundred dollars and another nice trophy belt buckle. It would be the third time out of three attempts that I had successfully ridden that NFR bucking bull. It would also be the second time that I won first place and another nice trophy belt buckle as a result of riding him.

A newspaper reporter, Siri Stevens, from a local publication called the *Fence Post* did a story. There was also a write up about me and my rodeo career included in the February issue because I had won the Bull Riding. The Cheyenne Tribune-Eagle ran a story on Sunday, January 14th titled, *Fort Collins Cowboy Top Bull Rider* that reported my big win at that event. Another newspaper called the *Wyoming Wrangler* also did an article in their February 1990 issue. The title of that one was, *Abe Morris is Winner of LCCC Bull Riding*.

My job had given me permission to take off and rodeo whenever I wanted, as long as I gave them ample notice. So, we went south to some of the winter rodeos again. Steve Bulke, Jess Grimes and I went down to Fort Worth. The go-rounds in the Bull Riding were progressive but I bucked off in the first round. I went to a few other rodeos but didn't do very well.

I went back to Rapid City, to defend my title from the previous year. I rode #7 Phantom, an NFR bull of the Burns Rodeo Company from Laramie, Wyoming. He had a good trip but I was only scored seventy-four points and placed fifth in the first go-round. I was disappointed because I thought that I should have been scored much higher. I qualified for the short go-round for the finals but I bucked off.

At this rodeo Rhonda Sedgewick from Newcastle, Wyoming,

Black Hills Stock Show and Rodeo, January 1990, Rapid City, South Dakota
#7 Phantom from the Pete & Hal Burns Rodeo Company
Photo: Dan Hubbell

interviewed me for a newspaper article. Rhonda had been the organist for several years at the indoor University of Wyoming college rodeo in Laramie. The article was later printed in the *Wyoming Wrangler* and *NIRA News* entitled, *Abe Morris—His Hat Still Fits.* I was very impressed with the article and personally thought that it was the best article that had been written to date about my rodeo career.

I went to the rodeo in Houston alone and stayed with Roz and Roy again. I didn't win any money at Houston. One night, I was driving back to Fort Collins and it was raining. I was aware that it was raining but I didn't realize that it was freezing rain. I had been gone for a while and I just wanted to get home. I was driving pretty fast at about 11:30 p.m. and I had my music turned up pretty loud in order to keep me awake. At that moment I was listening to a song called *Slow Down* by Loose Ends. I'd left Fort Worth that morning and was almost to the Texas/New Mexico state line.

I was crossing a bridge and there was a flashing yellow light on a sign warning that the bridge might be icy. My only thoughts were about getting home as soon as possible. I didn't realize that I was in trouble until it was too late. The first indication that I was in trouble was when I heard my tires start to spin out. All of a sudden, I was sliding toward the guardrail. I told myself, *don't hit the brakes, don't panic.*

I eased my steering wheel to the right. Then, all of a sudden, I was headed straight for the guardrail on the opposite side of the road. I continued to tell myself, *don't hit the brakes, don't panic.* I eased my steering wheel to the left. Then I started to fishtail back and forth, right down the middle of the bridge. *Then* I panicked and started to turn the wheel as fast as I could one way. I would then turn the wheel as fast as I could in the opposite direction. I'd lost control of my pickup truck and was doing all that I could to keep from crashing. It was a good thing that no one else was coming in the opposite direction on that two-lane highway.

I continued to move forward and fishtail back and forth down the middle of the bridge until I reached the end of it. Suddenly, I shot off of the road and down into a ditch. I mashed down on the brakes as hard as I could but didn't slow down at all. I was then sliding across the layer of ice that had accumulated on the grass. It was exactly like I was riding in a bobsled. I knew that if I hit a telephone pole or anything solid, I was going to be killed.

I thought to myself, *I am going to die!* Then my pickup truck somehow turned sideways. I could feel the truck start to roll. It rolled up on two tires and I thought, *here we go!* Then it fell back down on all four tires and bounced several times.

My engine had somehow shut off but my stereo was still blaring *Slow Down.*

I sat there for awhile with my heart racing. Finally, after realizing that I was still alive and not injured, I got out of my little truck to assess the damage. I had come to rest about seventy-five to a hundred yards or so beyond the bridge. I had a flashlight and I saw that none of my tires were flat and there was no visible damage.

I shut off my stereo and flagged down another pickup truck. I told the three guys what had happened and one of them said, "You mean to tell us that you slid off of that bridge way back there and you didn't roll your truck?" Then they asked if me if my truck would start. I didn't know because I hadn't tried to start it up yet.

I put the truck in four-wheel drive and it started up right away. It was already facing the highway. I drove it out of the ditch with no problems. I thought about stopping and getting a motel room for the rest of the night but I knew that I wouldn't sleep because I was too wide awake. Every time I crossed another bridge I would become terrified and squeeze the steering wheel very tightly. Every ice patch played its tricks with my mind.

I ended up driving non-stop from Fort Worth all the way back to Fort Collins. When I got home and told Carol what had happened, she laughed at me. I could have been seriously injured, paralyzed or even killed and all she could do was laugh. I didn't take it very well.

Later on, I found my sunglasses in between my door and the driver's seat. The sunglasses had been located in a pouch on the sun visor on the passenger's side of my truck. My truck had been tilted up on such an angle and so high in the air that the glasses had fallen out of that pouch and dropped in between the seat and the door. It was amazing and only by the grace of God that I didn't roll my truck. I also figured out that the reason I didn't roll was because my tires needed to grip the ground in order to initiate the rollover process. Because there was a coat of ice on the grass, my truck had glided across it instead of rolling.

I found some weeds that had become embedded in between the rubber and the rims of my tires. I'm sure this had happened when I was sliding sideways in that ditch. My truck had pieces of weeds stuck all over it. It looked like I had gone four-wheel driving in some kind of swamp. I had to take my truck to a tire place in order to get the weeds removed as I wasn't able to pull them out by hand.

After this incident, I refused to listen to that song, *Slow Down* for a couple of years. I also became very nervous on icy roads for several years afterward. It certainly served as a wake up call.

I was back on the trail about a week later and I won the Bull Riding in Wichita, Kansas. I rode #5- Sankey. He was the little red bull I'd ridden at the Circuit Finals. Sankey spun to the left again and I was scored eighty-one points. I won $987.00 for first place. I was spotlighted and introduced right before the Bull Riding event by the rodeo announcer, Duane Peterson. It felt good to come through after the big introduction.

The second week of March I headed out to Pocatello, Idaho to compete in the prestigious Dodge National Circuit Finals Rodeo. Johnny Shea from Delta, Colorado, who also qualified for the NFR in 1989 also qualified from the Mountain States Circuit. Johnny was the Overall Circuit Champion Bull Rider. Richard Rule from Washington, Oklahoma, who was then living in Loveland, Colorado, caught a ride with me. Richard had qualified as the Champion of the Prairie Circuit.

I bucked off of #104 Top Gun of the Hank Franzen (Powder River Rodeo Company) in the first go-round. In the second go-round, I rode #B52 Bomber of Dan Russell's string. He was a big black bull with banana horns who looked like an elephant standing next to the other bulls in the pen. He jumped and kicked pretty good and then he spun to the right. I spurred him but I didn't place in the go-round.

Cody Custer from Wickenburg, Arizona, who would later be crowned 1994 PRCA World Champion Bull Rider, rode #W7 Stinger of the Bob West (-W/ Rodeo Company) and won first place in the rodeo. It was the first qualified ride ever on that good bucking bull. Raymond Wessel from Cedar Point, Kansas, rode #171 Mr. T and won second place. It was only the third time that Mr. T had been successfully ridden. Ty Murray had ridden him at the rodeo in Rapid City, South Dakota in February. Cody Custer went on to win the Dodge National Circuit Finals Rodeo for three consecutive years.

After the National Circuit Finals I worked a lot until late May, then hit the trail again. That time Byron Juma from Torrington, Wyoming decided to travel with Todd and me. We started going to rodeos in late May and we traveled together on a regular basis for most of the summer. I continued to take my VHS camera and use it whenever I could.

My grandfather, Roosevelt Pope, died in late June. Carol informed me that she was leaving at the end of the summer to move to Alaska. She wanted me to take the whole summer off from rodeo and go with her. I refused. I didn't want to take a whole year off from rodeo because if I did, then I figured it might signal the end of my rodeo career. And I was not yet ready to throw in the hat.

On the way to Reno, Nevada, we stopped at a convenience store in Salt Lake City during the day. Some guy kept staring at Todd for some unknown reason. When we were about to leave, his buddy confronted Byron asking, "Are you guys looking for any trouble?" Byron said, "No." Then one of the guys ran to the car and pulled out a piece of PVC plastic pipe and was trying to egg on a fight. His buddy refused to get out of the car but was reaching under the front seat for something. We managed to get out of the parking lot without further incident. After we left, we wondered aloud if the guy in the car had a gun concealed under the seat. We were glad we hadn't stayed around to find out.

At one of the weekly summer rodeos in Steamboat Springs, Colorado, I bucked off of NFR bull, #11 Heckle. He was a good, black, muley bull of the -W/ Company that would get it on to the left right there in the gate. When I landed, I separated my right shoulder. I knew immediately that something was wrong and I climbed the fence using only my left arm. By the time Heckle left the arena and it was safe to get down off of the fence, my shoulder had slipped back into place. It was strange.

During the Fourth of July run, we went to ten rodeos in eleven days. I had a horrible Fourth of July run. I drew good bulls at several of the rodeos but could not get them ridden. I'm sure that part of the reason was that I was brooding over the loss of my grandfather and of Carol.

At Cody, Wyoming, I drew #13 King Dong, an NFR bull belonging to Ike Sankey. He was yellow and white paint colored and was one of the meanest bulls in the PRCA. I had seen him knock Scott Wheatley unconscious at the Circuit Finals. His spinning motions had a centripetal force and tended to suck cowboys down toward the inside of the spin. He was stout with long flat horns and he knew how to use them with authority. He was scary.

The bulls were loaded and I was going to be the first rider. Right before the Bull Riding was to start, the arena lights went out. They were those mercury vapor type that needed to warm up and would gradually get brighter. Finally, the lights started to come back on in the arena. The committee men wanted to get the rodeo going again and told me to get on my bull.

It was still a little dark. I was getting ready to get on #13 King Dong and Bobby DelVecchio stopped me and threw a fit saying, "Hell no, it is too dark and too dangerous for you to be getting on this bull. None of these committee men would be getting on this bull under these conditions and you aren't either. You go and sit back down."

Because Bobby was well known and a top PRCA bull rider, no one was going to argue with him. So I sat back down for about ten more minutes until it was brighter in the arena. The bull turned back to the left and had me a little in the well. I strained to get out but then he bucked me off to the outside of the spin and I got away cleanly. I hated to buck off but at least I didn't become another notch on this bull's long list of mauled victims.

We ended our journey competing in Prescott and Window Rock, Arizona. I bucked off at both places. I was financially broke and was glad to be headed back home again.

My summer continued to go downhill. In late July at Cheyenne I drew a good NFR bull #T50 Copenhagen Overall of the Alsbaugh Rodeo Company in the first go-round. I knew I could place pretty high in the go-round if I could ride that bull. Right before I was to climb on him, it started to hail pretty hard. The producers of Prime Sports Network were on hand and asked me if I would be willing to wear a cordless microphone during my bull ride.

Overall I had a good trip. He blew into the air and then he spun to the right. I moved too far to the inside of the spin when he turned back and he bucked me off into the well. Before I could get up and run he hit me with his horns and blasted me for a short and free ride. As I was flying through the air the cordless microphone fell out of my shirt pocket. This ride and wreck was later featured on the *Rodeo Bloopers Two* Video series. It was also used in a commercial on television to advertise *Rodeo Bloopers Two*. Several years later my nephews and niece, Michael, Coley and Tannah Morris, discovered that I was on this tape. They would watch it over and over until finally the VHS tape wore out and broke.

At home, Carol was pretty disappointed with me for bucking off. There was no way that she was more disappointed than I was, though. I made a brief appearance on a TV show from Cheyenne Frontier Days for Prime Sports Network and was interviewed about my ride on #T50 Overall and the upcoming final go-round. I would be a color commentator again along with Drew Goodman for the Sunday championship round.

A week after Cheyenne I hung on the side of a bull at Rock Springs, Wyoming, and he bucked me off right underneath him and walked all over me. I had always known better than to hang on to the side of a bucking bull. For bull riders this was always considered a bad idea. The price I paid was some broken ribs.

When I tried to get up to run, I was in so much pain that I got to my hands and knees and then I just froze up. I could not move and was just hoping that the bull wouldn't come after me. I was put on a stretcher, into a waiting ambulance and then transported to the hospital. It was a very embarrassing moment for me. It was to be the first time that I was carried out of a rodeo arena on a stretcher. This was something I had told myself that I never wanted to have happen.

It was an agonizing ride to the hospital. I felt every single bump in the road. My X-rays confirmed that I had broken four ribs. The pain was intense. There was nothing that the medical staff could do for me except to give me some painkillers. After a couple of hours in the hospital we headed back down the road to Fort Collins. I took the painkillers at first but then decided to tough it out.

This pretty much put me out of commission for the rest of the season. For the next few weeks I was very sore. It hurt to cough or sneeze. Whenever I had to sneeze I would do my best to block it and brace myself but it still hurt like crazy.

My mom had already planned a visit to Fort Collins and it was just a coincidence that I was injured right before she arrived. My whole family sent me get well cards and called to check on how I was doing. I even received a get well card and letter from Virginia Honeycutt, the rodeo secretary who had worked at the Rock Springs Rodeo. She was the wife of Roy Honeycutt, the stock contractor from Alamosa, Colorado. My cousin, Johnny Harp, called and we laughed as usual. I was laughing but it was killing me. I told him that if he didn't quit, I was going to hang up.

One night, my mom and I were watching a standup comedian on the TV. The guy was very good and was making fun of some of the Kung Fu type movies of the 1970s. We laughed so hard. I was obviously in a lot of pain and my mom was laughing and trying to say, "Turn the channel. Turn the channel." My reply was, "I can't. He's too funny." I couldn't tell if I was dying from pain or from laughing.

It was killing me to continue to watch this guy perform but at the same time he was so funny that I didn't want to change the channel and as a result I suffered through his whole performance. Afterward Mom said, "You should have turned the channel." I said, "I tried to but he was too funny."

My mom went with me to the television studio so we could put the final touches on the Cheyenne Frontier Days Rodeo broadcast. She met Drew Goodman and took a few pictures. I could tell that she was sure proud of her son for reaching a level in his rodeo career where he could be featured as a color commentator for an international broadcast of a world famous rodeo.

In late August, Carol flew to Alaska to live with her old friend

Julianne McGinnis, who was also originally from New Jersey.

Carol and I had gotten along very well over the years. We hardly ever had any disagreements or arguments. There were many times that I thought we would marry because we had a good relationship. We had traveled all over the country together and everyone in my family really liked her. Carol was also a very talented seamstress. She made several very nice western shirts for me that I proudly wore during my rodeo career.

Carol told me that leaving was an extremely difficult thing for her to do. We both cried when it was time for her to go. I dropped her off at the airport and watched her walk away until she was out of sight and out of my life as well. We had been together for five years and had lived together for four. I was sad to see her go.

In September, I attended a University of Wyoming Rodeo Team Reunion in Laramie. It was nice to see several of my rodeo friends from a bygone era. We all had a good time. A student from the UW Communications and Media Department was covering the event and conducted an interview on camera with me concerning my college and professional rodeo careers.

I continued to work at the pipe coating factory although I hated the job. The pay was not very good. The place was very dirty and extremely noisy. We had to wear earplugs and goggles to protect our eyes. It was extremely hot in the summer and bitter cold during the winter. Besides, I always told myself that I had earned a business degree and it wasn't to end up working in a place like that.

I would wear the same work clothes for a whole week because at the end of the day I would be filthy. I had cloth seats in my pickup truck and I put a towel on the seat so that it wouldn't get dirty. Sometimes I would stop at the Healthworks Club to work out on my way home from work. I refused to put my work clothes in a nice clean locker so I would put them in a big garbage bag and throw them on top of the lockers. I knew that no one was going to steal them. I was so dirty after work that I looked like I was homeless and was embarrassed to set foot in the club.

In October I competed in Casper, Wyoming, at the season finale rodeo on a bull named Abe. Byron Juma, my traveling partner, had a few bucking bulls at the rodeo and had named this black bull after me. I was very nervous considering that the previous bull I had attempted to ride had stepped all over me and hurt me pretty badly. I made a qualified ride with no problem. It always felt good to be able to walk away safely after competing.

In November, Todd and I went to the rodeo in Kansas City. Even though it was held in November before the National Finals Rodeo in December, the points usually counted for the next year in the PRCA standings. I told Todd that I hated my job and that I was already looking for something else.

A couple of weeks later I was laid off because our production had come almost to a standstill. We did more cleaning up than coating pipes. Several other employees were placed on a reduced workweek schedule. My boss said that more than likely I would be hired back in the spring. When I cleaned out my locker there was no doubt in my mind that I would never again return to work at that place. The song that was playing on my truck radio when I started it up to leave was *It Feels Good* by Tony Toni Tone. I turned it up loud as I drove out of the parking lot. I was making a statement.

I was eligible for unemployment but I did not enjoy sitting around the house all day. I was always one who got bored very easily. Even working out regularly, I got bored.

I chatted with a friend Joe Cuddemi from the health club who was a school teacher in Loveland. He asked me to speak to his students about my rodeo career on the last day of school before the Christmas Holidays. I took my photo albums, VCR tapes and my rodeo equipment.

As I was speaking to his class of seventh graders I could sense that I really didn't have their undivided attention. It was not until I started showing them the tapes of my television appearances that I got them to perk up their ears and pay attention to me. Some of them would look at the tapes on TV and then glance back at me. They wanted to make sure that it was really me on the television screen.

When we were finished, Joe said, "We have about ten minutes left in the class so we can have a question and answer session." One student went right to his notebook and ripped out a page and headed in my direction saying, "I want to get his autograph!" The other students followed his lead and soon were lined up. So for the remainder of the class I signed autographs for all of the students. It was just what the doctor had ordered for my self-esteem. Things had not gone very well for me personally the previous few months. It really made me feel good that they wanted my autograph.

Joe asked me if I could hang around and speak to his other class, too. I gladly obliged. It turned out to be a decent Christmas present for me since I would not be going back to New Jersey for the holidays because I was broke.

Another friend from Healthworks asked what I had done for Thanksgiving. I told him that I'd spent the holiday alone. Tracey Foster said, "We are not going to allow you to spend Christmas Day alone." So he invited me to his parents home for Christmas dinner. During dinner Tracey said that I had become their "foster child" for the day. They even surprised me with a few small presents under the Christmas tree. I still have and use the workout gloves that were given to me.

I had a new roommate, Tim Steffans, a Colorado State University student from Texas. He went home for the holidays and asked me to feed his horse. We had a severe arctic air blast that moved through the area and settled in for a few days. It was bitter cold outside. I lived in an old house and did all I could just to stay warm while I was inside. I would bundle up and even put on coveralls whenever I went out to feed his horse. I would run outside and hurry as fast as I could and I would still be freezing cold before I could get back in the house.

32

1991

I could not afford to pay my PRCA dues and couldn't enter the rodeo in Denver. I was able to scrounge up the one hundred dollar entry fee for the Open to the World Bull Riding jackpot in Cheyenne. I felt like I was at a crossroads of my bull riding career. It could continue or would very soon come to a grinding halt.

I had drawn a good bull. He jumped out and spun hard to the left but he was kind of flat and did not kick a lot. I spurred him pretty good and afterward I felt great. I also placed fifth in the Bull Riding. I realized that I had a few good years left and that the burning desire was still there. I really needed to know my potential at that stage in my career.

I worked for a temporary job service for a couple of months. One day I saw an ad in the Help Wanted section of the paper for a company called Marketing and Management Corporation of America. I went to a recruiting meeting and was hired. It was a financial services company that marketed life insurance and annuity products.

I came on board with MMCA in April of 1991. I attended their three day training school in Longmont, Colorado. At the end of the school, everyone in our class received their certificate of completion and said that they were going to set the sales world on fire. I simply got up and said, "I will do my best. One of the biggest reasons that I am happy to be with this company is because I can still maintain and continue with my other career." I did not divulge what my other career was. My regional manager, Mike McVicar from Denver, became very curious after I made that statement.

I went to a few meetings in preparation but I knew that as soon as the rodeo season was in full swing, I would be off to the races again. I was going to have to study and then take a test in order to get my insurance license for the state of Colorado. I'd told my direct manager Dave Menard, who also lived in Fort Collins, that I was going to take a break during the summer but that I would be prepared to take off and go all out in the fall. He didn't believe me because sales organizations suffer from revolving door syndrome.

I rodeoed again with Byron Juma. We started with the rodeo in Fort Smith, Arkansas. I practiced my sales presentation on the road with Byron Juma. When we returned to Colorado he told me that he had been seriously considering getting involved with some products for his financial future. All along I thought that he was just doing me a favor by pretending to be a live client on a sales appointment. I called up Dave because I was not yet licensed and Byron became my very first client.

That June, Byron and I were driving my small Nissan truck to the rodeo in Grand Junction, Colorado. The truck had a camper shell and there was a mattress in the back in case someone wanted to catch a few winks during our trips.

I always told people that my dog, Kato, owned the pickup truck but he let me drive it. Kato was very possessive and protective.

We were in the mountains and we got caught in a vicious hailstorm. It was coming down so hard and fast that we could not see and had to pull off to the shoulder of I-70. All of the traffic came to a grinding halt.

There was a sliding glass window between the camper shell and the cab of my truck. The hail was hitting so hard that it sounded like someone was banging a hammer. I was sure that any moment it was going to crack my windshield. I told Byron to close the sliding glass window to the shell and he couldn't even hear me for the racket.

When it finally ended, we drove to the rodeo grounds in Grand Junction. I was very anxious to assess the damage to my little Nissan truck which was my pride and joy. It was the first brand new vehicle that I had ever owned. I stared at it. It looked like it had been involved in a helicopter fly-by shooting. It was a disaster. When I took it in to my insurance agent he asked me why I didn't just keep driving so I could have gotten out of the hail of bullets. It made me a little upset. He acted like my idea of a good time was sitting in a hailstorm knowing that my vehicle was being beaten to death.

A reporter at the Grand Junction Rodeo interviewed me for a newspaper article that was printed in *The Daily Sentinel* on Saturday, June 22nd. The article was titled, *Morris Bucks Bias on Rodeo Circuit*.

Byron and I chose not to go helter skelter during the Fourth of July that year compared to 1990. We went to Cody, Red Lodge, Greeley and a couple of other rodeos. We drove up to Red Lodge, Montana. We were up in the Bull Riding on the final performance and I had a cute little brindle bull that was virtually unknown.

My cousin Gene Walker and his family happened to be in the vicinity. Gene was on the set making a movie, *Far and Away* with Tom Cruise, teaching the star how to ride a horse. The movie was shot on the

Pryor Ranch just outside of Billings.

Gene had also been in Billings the previous summer during the filming of a made for television movie, *Son of the Morning Star*. It was also filmed on the Pryor Ranch and was a story about General George Armstrong Custer. My cousin had a small part in both movies.

Gene was not able to come to Red Lodge on July 4th. It was only about a hundred miles from Billings but he was working on that particular day. His wife, Carol, and children, Deana and Jason, were able to come to Red Lodge to watch me compete. Tom Whitely, a retired bull rider originally from Nebraska, pulled my bull rope for me. My bull was just plain cool. He went a few jumps and then he turned back to the left and had a nice trip. I tried to dress him up and made some big sweeping, stylish moves with my free arm. The crowd and the judges really liked it. I was scored seventy-nine points and was leading the event.

The very last bull rider with a chance to beat my score was Brent Thurman, a NFR bull rider from Austin. Brent rode a good NFR bull, #-1 Bad Intentions of the Ike Sankey Rodeo Company, and tied my score of seventy-nine points. We split first and second place monies for a total of $1,266.86 in the event. I didn't place in the Bull Riding at Cody on that evening but at least I won a day money check for $208.00. I was on a roll, a one hundred and eighty degree turn around from my performance a year earlier.

At Cheyenne, I drew #11 Hot Licks. He was a good little white bull with tiny spots on him. I was very excited to have drawn him because Butch Kirby had ridden him for about ninety points at some other rodeo. I knew that I could win a lot of money on him if I could ride him. To my disappointment, he stopped bucking altogether and parked it about four seconds into the ride. Though I was awarded a re-ride by the judges, it ended up not being my day.

I didn't win any money at Cheyenne. Nick T. Buckley, another black bull rider, went with me to a couple of rodeos in the Prairie Circuit during Cheyenne Frontier Days. Nick was originally from Laramie and had also graduated from the University of Wyoming. We went to Manhattan, Kansas, and then to Burwell, Nebraska.

We were not very readily accepted at the rodeo in Burwell. When we arrived at the rodeo there was a guy directing traffic and parking cars. We showed him our PRCA cards and asked him where the contestant parking was and he lied to us saying, "Hell I don't know." We could tell the locals just did not care much for black people in general. It was sad because all we wanted to do was to win some money, just like all of the other contestants. I had always wanted to go to Burwell because of the old rustic wooden chutes and I had seen pictures of other cowboys competing at that rodeo. We were shocked and very disappointed in the way that we were treated and we both vowed to never enter that rodeo again.

We were glad to leave and head back to Cheyenne. Nick had qualified for the finals in the Bull Riding event and I was slated to do the television commentary again for Prime Sports Network.

The following week, I attended a three day class in Denver to prepare for the insurance examination for the state of Colorado. While I was in the restaurant during a break I saw Clay Jowers, a saddle bronc rider from Florida. He was on his way back home from Cheyenne. I knew Clay but I knew that he would not recognize me because I was incognito and out of "uniform." I started messing with him in the restaurant and he got a little miffed until he realized that it was me. I was known to do this to other cowboys from time to time because I knew that they wouldn't recognize me away from the rodeo.

I passed my exam on Saturday morning and then drove up to Steamboat Springs that afternoon for the weekly PRCA rodeo. I was feeling pretty good about myself because obtaining my insurance license would open the door to a whole new and exciting career. I had no idea at the time but I was going to have a long and very successful run with Marketing and Management Corporation of America.

That night in a bar, I met a woman who told me that I looked exactly like a guy that she had gone to high school with in Florida. After a long question and answer session it turned out that the guy just happened to be my first cousin Paul Thompson from New Smyrna Beach, Florida, where I was born. What a small world. His mom, Pearlie May Thompson, is my dad's sister.

I stayed overnight in Steamboat Springs and could not wait to call home to tell my family the good news about passing the insurance licensing exam. I told my mom I thought this was a major achievement in my life and who knew what it could lead to later. At that point, Mom told me something I will never forget. She said, "I've always thought that you are one of the most talented black men in the whole world."

For the next couple of weeks, Byron, Nick and I traveled together. I usually kept the books and did all of the scheduling and entering for our group. We had entered at Gillette, Wyoming. Byron called me at home and asked if I'd called back for stock at Gillette yet. I told him, no.

Then he said, "If you don't go, I won't blame you." I immediately knew that I must have drawn a dreadful bull. Hank Franzen had purchased a bull, #50, from Dan Russell out of Folsom, California. The bull had a scary reputation because he had stepped on Jeff Crockett's head and killed him at Yerington, Nevada in August 1988. The next year in June, at Reno, he had stepped on World Champion Charles Sampson's head and torn off his ear.

I made up my mind right then and there that I was going to go and get on him. I told myself that if I rode him right and got off properly that he couldn't step on my head. I was very nervous but it was something that I knew I had to go through with. Number 50 had a good trip and I rode him well. I made a good dismount and landed on my feet. The Bull Riding was a little tough though and as a result I didn't place on him. But I was proud of myself for staring adversity in the face and not backing down.

At Deadwood, South Dakota, I got on #91 Terminator, a NFR bull of the Sankey Rodeo Company. Terminator was blind in his left eye. I anticipated that he would not turn back to the left for that reason and I set a trap for him to spin to the right.

Terminator fooled me and caught me completely off guard. He turned back right in the gate and spun to the left. He bucked me off pretty hard and also severely aggravated my left groin muscle again. Afterward, I was limping pretty badly.

I considered taking a doctor's release but that meant a mandatory fourteen day layoff as a PRCA rule sanction. I did not want to sit out for the next fourteen days because there were several good circuit rodeos scheduled in the next couple of weeks and I didn't want to miss them. I knew I needed to win enough money to secure a berth at the Mountain States Circuit Finals. To me, it was a big deal not to qualify for the Circuit Finals. I felt I deserved to be there every year.

I decided to wait and see what I drew at Eagle, Colorado before I made a decision about taking a doctor's release. I drew #-7 Simply Irresistible of the -W/ Rodeo Company. Todd Steinbock had always referred to him as "duck soup" because he looked good while he was bucking. Number -7 really was not all that difficult to ride. His usual trip was to turn back and spin to the left, right in the gate. Many guys were able to spur him and get a few extra points from the judges. A lot of money was won at the Bob West rodeos on that neat bull. But just like any other decent bucking bull, #-7 was capable of bucking a guy off if he got lackadaisical and "stubbed his toe."

Simply Irresistible had his usual good trip and spun to the left right in the gate. I was able to spur him to the tune of eighty-one points. I won over a thousand dollars and first place in the Bull Riding but I aggravated my already painful groin muscle. I should have made the decision to call it quits for the season but I chose to tough it out and continue getting on my other bulls.

Next we went to Colorado Springs. I made the whistle and won some day money but I didn't place in the overall top eight at this rodeo. I bucked off of bull #5 Gator, of the Burns Rodeo Company at Wheatland, Wyoming on Saturday afternoon. I also bucked off of my bull at Riverton, Wyoming, during the performance on Saturday night. During the rodeo, I was interviewed for a story that ran in the *Riverton Ranger* newspaper on August 12th. The story was titled, *Living On, and Off, Bulls*. The subtitle was, "Abe Morris, bucked off in Riverton, isn't typical." There was also a picture of me competing during the rodeo performance. The article focused on the dilemma of me trying to compete with a severely injured groin muscle.

The bottom line was that the best therapy for my groin muscle was to obtain a doctor's release and turn out the remaining bulls on my rodeo schedule and just let it rest for a while. I was not having any success in getting any more of my bulls ridden for the eight seconds and all I was doing was constantly aggravating my injury.

I decided to give it one more attempt. I got on my bull at Castle Rock, Colorado, and bucked off when he turned back and started spinning to the left. Part of my riding style was to always get good solid holds with my feet. I could not take hold of any bulls with my left foot because it shot pain up my leg.

I had drawn Roger Rabbit of Bennie Beutler's bulls at the rodeo in Loveland, Colorado. I would have had a lot of difficulty riding him, even if I were a hundred percent healthy. Roger Rabbit was considered to be an eliminator bull and the bull riders hated to draw him because he was so hard to ride.

I finally made a decision to get a doctor's release. While I was on the injured reserve list I announced a Bill Pickett rodeo production that was held at the Adams County Fairgrounds in Henderson, Colorado. The Bill Pickett Invitational Rodeo Association, based in Denver, consisted of only black cowboys and black cowgirls and had a tour of about twelve cities throughout the United States.

I cracked out again at the rodeo in Keenesburg, Colorado, a couple of weeks later. I ended up splitting third and fourth places in the Bull Riding. Terri Hart caught a ride with me back to Fort Collins. She told me that Ronnie Rossen, the 1961 and 1966 RCA World Champion Bull Rider from Broadus, Montana, had been killed in a Senior Pro Rodeo in Rocky Ford, Colorado. He had won first place in the Bull Riding and had been stepped on in the chest after he dismounted.

I continued on to Douglas, Wyoming, where I had a rematch with #91 Terminator, who had initiated my groin injury a couple of weeks earlier.

This time, Terminator had a dynamite trip and turned back right in the gate to the right and started spinning. The first round I thought that I was a little late and out of position so I shifted my butt a little to the right. That move proved to be an almost fatal mistake. I knew that I was a little ahead of him and I kept scratching and clawing and trying to ease back a bit to the left. He was bucking very hard.

I did all I could to try to get back to the center but to no avail. I even tried to look out and toward the left with my head hoping to get out of the well. Finally, he dropped me in the well and stepped on the brim of my cowboy hat which was still on my head. Terminator also stepped on my right shoulder. My traveling partner, Byron Juma, told me later, "Man you scared me to death when he stepped on you. I could have sworn that he stepped right on your head. I was so relieved to see you get up to run. I didn't think that you were going to get up. I thought he'd killed you."

The bull's hoof had come so close to my head that it had smashed my cowboy hat down over my eyes. When I jumped up I knew that I had been hurt because my shoulder was killing me. I could not see where I was going. The first thing I did was to reach up with both hands and rip my hat off of my head so that I could see where to run to get out of harm's way.

The chute gate was still open. I took a couple of steps and ran back into the same chute that I had just come out of. Then I bent over because I was in excruciating pain. The gate men alertly closed the chute gate behind me so that Terminator couldn't get to me. I knew immediately that my right shoulder had been separated and that I would have to go to the hospital in order to get it fixed.

I spent quite awhile in the hospital. First I had my shoulder X-rayed and then the doctor put a weight on my arm in order to ease it back into its proper place.

They loaded me up with painkillers and a sling for my arm and I was finally released. I stayed overnight with the Huxtables in Douglas. I had known their family for several years during my college rodeo career and had spent the night with them in the past. Howard, Gary, Jimmy and Dixie had all been involved in rodeo for many years. Dixie had given me a ride to the hospital because I'd refused to go in the ambulance.

I was pretty disappointed because I would have won first place in the Bull Riding very easily. Tommy Keith, one of the PRCA judges, said, "You were 7.8 seconds on the stop watch and you would have been ninety points for sure on that bull." This injury closed out my 1991 season and dashed any hope I had of qualifying for the Mountain States Circuit Finals again.

With my rodeo season now over I started to concentrate on my financial services and sales career. My very first month with MMCA I ended up in seventh place in the nation based on premiums and sales generated. That meant I'd made some decent money. From that point forward, I knew that it would be a great career for me.

I had a little difficulty driving my pickup truck because it had a manual transmission and a stick shift. I had to hold on to the steering wheel with my right hand and cross over with my left hand to shift.

When I went to the HealthSouth Rehabilitation Center in Fort

Collins, the doctor suggested surgery on my right shoulder. He said that it would only get worse. It happened to be the second time that my shoulder had been separated and each time it would become more susceptible to popping out again. I told him that I played racquetball on a regular basis. The doctor told me that if I did an overhand smash, then my shoulder could become separated again just by swinging at the ball.

I decided not to have surgery but to do a lot of exercises at the health club in order to strengthen my shoulder. Because I rode bulls right-handed, there was less of a chance of my right shoulder popping out again. Whereas if it had been my left shoulder, the chances increased because I would be making big sweeping moves with that arm.

I started wrapping my shoulder and my chest with a long, wide ace bandage before each of my rides. Eventually I purchased a shoulder harness from the rehab facility that I wore underneath my shirt for the rest of my bull riding career. Between the exercising and the shoulder harness, I was fine. My shoulder didn't come out again during the remainder of my bull riding career.

I spent quite a bit of time in the health club working out and also playing racquetball. Whenever I did an overhand shot, I was aware of what the doctor had told me. I met Mike Bond at the Fort Collins Pulse Health Club and we started playing racquetball together on a regular basis. We were great competitors on the court and became great friends off of it. I would join him and his family for several holiday dinners in the future.

I spent the fall concentrating on my MMCA career. It was a good niche market for me. There are a lot of people that were involved in rodeo who didn't have life insurance or retirement products in their portfolio. This was my target market and I pursued and got many of them to get involved with our company and have me as their life insurance agent. I had an excellent quarter in MMCA.

In December I was fortunate enough to be able to go to the National Finals Rodeo in Las Vegas, Nevada, for the first time. I

traveled with Gerry Strom, Hal Burns and Charlie Marker. I ran into a
lot of old friends that I hadn't seen in a few years. It was a blast.

After each performance we would go up and hang out in the
concourse area. Fred Whitfield, a calf roper from Hockley, Texas, and
Ervin Williams, a bull rider from Tulsa, Oklahoma, were the only two
black cowboys who had qualified for the Finals. There were very few
African-Americans in attendance at the rodeo performances. Many fans
apparently thought that I was one of those two contestants. I was
wearing one of my Dodge National Circuit Finals jackets with my name
on it.

As we were standing around the concourse area, rodeo fans
would walk by me and stare at my jacket to see the name on it. I noticed
it right from the beginning. Finally Gerry Strom said, "Am I
imagining it or is everyone who walks past you staring at you, Abe?"
My reply was, "No you're not imagining anything. Everyone who walks
past me just stares at me and reads the name on my jacket to find out
who I am."

33

1992

In December of 1991, I got to go back to New Jersey for Christmas and the New Year's holidays. While I was there, my sister Patricia went on the campaign trail on my behalf. She wanted to promote my success in the sport of rodeo. She contacted two of the local newspapers in the Salem County area and set me up to do interviews. My sister also wanted the stories to include the fact that I was single and available!

One of the articles was printed on the front page of the *Today's Sunbeam* on Wednesday, January 1, 1992. The article was titled, *Woodstown Native Loves the Rodeo*. The other article printed on the front page of *The Sampler* on Wednesday, January 8th was, *Beating the Odds, Woodstown Cowboy Makes Name in the West*. *The Sampler* was distributed in Salem, Gloucester and Cumberland counties.

My family and I were very pleased with both articles. After the earlier article, *Abe Morris—His hat still fits,* that *Sampler* article written by Susan Walker became my second favorite newspaper article about me and my rodeo career.

In January, at the Mid-Winter Open to the World Bull Riding jackpot I got on a bull that came out of the chute backwards. I tried to get my leg out of the way but he somehow caught my spur on the side of the chute. I was strung out and in a very precarious position. I reached down and grabbed my wrap and untied myself. My right ankle was badly swollen and I thought for sure that it was broken.

I went to the hospital and the X-rays were negative. The shank on my spur was horribly bent and broken in the process. I had to take my spur to a welder to have it fixed. I got my crutches out of the garage and hopped around on them for a couple of weeks. Luckily my mishap did not interfere with my sales appointments.

I continued to be very successful with MMCA and became a regular in their monthly production reports and national newsletters. I went to a few of the winter rodeos but didn't set the world on fire. Byron Juma and I went to a few rodeos including Fort Smith in May. I did okay and won a little money.

In June, Byron and I went to the Earl Anderson Memorial rodeo in Grover, Colorado. We were also up in the Bull Riding that night in Grand Junction. In order to make it on time, we had booked a commuter flight out of Denver to Grand Junction. We were late arriving at Stapleton International Airport in Denver and had to run through the airport. We decided to carry our gear bags on board because we knew that if we sent them through with the regular baggage that they would not make it on our flight.

I had carried my rigging bag on board in the past and didn't think that it would be that big of a deal. And though this was long before the heavy security we have today, the security agent made me take everything out of the bag and decided that my bull rope and spurs could be considered dangerous and used as a weapon. She was not going to allow me to carry them on the airplane. I finally convinced her that if I didn't have my bull riding equipment, there would be no sense in me going to the rodeo to try and compete.

She said that the only way that I would be allowed to take them on board would be with the approval of the pilot. So she personally escorted me to the airplane and had me show the pilot what was in my gear bag. What bothered me was that during this whole escapade she never even asked Byron to open his gear bag. It also had gone through the X-ray machine and Byron had the same things in his gear bag that I had in mine.

Byron was never even questioned as he stood right next to me with his gear bag in his hands. I was sure that it was because I was black. It would not have bothered me if she had searched Byron's bag as well, but she acted like he wasn't even with me. I was the bad guy and Byron was the invisible man. Only me and my rodeo equipment needed to be scrutinized and subjected to a detailed interrogation and inspection.

Without any hesitation the pilot granted me permission to carry my gear bag on board his airplane. He also wished Byron and me, "good luck" at the rodeo after we landed in Grand Junction. We met a total stranger at the airport who offered to give us a ride to the rodeo grounds.

I rode a good bull that spun to the right. I got a little out of shape right before the whistle and Richard Rule, the judge, disqualified me for slapping my bull with my free hand. It really irritated me because I probably would have won first place in the Bull Riding event. There was no doubt in my mind that I hadn't touched the bull. I told Richard that he was wrong and that he should have given me the benefit of the doubt. He could not have seen me slap this bull especially if I didn't do it. Any bull rider knows immediately when they touch a bull with their free hand because it totally breaks their concentration.

There was a rank bull, #H owned by Doug Vold, at the weekly

Steamboat Springs Summer Series Rodeo that had not been ridden. He was a very pretty black and white spotted bull and he really blew into the air just like a bareback horse and then he would drop and kick over his head. He had a habit of jerking cowboys down on his head. I remember him jerking Randy Lopez down and popping him with a horn right in the chest. Randy removed his shirt after the rodeo and we could see a big mark where #H had blasted him in the chest. This was a few years before bull riders started to wear protective vests.

I made a comment to Byron that I would sure like to draw that #H because I thought I could ride that bucking son of a gun. The very next week was the special Fourth of July rodeo at Steamboat Springs when there was a huge increase in the prize money. When I called back for my stock, I was told by the operator at PROCOM that I'd drawn bull #H.

Then it became "put up or shut up" time for me. I had opened up my big mouth and now it was time to show what I was made of. I really wanted to perform well since I'd had such a horrible Fourth of July run in 1990.

Byron and I started out our run in Greeley. Next we went to Belle Fourche, South Dakota. I made the whistle there but I did not place. Byron was making a good bull ride and all of a sudden he seemed to jump off for no apparent reason. He grabbed his arm and said that he had done something to his riding arm. After he rolled up his sleeve you could see a lump on his arm. During the ride, the ligaments that held his bicep muscle to the bone had been torn and his bicep muscle had rolled up into a knot.

Byron would have surgery on his riding arm and have the ligaments stretched and stapled to the bone to re-attach them. That would end his rodeo season for 1992. I would have to travel alone for the rest of the Fourth of July run and the rodeo season. I

At Steamboat Springs #H had a terrific trip. He bucked hard and threw everything that he could muster at me but I handled it well. I rode him farther than any other bull rider had gone on him. Number H got stronger and more rank on each jump. At about the six seconds mark I really bore down and tried extra hard because I didn't want to buck off at the last second. Finally, the whistle sounded and I opened my hand and let him buck me off. I had had enough. I landed kind of rough and I was in a lot of pain. I did not get up right away and by the time that I did, J.D. Hamaker, a saddle bronc rider from Laramie, came out to help me. I told him that I was okay but that I must have strained some muscles on my rib cage because they hurt like crazy.

I was scored seventy-eight points and I ended up winning first place and over a thousand dollars. Since I was traveling alone now, another bareback rider, George Harty from Lusk, Wyoming, caught a ride with me to Douglas, Wyoming. He was also a large animal veterinarian. From there I drove alone up to Red Lodge, Montana.

I had drawn NFR bucking bull, #5 Mucho Dinero, of the Ike Sankey Rodeo Company He had a very good trip and made me bear down and try my butt off. I knew that he was bucking pretty hard because I could hear myself screaming again. I made the whistle and when I jumped off the crowd was going wild. I reached for my cowboy hat and launched it skyward out toward the middle of the arena.

It was pretty cool that day in Red Lodge on July 4th and there was a good breeze blowing. I had worn my down-filled vest during my ride in order to try and stay warm. Ike Sankey, the rodeo stock contractor, was standing on the back of the bucking chute where I'd come out. My cowboy hat sailed through the air, the wind caught it and blew it back towards the bucking chutes and Ike caught it for me.

When the announcer relayed my score of eighty points to the crowd, they went wild again. I won first place in the Bull Riding and a check for over a thousand dollars. I had now won the Bull Riding at the rodeo in Red Lodge for two years in a row.

I had a good brindle bull at Cody, Wyoming, that night that bucked hard, turned back to the left and spun. I was a little late in "getting around the corner." In other words, I was late in making my move as he initiated his turn back to the left. As a result, I was bucked off and got a little angry at myself for not being more aggressive. I would have placed on that good bull.

Next, I finished up my Fourth of July run by getting bucked off of a good, little blue spotted muley at Crawford, Nebraska. The thought of taking a "visible injury" exemption and just paying my entry fees and turning him out had crossed my mind. But when I found out he was a good bull and that I could possibly win first place on him, I decided to go ahead and get on. If the bull I had drawn had not been a good bucking bull, I probably would not have competed there.

As it turned out, I had a good seat and a good hold of the bull with both of my feet and he still managed to jerk me down on his head. He bucked. As I was bucking off, I caught my left spur in the jeans of my right leg and ripped a pretty good size hole in them. By the time I got on that bull my riding arm was killing me.

In July at the Cheyenne Frontier Days Rodeo I rode a red brindle NFR bull, #110 of the Rudy Vela Rodeo Company, for seventy-seven points in the first go-round and won sixth place and a check for $789.45. The bull spun to the left right in front of the chutes and then jumped out of it right before the whistle. My ride was shown on the Rodeo Round Up show that evening. I taped it and thought that it was as solid a bull ride as I had ever made. I put it on slow motion and my moves and body position were textbook and picture perfect.

I was thrilled with the possibility of qualifying for the Finals again. The television producers at Prime Sports Network were also well aware that I might make the Finals. There would be a conflict since I was scheduled to do the color commentary.

In the second go-round I rode Poppin' Joe of the Dan Russell bull string, right to the whistle before I bucked off. I was making a super ride. The bull had jerked my bull rope to my fingertips on the second jump out of the chute. I knew that I was in trouble right away. I squeezed

Cheyenne Frontier Days Rodeo, July 19,1992, Cheyenne, Wyoming
#110 from the Rudy Vela Rodeo Company
Photo: Randall Wagner

as hard as I could to hang on. I'd bucked off of several bulls during my rodeo career because the bull rope was jerked out of my riding hand.

Number 564 Poppin' Joe, a NFR bull, turned back to the left and got it on. I bucked off of him right at 7.9 seconds into the ride and landed very awkwardly on my head. I layed there motionless, much to the concern of the hushed crowd. I had been knocked out for the third time in my Bull Riding career. It was also the second time that I was knocked unconscious at Cheyenne Frontier Days. Tommy Keith, the PRCA pro judge, later told me that I probably would have won first place in the second go-round on this bull.

There was a newspaper reporter at the rodeo from Fort Collins who interviewed me for a story that was printed in the *Fort Collins Coloradoan* on Saturday, July 25, 1992. The article was titled, *Bull Rider Thrown Down, But Not Out*. It also included a photograph of two first aid workers helping me to walk out of the arena after regaining consciousness. It was a very embarrassing moment for me.

I did the color commentary for Cheyenne Frontier Days again for Prime Sports Network with Drew Goodman. I was disappointed because I had missed a golden opportunity to qualify for the CFD finals and possibly win the championship in the Bull Riding for the Mountain States Circuit as well. The circuit year-end titles were based on total money won in the circuit and Cheyenne was the perfect place to win a huge paycheck that would count for the circuit standings.

The next week was the beginning of August and I headed off to Hill City, Kansas. Nick T. Buckley caught a ride with me. I rode bull #777 for seventy-six points and won first place and a check for over a thousand dollars. He jumped and kicked and had a little hang time. The bull was pretty strong and also showy and the crowd and the judges loved it. I was pretty fond of the ride myself. The next night we went to Colby, Kansas and I won third place.

In the next couple of weeks I was pretty consistent and won first place in Riverton and also third place in Eagle. At Eagle I rode #4

Texican of the -W/ Rodeo Company for eighty-one points and placed third in the rodeo. Texican had a nasty reputation for listening for the chute latch to open and then he would buck right in the chute before coming out. He would catch a lot of cowboys off guard and buck them off right away. Texican was kind of a cheap shot artist and it often worked in his favor.

When I arrived at the rodeo, Scott West said that he would open the latch and tie a gate rope on the chute before I got on #4 so that he would not "cheap shot" me. Right before I was ready to climb down on him, Scott backed off and said that he would be very quiet and sneak the chute latch open in order to surprise Texican. I said, "No, you said that you were going to tie a gate rope on the chute."

Because I knew Scott pretty well and figured I could get my way with him, I said, "I'm not getting on him until you tie a rope on the chute gate." I had seen Texican jerk guys down on to his head right there in the bucking chutes. He was a very dangerous bull and he would hurt you. I was not about to take any unnecessary risks with him. Texican was also a good bucking bull and good bucking bulls do not allow cowboys to make mistakes.

Scott tied the gate rope and Texican bucked hard as usual. I had never seen that bull have an off day. He was, as the bull riders would say, "a handful." I was proud of myself because I rode him well and solid.

In Castle Rock I drew #777, the same bull that I had won first place on in Hill City, Kansas, a few weeks earlier. Number 777 had a better trip and spun to the right this time. I rode him well and won first place on him again. This time I won over six hundred dollars.

I placed fifth in the Bull Riding at the State Fair in Pueblo, Colorado. I rode #18 Goonie for seventy-five points in late August. In September Todd Steinbock, Dan Wolfe and I went to Hastings, Nebraska.

We also went to the NILE rodeo in Billings in October. All three of us placed in the Bull Riding event.

Since the rodeo season was slowing down again, I concentrated more and more on my financial services work and continued to have quite a bit of success. I became a regular in the MMCA national newsletter for monthly production and sales. The competitive aspects of my bull riding career carried over to my sales career. I was fortunate enough to be able to venture home to New Jersey for Christmas again.

30

1993

The Mountain States Circuit Finals rodeo in Cheyenne was moved to January. I rode my first two bulls and was in a great position to ride my third but he stumbled and I ended up bucking off. That turned out to be just another one of the breaks of the rodeo game. Sometimes you get lucky and sometimes you don't. You win some and you lose some. Not placing in the Mountain States Rodeo meant that I wouldn't qualify to go back to the Dodge National Circuit Finals Rodeo again.

One of the highlights of the rodeo was that the bull riders were given some very nice jackets for qualifying for the Circuit Finals. When I arrived at the rodeo I saw Dan Wolfe and said, "Man that sure is a nice jacket. You lucky dude where did you get it?"

Dan said, "Oh you like my new jacket huh?"

I said, "Yes."

Then Dan said, "Well go and get yours."

I made a beeline to the rodeo office so I could pick up my 1992 Circuit Finals jacket. I would get many comments on that jacket over the years.

I went down South to some of the winter rodeos. I didn't do very well and only won some day money. In Fort Worth, Texas, I rode a good bull, Ghost Buster, of the Neal Gay Rodeo Company. I was scored seventy-six points on him and he had a good trip spinning to the left. Afterward, in the locker room a friend, Buddy Gulden from California, told me he thought that I should have been at least eighty points on that bull. I agreed. It took seventy-seven points in order to place in the first go-round.

At the rodeo in Rapid City I rode a small white bull, Grim Reaper of the Korkow Rodeo Company. He came out spinning very fast to the right. Grim Reaper made several rounds and the crowd went wild. He was the fastest spinning bull I had ever ridden in my life. After the whistle sounded, I could not get up and run. I was very dizzy. I half stumbled and trotted over to the fence and when I got there, I fell into it.

I was scored seventy-six points. After my score was announced, the crowd booed the rodeo judges vociferously. Because I had my VHS camera with me, I was able to watch this ride several times afterward. It's funny watching myself trying to get to my feet. I still laugh, watching myself falling into the fence at the side of the arena.

I won fifth place in the first go-round and qualified for the short go-round (finals). I rode my second bull as well, but he was kind of sluggish and I didn't place in the go-round or the average.

Todd and Dan chartered a flight with Johnny Morris and flew back to Fort Worth to get on their second bulls. I didn't want to invest the money in airplane fare and so I opted to turn out my second bull at Fort Worth. I hadn't drawn a good bull.

I jumped in with Tony Stoddard from Lagrange, Wyoming, and

we met Todd and Dan at another rodeo in Texas. I didn't really enjoy myself during this trip because I wasn't winning and after a few more rodeos I flew out of the Dallas/Fort Worth airport back to Denver.

Next, Todd, Dan and I went to the rodeo in Tucson. A television crew there was just starting the filming for the movie *8 Seconds* about the life of Lane Frost. It was originally titled, *8 Seconds to Glory*. Tuff Hedeman was competing in the performance and introduced us to the film director.

The film director met with all of the bull riders before the Bull Riding event started. There were several black hats with feathers in them and several pairs of chaps that were replicas of the ones that Lane wore. They were going to get as much footage as possible to simulate Lane's rides. The director said, "Anyone who will wear the chaps and one of the black hats while competing, I'll give you a fifty dollar bill." He also said, "If we use your ride in the final film production, then I'll pay you an additional five hundred dollars."

Most of the bull riders started to grab a pair of chaps and pick a black hat that would fit them.

I knew that I would not be asked to wear the attire because I was black and Lane was white but I acted like I was going to, regardless. I stepped up to try on a pair of chaps and the film producer said in a hesitating voice, "Hold on there a minute. I don't think that we will be able to use you." So I looked back at him with as serious a voice as I could muster and said, "That's not fair. You're going to pay everyone else fifty dollars to wear the hats and chaps. Why can't I? That is just plain discrimination."

I didn't push the issue. I just wanted to see what kind of a response I would get from the film director. I probably should have insisted that I get paid like all of the other bull riders but I didn't. I have always been very easy to get along with and was not looking to stir up anything. It still made me sad to think back to the day that Lane Frost was killed.

That spring I focused my energy on my MMCA career instead of going to a few rodeos. Byron and I went to Fort Smith again in May. I had a good bull, #M of Sammy Andrews Company. He really blew into the air but lost his footing on one jump. It tilted me a little out of shape and I bucked off. It was just bad luck but a little disappointing, nonetheless.

My roommate, Tim Steffans, got his doctorate degree from Colorado State University and moved out. In May, right after Tim moved out, I decided that I would rather live alone and pay the rent by myself. I was making good money selling life insurance and annuities. And I preferred to live alone and have the whole house to myself.

The week that Tim moved out, I won the jackpot on a bull named Cisco. John McDonald from Wellington, Colorado, was producing some small bull riding jackpots at the Sundance Dance Hall and Saloon in Fort Collins. The events were held in the parking lot at the rear of the bar in April and May.

I thought that it was perfect timing because I could surely use the extra money and it would take some of the pressure off. The next evening I won the Bull Riding again on the same bull. Altogether, I won over five hundred dollars for the sixteen seconds of work. It also served as a confidence builder going into the summer rodeos.

Bob West and the -W/ Rodeo Company had a summer series rodeo at the Jefferson County Fairgrounds in Golden. The rodeos were held on Tuesdays and Wednesdays of each week so there would not be a conflict with other rodeos that were held during the weekends. The rodeo committee was to award trophy belt buckles to the event winners at the end of the season based on a point system.

I didn't have a very good Fourth of July and was a little low on cash again. I was on my way to one of the weekly Golden rodeos and debating whether or not to cut back on my rodeo schedule for awhile. I was listening to a cassette tape by Rance Allen and a song titled, *Ain't No Need Of Crying When It's Raining*. The lyrics in the song were, *have a little faith in yourself, that's all you need to do you some good...look real hard can't you see the sun shine...thank the Lord above for the strength to see...it's gonna be alright.*

I listened to this song over and over on my drive from Fort Collins to Denver. By the time that I arrived at the rodeo, I was pumped and ready to put this song to the test. I had drawn bull #28 Renegade. I didn't like that bull because even though he usually spun, he would hardly kick. He was kind of hard to ride. I made the whistle and I was very proud of myself.

The song really worked for me. In the years since then, I have often thought of that song and that ride when I have to dig down deep in order to succeed. That proved to be a major turning point in my season.

The rodeo judges scored me seventy-six points and I ended up winning first place, much to my surprise. I honestly felt like the judges had loaded me. There were not many times when I felt that I was scored too high, but that time I did.

We cowboys forget the times we think we got "loaded" or gifted by the judges as soon as we cash our prize money checks. Every time that we feel "slighted" by the judges, the stories live on and on. We tell as many people as will listen. I was no different than anyone else when it came down to my feelings about getting slighted. But in this case, I was well aware that I had been scored a few extra points.

A couple of weeks later at Golden, I won first place again along with a check for $638.00. This time it was on a bull named Grover. He was a black muley that spun either way. Grover had been bucking everyone off at that rodeo. I knew that I could ride him as long as I had a good seat on him when he turned back. It had been raining and the arena was muddy. When the whistle blew I took the cowboy hat off of my head and faked like I was going to throw it and then put it back

Cheyenne Frontier Days Rodeo, July 30, 1993   Bullfighter in background is Dwayne Hargo)
Photo: Randall Wagner

on my head. I did not dare throw my nice hat and get it all muddy.

Earlier that same day I had won third place and $413.00 at an afternoon rodeo in Estes Park. My total for the day was more than a thousand dollars. After the rodeo in Golden that night, I stole a line from a popular and current hit song by Ice Cube and told Byron, *Today was a good day.*

A week after the Cheyenne Frontier Days Rodeo I drew #11 Heckle, an NFR bull. Marty Staneart had ridden him for eighty-four points and placed in the first round at Cheyenne. Heckle had gone both ways with Marty. He had spun in one direction and then reversed it and spun in the opposite direction. I was in Cheyenne on that day and watched the ride.

In Golden, with me, Heckle spun to the left right out of the bucking chute and then he stopped for a split second. Whenever a bull stops bucking before the eight seconds whistle, a cowboy has a tendency to relax. But I knew this bull and I had expected him to go both ways before I even got on him. So instead of relaxing when he stopped, I really clamped down on him. I was not at all surprised when he gassed it the other way. I was ready for him.

Heckle got it on to the right and I opened up with my left foot and really spurred him. When the whistle sounded I was too aggressive and was a bit to the inside of the spin. I dropped into the well. I don't know if he smacked me or if I landed in an awkward position. I was stunned and didn't move. I am pretty sure though that he did not knock me unconscious. I momentarily blacked out and didn't remember what happened next. Another cowboy quickly stepped in and picked me up by the shoulders and dragged me to the chutes and out of harm's way. Heckle was not a mean bull but he would run over you if he got the opportunity.

The judges scored me seventy-eight points with the option for a re-ride because Heckle had stopped for a split second. I turned down the re-ride and ended up winning second place in the Bull Riding for the weekly rodeo.

That summer series of rodeos turned out to be truly Golden for me. I ended up as the number one ranked bull rider and was awarded another nice trophy belt buckle for my efforts. The belt buckle had *Mile Hi Pro Rodeo Classic (Bull Riding) Champion 1993—Summer Series* engraved on it.

I continued to be pretty consistent and ride well for the rest of that summer. However, in Loveland I had drawn #81 of the Burns Rodeo Company. Number 81 was one of the meanest bulls that I had ever known. It was raining on the evening that I had to get on him. My rope was slick and I knew that there was no way that I was going to be able to hold on to it. I told Hal Burns that I might have to run the tail of my bull rope in between my ring finger and my little finger (the split tail wrap). Hal said, "I don't know if you really want to do that on this mean old son of a buck." I knew that he was right. If I hung up to that bull, he was going to hurt me pretty badly. I decided not to risk getting hung up by taking a suicide wrap.

Number 81 was a good bucking bull. He jumped out and turned back to spin. Sure enough, my hand popped right out of my bull rope and I was bucked off. Before I could get up and run I knew that he was going to get me because I could hear the reaction from the crowd. I was still on my hands and knees.

My back side was facing #81 when he completed his round and saw the bull's eye on my butt right in front of him. He stuck a horn right in between my legs and it was blast off time. Number 81 lifted me up off of my feet and launched me toward the bucking chutes. It didn't hurt but it sure scared the heck out of me. Afterward, Kevin Rich, the bullfighter from Windsor, Colorado, apologized to me. I assured him that it wasn't his fault that the bull had hit me. I had been bucked off in a bad spot.

In September at the Colorado State Fair and Rodeo in Pueblo, I bucked off of a big black muley of Harry Vold's, #13 Black Jack Skoal.

As I bucked off, I hit the bucking chutes. It looked like I was slammed pretty hard against them. It looked a lot worse on the large instant replay screen than it really was. It did not hurt me.

Continental Airlines was awarding a free round trip airline ticket to the winner of the "hard luck cowboy" again, based on the worst wreck of the rodeo. The fans voted on this award based on an applause meter during the final performance. I won the the ticket.

I used it to fly to New Jersey for the Christmas holidays. The day of my flight, I was rushing through Stapleton International Airport and I heard someone say, "Abe." I was in a hurry and was going to ignore it, thinking that someone had said, "Hey." People say, "Hey" quite often and I always look because it sounds so similar to "Abe." Reluctantly, I looked around to see who it was. I saw a cowboy hat and immediately knew that I'd heard, "Abe."

It was Hadley Barrett, a well-known PRCA rodeo announcer from Kersey, Colorado, and his wife Leigh. We chatted for a while because my plane was delayed due to a major winter snowstorm. Leigh worked for Continental Airlines and she got my ticket upgraded to first class. We were delayed for quite awhile getting the wings of the airplane de-iced. I decided to have a few drinks and got to fly home in style. It turned out to be a very nice trip. Although my heart was in Colorado and the West, I always looked forward to going home to New Jersey to visit my family.

As a result of a good summer rodeoing in the Mountain States Circuit I again qualified for the Circuit Finals to be held in January, 1994 in Cheyenne.

31

Bull Riders Only

Bull Riders Only was the predecessor of the very successful Professional Bull Riders (PBR) tour. In the early 1980s one of my roommates in Laramie, Shaw Sullivan from Cheyenne, had mentioned that his goal and dream was to start a Bull Riding Tour for the rodeo cowboys. Shaw had toyed with the idea of Bull Riding becoming a stand-alone event because it was the most popular in rodeo. This is the reason Bull Riding is always the last event on the program.

The tour paid out very lucrative prize money and cut down on the traveling and the time away from home for a rodeo cowboy. About ten years later, the first Bull Riders Only event was held in Tacoma, Washington. It was nice to see a former roommate achieve a huge goal and the bull riders given the opportunity to enjoy the fruits of their efforts and labor.

My first Bull Riders Only event was in April of 1992 in Denver, Colorado at McNichols Sports Arena. I toured with this group for about two years. It was a blast. There was no entry fee and the overall winner won ten thousand dollars. The top bull riders from the PRCA would participate in these events. The only costs to us were traveling expenses. The events were by invitation only from the BRO Corporation and were usually held on a Saturday night. They would all be televised, usually about two weeks later, on Prime Sports Network.

One of the highlights of my tour with BRO was when I rode a bull named Levi in Casper for eighty-six points and won six hundred dollars and second in the first go-round in May 1992. He turned back to the right and spun. I made a wild spurring ride on him. The crowd went crazy and instead of tossing my hat, I tipped it to them and acted as if it were simply another day at the office. That qualified me for the next round but I was bucked off and didn't make it to the ten thousand dollar championship round.

During my tenure with Bull Riders Only, I went to a number of events. These included Denver, Casper, Rapid City, Tacoma, Washington; Wichita, Kansas; San Diego, Long Beach, Chicago, St. Louis, and Salt Lake City.

The Bull Riders Only contestants were given free, very stylish western shirts at each event. Roper Western Wear was a major sponsor. We were allowed to pick a new shirt from an assortment of shirts that had not been released yet to the western stores. I always selected a "Flash Gordon" shirt in which to compete.

Because I was also involved in my financial services career, I would wear these wild outlandish shirts to my weekly team meetings and personal sales appointments as well. Someone liked one of my shirts and asked me, "Where do you do your shopping? I would surely like to know." My reply to them was, "You do not want to shop where I shopped in order to get my hands on these kinds of shirts."

Bull Riders Only also gave us very nice contestants jackets that had an official BRO logo on the back. It was a lot of fun to show up at rodeos and have different fans tell me, "Hey I saw you on TV on Bull Riders Only last week."

In August 1993, Jeff Cathcart and I showed up at the rodeo in Douglas, Wyoming. It was apparent that two boys had been waiting for us to get there so they could get our autographs. BRO had made us celebrities. It made both of us feel very good.

We signed autographs at the conclusion of each event. We got to know some of the fans on a personal basis. At some of the events we were individually and formally introduced to a cheering crowd before the event kicked off. Then we usually congregated at an official bar or saloon for an after the events celebration. Sometimes we were transported to and from the bar on a bus. We had a blast. I always enjoyed getting to know the rodeo and bull riding fans.

BRO was entertainment at its best. It pitted the best bull riders in the world against some of the best bucking bulls in the world. Sports writers voted Bull Riding the most dangerous event on the North American continent and the rodeo fans' favorite.

A lot of the draw is the danger, the same reason that car racing is so popular; people don't want to see someone in a huge crash but if it is bound to happen, then they don't want to miss it.

At the event in St. Louis in May 1992, I was interviewed for a story that appeared in the June edition of a local African-American newspaper called *Limelight*. The title of the story was, *Abe Morris – Modern Day Bill Pickett – Top Black Bull Rider*. It was a good write up. I was hoping that it would stimulate interest in a sponsor to help extend my bull riding career. Sad to say, it never happened.

At the event in Tacoma in June 1993, a news crew from *Inside Edition* showed up in order to do a segment on the dangerous sport of Bull Riding. I qualified for the ten thousand dollar championship final round, but I was bucked off right out of the chutes. During a break in the action I was interviewed by Rolanda Watts.

The segment was aired on national television between the Christmas and New Year holiday break in 1993. I happened to be in New Jersey at the time and I knew when the segment was going to be aired. My whole family was gathered around the television to watch the show. Rosalyn and her family were visiting from Fort Worth.

All of a sudden, my face filled the television screen. A huge roar went up in the house. Even though I was speaking, all you could see were my lips moving because everyone in the house was so loud. "Ahhhhh, there he is, there he is!" Luckily, my brother David had taped the show on his VCR, otherwise I would not have known exactly what I said during the interview.

The ironic thing was that Billie Baker, the wife of Carlos Baker (the CEO of MMCA), was also watching that particular show in St. Petersburg, Florida and commented to her visiting guests during the lead up that, "We have an agent who works for us that participates in the Bull Riding events." Then, low and behold, there I was, right there on the TV screen being interviewed. What a coincidence.

I qualified for the 1992 BRO Finals which were held in October in Denver. I bucked off of my first bull and did not advance to any other rounds. Cody Custer from Wickenburg, Arizona, was crowned the 1992 BRO World Champion when he rode Burns' #73 Copenhagen High Five (a son out of the great bucking bull Mr. T). He was crowned as the Dodge National Circuit Finals champion and the PRCA World Champion Bull Rider as well, to cement the Triple Crown in 1992.

The event in San Diego in March 1993 was staged on two separate days. There was a preliminary qualifying round on Saturday prior to the main event on Sunday afternoon. I was fortunate enough to be seeded to the main event on Sunday. During the Saturday event there was a local cowboy who was running the out gate. He was letting the bulls out of the arena after each one was bucked.

This guy was being extra cool in handling his duty that day. Each time that he would open or close the gate he would do a little pirouette. He could have simply opened and closed the gate but no, he had to add a little extra pizzazz to his job. He was getting some attention and seemed to be relishing his appointed gatepost duty.

One particularly cantankerous bull gave him a lot more attention than he had bargained for. Instead of exiting the arena, that bull decided to take out his frustration on the cool gate man. Somehow, the gate man got hung up in between the fence and the gate. That bull started hooking him with his horns and there was no way for the guy to get away. He was holding tightly onto the gate and didn't dare lose his grip. If he had, and if he'd fallen into the arena, he would have had to give up his role as a nimble ballerina, and become a gladiator instead.

Finally, the bull got fed up with working that poor guy over as he clung to the fence for dear life. In the process, the bull had ripped a gaping hole near the groin area of his jeans. Well, the guy was not wearing any underwear! After the bull had exited the arena, the guy stepped down from the fence and his entire private package was hanging out of his jeans. The gate man was very embarrassed and immediately stashed his unmentionables back into his pants. Then he twisted his jeans to the side to keep himself covered.

Jeff Cathcart and I were standing in the audience area near the out gate. We had been noticing this cool acting guy during the whole performance. When the guy's pants got a little extra air conditioning, I had to leave the area because I was laughing so hard. Now, the guy had to make very careful movements opening and closing the gate lest he be exposed again.

I repeated this story to my family and friends several times and I would laugh just as hard each time.

On Friday, October 1, 1993 the *Rocky Mountain News* printed a story about me in the sports section of their newspaper. The article was titled, Black Bull Rider Packs a Loaded Briefcase. The subtitle of the article was, "Fort Collins cowboy runs financial planning company when he's not on a rampaging animal." The article discussed my rodeo and financial services careers and also served as an introduction to a BRO event that was going to be held in McNichols Sports Arena the next night. Mike McVicar from MMCA read the article and called me at home to congratulate me.

That same day a job recruiter from Denver called and offered me a position with a financial services and pension company TIAA-CREF (Teachers Insurance and Annuity Association—College Retirement Equities Fund) which had a large office in downtown Denver. I told him that I really liked my job, even though it was all commission based sales. Besides, I figured that I still had a few good years left to rodeo and I was not ready to let that go yet so I turned him down. Ironically, I did finally go to work for that company on June 12, 2000.

Later that October we competed in a BRO event in Chicago at the Rosemont Horizon. Terry Don West won the competition on a bull, Achey Breaky of the Sammy Andrews Rodeo Company. Ervin Williams won second on a bull named Skoals Outlaw Willie, also of the Andrews Rodeo Company. Oprah Winfrey and Stedman Graham attended that event. I didn't personally meet Oprah, but Stedman attended the after party and I was able to chat with him. I also saw Thryl and Mike Latting from Robbins, Illinois, two black cowboys who produce IPRA rodeos in the Midwest.

I qualified for the BRO Finals in Long Beach in November 1993. All of the qualifiers were presented with very nice rodeo gear bags. It was an excellent competition. Tuff Hedeman, the three time PRCA World Champion Bull Rider, made one of the best rides that I've ever seen. He rode #J31 Bodacious, of the Sammy Andrews Rodeo Company, for ninety-three points and the BRO World Championship title.

I bucked off of a NFR bull branded #X55 and named Sir

Barkley in the second go-round. After I returned to Fort Collins, the local television news station, Channel 14, did a short segment on me. It talked about my start in New Jersey and then coming out West in order to compete in major rodeos.

In 1994 I only competed at a couple of BRO events. One event was held in Tampa Bay. My Uncle R.C. and Aunt Pearlie May Thompson came down from New Smyrna Beach to watch. I bucked off. After the event, I went with them and spent a couple of nights at their home. I got to visit a lot of my relatives in New Smyrna Beach before I flew back to Denver.

I did not do very well in the BRO events in 1994 and as a result I was cut from the traveling squad.

32

1994

I went to a few of the winter rodeos but I didn't do very well. In 1994 I chose to concentrate more on MMCA and a little less on riding bulls. I was having a great deal of success with my financial services career and finishing in the top ten nationally each month in sales production.

Many of my fellow agents became more concerned with trying to beat me than they were about reaching a certain level of production based on new premiums. I realized that my Bull Riding career was winding down. The same competitive fire which had made me successful in the rodeo arena spurred me on in the business field.

One evening in the spring I was talking to Clay Keller, a PRCA saddle bronc rider from Fort Collins, in the Sundance Saloon and Dance Hall. We were discussing the upcoming summer rodeos and trying to decide how much longer we were going to compete. Ironically, we were both able to answer this question a lot sooner than we anticipated.

At the Elizabeth Stampede in June I rode #72 of the Burns Rodeo Company. He was a big strong white bull that was a son out of the great NFR bucking bull #7 Phantom. He had a really good trip and spun to the left. I made a good bull ride and was scored seventy-eight points I ended up winning second place and received a check for $785.25.

I had a potential client who wanted to talk business right before I got on my bull. I already had my chaps on and was just about ready to ride. So I handed him a clipboard with a financial survey on it so I could contact him later to set up a personal appointment. I became very adept at playing the role of both rodeo cowboy and businessman.

Word of mouth helped me a lot. People started to ask me about the program and some signed up with me just because their friends had. I didn't even need to give them a sales presentation, I'd just pull out a program application and sign them up right on the spot.

That night after the rodeo in Elizabeth, I was able to get a couple of cowboy friends to start life/annuity programs. They all had known me for years and were very comfortable with my recommendations. Many of those cowboys were leery of the "suit and tie" businessmen and preferred to do business with one of their own. I was also able to set a couple of successful appointments for the following week. One appointment was with Gary Wood from Denver. A few years later Gary would be the World Champion Bull Rider in the Senior Pro Rodeo ranks. It turned out to be a very productive weekend.

I started conducting my MMCA business prior to and after each rodeo. I got into the habit of taking my insurance applications and other necessary paperwork with me. I talked to my rodeo friends and convinced them to do business with me before the rodeo. Some of the cowboys that I signed up at rodeos included Buddy Gulden, Eric Christensen, Thor Hoefer, Mike Mason, Tony Stoddard, Dwayne Hargo,

Troy Pruitt, George Harty, and Sean McRoberts. The list goes on and on and on. I signed up Myron Duarte, a NFR bull rider, who was originally from Hawaii, on an airplane while we sat on the runway at Denver before taking off for a Bull Riders Only event in Chicago.

That summer Jeff Cathcart and I had been traveling to some of the Bull Riders Only events together and so we started going to a few PRCA rodeos. At the age of thirty-eight I had become one of the senior bull riders in the Mountain States Circuit. Most of the guys that I had traveled with such as Zane Garstad, Hap Kellogg, Gerry Strom and a few others had already hung up their bull ropes and spurs and had been turned out to pasture.

Jeff did well over the Fourth of July placing at both Greeley and Cody.

At Red Lodge, Montana, I experienced my first loss as a life insurance agent. A friend and fellow bull rider, Mike Mason, was killed at a rodeo in Folsom, California. A bull had jerked him down and hit him in the chest. This happened at about the same time that many bull riders were starting to wear protective vests. Sadly, Mike wasn't wearing one. I was told of Mike's death by another friend, Sean McRoberts, who was also from California.

Although Mike and I were not close, it still affected me because he had been my client. Whenever another cowboy was seriously injured or, as in that case killed, the news hit me hard. I got very sad. And I hated that I still had to get on my bull right after I found out about Mike's death. On top of that, I was going to have to follow up with a notification of death to my life insurance company. I had never had to do that before. It was a sad but necessary part of my business.

Mike had gotten married since I'd originally signed him up. When I spoke to his father in California, he was shocked that Mike had even taken out a life insurance policy.

During that summer, I made the very difficult decision that it would be my last year to ride bulls. I also finally changed my wrap because several bulls had jerked the bull rope out of my hand. I would be in great shape and then all of a sudden, pow, my hand would come out of the rope and I would buck off.

At Laramie in July I rode #907, of the Burns Rodeo Company. I was very proud of myself because it was the first time that I experimented with the new wrap and it worked well. Number 907 was a good size red bull that had a reputation for jerking bull riders down on his head. I really bore down and rode him well.

After my ride was completed one of the rodeo announcers, Randy Taylor, a UW graduate and former NFR bareback rider who was on horseback, interviewed me while I was still in the arena. Randy said, "Now Abe, you have been at this sport for several years. How much longer do you think you'll continue to rodeo?" My response and thus my first public announcement was, "I've already decided that this is going to be my last year to ride bulls."

When they heard this, the Laramie fans gave me a huge send off. I tipped my hat and waved goodbye to them because Laramie had given me a lot of good memories. I was a little sad as I walked across and then exited the rodeo arena at the Albany County Fairgrounds for the final time.

Jeff and I went to the Cheyenne Frontier Days Rodeo on Sunday July 24, 1994. I bucked off of #727 Totally Teed Off, of the Burns Rodeo Company. He was a son of the great bucking bull Mr. T. Number 727 had a miserable trip and I was not at all impressed with him. During the rodeo I was interviewed by a reporter from the Associated Press. Jon Sarche wrote an article titled, *Morris: No Regrets, But Judges Aren't Color-Blind*. The article was printed in the *Laramie Daily Boomerang* on Tuesday July 26, 1994. It talked about my rodeo career and the fact that it was a little tough at times to get the scores that I thought I deserved from the judges. The article also talked about my current financial services career with Marketing and Management Corporation of America and my business degree from the University of Wyoming.

I had never attended an MMCA National Convention because they were always held during the last weekend in July. This conflicted with Cheyenne Frontier Days and I was not going to miss that prestigious rodeo. A lot of people in MMCA were very anxious to meet me because my name regularly appeared on the national newsletters and the bull riding added to my mystique.

I was scheduled to ride my second bull on Friday, July 28th. I had decided that if he was not a very good bucking bull, I would turn him out and instead attend the MMCA convention in St. Louis. I had qualified for "Top of the Line." It was a black tie affair to honor the top salespeople in the nation for the year.

I did not draw a very good bull and opted to go to St. Louis instead. Before I went, I had a telephone conversation with Sue McNamara, an office employee at PFL Life in Little Rock, Arkansas. She said that she would be at the convention and had asked me to describe myself. I refused. So she said, "Let me guess, I bet that you have blonde hair." Then I knew that she was way out of the park. I almost told her that she was right.

My response was, "I will definitely stand out in the crowd and once you see me, you won't forget me." She got a little miffed and wanted to know why I thought I was so special. I assured her that she would be shocked when she finally met me.

I was up on the stage to give a short speech when these two ladies walked into the room. I knew right away that it was Sue because she had described herself to me on the telephone. She had said that she and her co-worker, Janet Carroll, would be together and they both had long blonde hair. Another co-worker, Jennifer Dizmang-Smith from

Windsor, Colorado, was giving her speech and mentioned my name. I waved at Sue and Janet and watched the two of them laugh hysterically after they realized that I was black.

I had a blast at the convention. PFL and MMCA rolled out the red carpet for their top producers. I was wined and dined and I also had a free motel room for the weekend. I attended a large banquet decked out in a tuxedo on Saturday night and then caught an early flight back to Denver the following morning.

I had to be back in Cheyenne to do the broadcast commentary for Prime Sports Network. That year would be my first to work with Jerry Schemmel, who was also the in-house voice for the Denver Nuggets NBA basketball team.

I felt pretty blessed to be versatile enough to don a tuxedo and be honored with the top players in my business organization and then turn around the next day and feel right at home again in a pair of Wrangler jeans and a cowboy hat. I thanked God that I felt at home in front of a television camera. It added a wonderful dimension to my life.

The first week in August, Jeff and I went to Wheatland and then to Riverton, Wyoming. I bucked off of a good bull, #G29. He spun into my hand and I got behind and was not able to catch up. I got strung out and eventually bucked off. I was disappointed. But then again, I was always disappointed whenever I bucked off. It cost me first place in the Bull Riding at that rodeo.

The next night in Riverton, I rode #1 Too Tall, of the Powder River Rodeo Company, for a whopping eighty-five points. He was a big tall gray Chianina bull that usually blew in the air and kicked hard. Charlie Needham from Riverton pulled my bull rope for me. Before I got on, he gave me a hard time about being too old for the sport. Charlie had qualified for the NFR in the Bull Riding twice in the 1980s and had been retired for about five years.

Ninety-nine percent of the time, when I was almost ready to nod my head to the gate men, I would have to reach up with my free hand and grab hold of the chute to pull myself forward as close to my bull rope as possible. This bull was so big and tall that I had to reach down to the top rail of the chute in order to slide forward. At the time he was one of the larger bulls in the PRCA.

Too Tall really bucked. He went about two jumps and then he spun to the left. At about the seven seconds mark he really bailed into the air and gave me a big mambo. I handled it well. I made a solid ride and was mighty proud of my effort. When the whistle sounded I jumped off, landed on my feet and reached for my cowboy hat and launched it skyward.

The crowd roared. When my score was announced I threw my cowboy hat again as they exploded again. I won first place and a check for over five hundred dollars. The next day a picture of me competing on Too Tall and an article about the rodeo appeared in the *Riverton Ranger* newspaper.

On the ride back to Cheyenne, Jeff tried to convince me to rodeo for one more year. He said, "If you quit then I won't have anyone to travel with next year." I said, "Let me see how I do the rest of this year. I might change my mind and compete for one more year." I knew I was going to have to have a stellar performance to keep the fire burning for one more year.

I was not getting any younger and I'd always told myself that in the end, I just wanted to be able to walk away. I did not want to be one of those bull riders who hung around too long and then got seriously injured or even killed. I worried about a debilitating injury that would prevent me from participating in the other sports I loved —racquetball, basketball and softball.

The following night we competed in Casper. I had drawn a bull that had not been ridden in 1994. He was #26 and was a Dodge Bounty bull. The Bounty program was part of the Dodge Trucks program and a cowboy could win a bonus if the animal was successfully ridden at certain designated Dodge sponsored PRCA rodeos. Casper was not listed as an official Dodge rodeo and there would not be bonus money up for grabs.

During the rodeo performance we were chatting with the bullfighters Eddie Hatfield and Rick Chatman. Eddie asked what bull I was getting on and I told him #26. His reaction was, "Whoa, are you going to be in trouble." So I said, "I suppose I'm going to need my PF Flyers." Eddie told me I was going to need a lot more than PF Flyers. Then they let me ponder my situation for a while.

Before the Bull Riding started, Eddie found me and assured me, "You're not going to have to worry, because we'll be there for you."

When I sat down on that bull, he was fighting the chutes and would not stand still. Jerry Dorenkamp, the flank man for Mike Cervi said, "Make sure that you pick your spot when you decide to get off." That is a term often used when a bull is bad and will hunt you down. He also said, "When you hit the ground, you'd best be running because this son of a gun is BAD."

Jerry told the two bullfighters to get as far away from that bull as possible. They said, "Way out here?" and Jerry said, "Yes, because if he sees you, then he won't turn back and buck."

I finally nodded my head and was able to get out (of the chutes) on him.

Turning back and bucking was the farthest thing from #26's mind. He scattered across the arena like an untied balloon filled with helium and then suddenly released. I could feel my bull rope being jerked to my fingertips and yet I still tried to hold on for dear life. It was futile. Pow!—the bull rope was jerked out of my hand and I hit the ground.

I immediately jumped up because I knew that he was going to be on the hunt. I was far away from the bucking chutes and I didn't know where the bull was, but I wasn't going to waste any time glancing around and trying to locate him. I made a beeline for the chutes.

I was only about four or five steps from the chutes when, out of the corner of my eye, I saw him coming. But it was too late. The rodeo bullfighters were not in a good position to save me. Number 26 was like a locomotive with a full head of steam. I was like a small running back on a football field. I was about to be hit by the biggest and the meanest defensive player from the opposing team. I kept on running and then braced myself for the hit. This probably made it a lot worse for me.

Blast off! He hit me on a dead run and sent me flying into the night sky. I landed like a sack of potatoes. I was in a lot of pain but I was not going to hang around so that he could add further insult to my injury. Somehow, I made it to the chutes. I didn't think that I could climb them and so I just held on until he left. Then I limped out of the arena. There was an instant replay screen and my wreck was shown over and over.

As I was putting away my equipment, the pain got more and more intense. Billy Zurcher, a bull rider from Mitchell, Nebraska, came over and asked me, "Are you alright Abe, because you don't sound like you're doing too well?" Evidently I was making some strange sounds.

After I put away my equipment, I told Jeff Cathcart and Colt Bruegeman, a saddle bronc rider, that I was going to go over to visit the Justin Heeler. I iced my groin muscle because it was always giving me problems. I figured that I had re-injured it.

Eddie Hatfield checked in on me. He felt really bad because I had taken such a vicious hit. He apologized saying that he and Rick were so far away to begin with that they didn't have a chance to get in there and distract the bull's attention away from me. I told him not to worry about it because I couldn't blame him. It was not his fault that #26 had decided to run off and have such a miserable trip.

When I got up to leave, I discovered that I couldn't walk so Colt went and got his pickup truck and backed it up to the trailer. I was bent over as I hobbled over to the camper and laid down on the bed. I was in excruciating pain.

I tried to go to sleep but I couldn't. Nor could I get comfortable.

I suffered all the way back to Cheyenne. When we arrived at Jeff's house at about two a.m., it took me a long time to get out of the camper. Finally Jeff yelled at me, "Abe would you come on!"

I took a couple of steps and then I stopped and leaned up against the truck exclaiming, "I can't walk!" Jeff said, "Hold on." He ran into the house and came out with a pair of crutches. I used them and ending up spending the night in Cheyenne. The next day I drove home to Fort Collins.

Sunday evening I went to the rodeo in Loveland and spoke to Dr. Jack Harvey and Chad Smidt from the HealthSouth Sports Rehabilitation Center. They told me to come over to their facility first thing the next morning. I continued to hobble around on my crutches. I could not lift my left leg to place it on the clutch in my pickup truck. So I had to pick up my leg with my right arm. I was able to push down with it. After I would put my truck in fifth gear, I would reach over with my arm and place my leg on the floorboard of the truck. Whenever I wanted to stop, I would have to reach over and place my leg on the clutch and repeat the process again.

The doctors at HealthSouth thought that I had a fractured hip but the X-rays proved negative. I was diagnosed as having a very severe and deep hip bruise. I was going to have to attend therapy sessions in a swimming pool several times a week for a month. Eventually, I used an underwater treadmill in order to learn to walk again.

I was given painkillers but I quit taking them right away because they didn't do me any good. When I had doubled up on the medication, I would just get a headache. Every morning I would wake up and stare at my crutches on the floor, realizing that I was going to have to endure another painful day.

During one of my rehab sessions at HealthSouth I saw Clay Keller. He had bucked off of a saddle bronc and torn the ACL in his knee. How ironic that we were both in physical therapy at the same time when we'd so recently been discussing how much longer we planned to compete in rodeos. It looked like both of our rodeo careers had reached the end of the trail at the same time.

When I showed up at the television studio in Denver for Prime Sports Network to put the finishing touches on the Cheyenne Frontier Days rodeo production, I was limping very badly.

I gradually improved and finally was able to put away my crutches. My hip continued to pop a couple of times a day for the next few months. I got use to the weird "popping" sound and I knew when it was going to happen again. It especially bothered me when the weather got cold in the fall. My hip popped every single morning for about a year and a half.

People started asking me if and when I was going to resume my bull riding career. I had always been in excellent physical condition and knew that I could return to the rodeo arena if I really wanted to. I contemplated my return for a very long time.

Finally a friend, Byron Murphy, a former rodeo clown, had a heart to heart talk with me. He said, "Abe, you have already proven yourself in the rodeo arena. You made a name for yourself." I responded that I would like to qualify for the Circuit Finals at least one more time. Byron said, "You've already gone about as far as you're going to go. If you get hurt and re-injure that hip, you're going to be in some serious pain and jeopardize your health and well-being for the rest of your life. It's not worth the risk. Besides it takes a braver man to walk away from the career than to make a major comeback."

I had been listening to several friends. Byron was the first to suggest that I not try to make a return to the inherently dangerous sport. I mulled over his advice for quite awhile. Then I made my decision. I announced my decision at an MMCA monthly rally in October in Frisco, Colorado. I said, "I have had a very successful career in this business but I have finally made a very agonizing decision that it is time to move on. I have made a ton of friends along the way and I will miss them."

Karen Ketcham from Wiley, Colorado had become one of my closest and dearest friends. I was trying to make all of my business co-workers think that I was leaving MMCA. It worked. I had their undivided attention and concern. Then I said, "I have decided to retire from the sport of rodeo and bull riding." They all felt a sense of relief, I could see it on their faces.

During the break following our meeting, they came up to me and said, "Man you sure had all of us going. We all thought that you were going to resign from Marketing and Management."

That same weekend I attended the Finals of the BRO in Denver. The event was won by Gilbert Carrillo from Stephenville, Texas on Playboy Skoal of the David Bailey Rodeo Company from Tahlequah, Oklahoma.

With my rodeo career behind me, I was able to concentrate on my MMCA and sales career. I ended up third in the nation at the end of that year. I was very impressed because I was also rodeoing during the year and had taken three months away from the business during the summer to concentrate on my bull riding. I had established a new territory record based on premium sales for the Rocky Mountain Region. I also earned an all expenses paid trip to Cancun, Mexico the following spring of 1995.

I continued to attend various rodeo and bull riding events throughout the region, but I refused to travel more than seventy miles just to watch an event. I had traveled from sea to shining sea and had no desire to continue running around. I could still get to watch plenty of rodeo action within my seventy mile radius.

I went home to visit my family again for Christmas and New Year's. I was a regular guest at my brother David's elementary school class in Salem, New Jersey. I would speak to his students and bring along pictures and VHS tapes. Then I would sign autographs.

33

1995-1996

I continued to do very well with MMCA and my financial services career. I was not looking forward to the summer because I figured that was when withdrawal would really kick in.

I picked up a summer job announcing a weekly open rodeo in Laramie, Wyoming for Curt Blake. The rodeo was held on Wednesday and Thursday nights at the Albany County Fairgrounds. It was a lot of fun and a good way to keep my announcing skills polished.

I had experienced a few problems with the transmission in my truck which then had over 180,000 miles on it. I got it repaired and bought a brand new Saturn. It was nice to own two roadworthy vehicles and I drove both of them regularly. Financially, I was doing well and felt like a rich man. My Nissan truck was silver and my new car was gold.

I had decided that when I retired from riding, I was not going to continue to run up and down the rodeo trail as a fulltime announcer. I was tired of being on the road all of the time. I was finished with being a "*road*-eo" cowboy.

I was sure that the summer of 1995 was going to be boring for me. But it turned out to be a very productive time. I did the television commentary with Prime Sports Network for Cheyenne Frontier Days Rodeo. I worked with Jerry Schemmel again. I also stayed busy and very productive with MMCA.

In the fall I made a decision to move. The rental house was like an icebox in the winter I had endured enough cold.

My MMCA sales career continued to flourish. I bought my first home and moved into it on June 24th, 1996, my birthday. It was by far the biggest birthday present I'd ever received. That night I almost felt like crying. I was very overwhelmed by the satisfaction of living in a home that I owned.

In July, I worked with Prime Sports Network on the telecast of Cheyenne Frontier Days Rodeo. That year I would be working with Hadley Barrett, a well-known and popular PRCA announcer from Kersey, Colorado.

In August, Bob Wilson, a black cowboy from Denver, and I attended the Hall of Fame induction ceremony for Charles Sampson and a few other PRCA cowboys in Colorado Springs. I talked to Bobby Steiner, the 1973 Bull Riding World Champion. I was surprised to discover that he already knew who I was. It made me feel good.

I also got to meet Gale Sayers. I got his autograph and tried to strike up a small conversation with him but got no response. I was very disappointed because he had always been one of my football heroes and yet he did not utter a single word to me. My sisters Patricia and Janice got a tissue box and cried their eyes out when *Brian's Song* was aired on television in the early '70s. I had always told myself that no matter how well-known that I became, I would still at least talk to all of my fans and admirers. I hope to remain true to that promise.

I attended a few rodeos and I was always searching for new clients. The rodeos became a prime hunting ground for new business. I had signed up a whole arsenal of rodeo cowboys and their wives to my company's life insurance and annuity program. I also judged a few Bull Riding jackpots throughout that summer.

I hadn't been home for more than a year so I went home to New Jersey for the Labor Day weekend. In the airport in Denver, I ran into Lyle Sankey, a former top ranked rodeo cowboy. He asked me where I was going. I told him I was going home.

Lyle said, "I thought that you lived here in Colorado."

"I do, but I'm headed to New Jersey to visit my family. I still consider New Jersey to be home although I live in Colorado. Where are you going?"

He said, "I am going to Laughlin, Nevada to judge a PBR (Professional Bull Riders) event."

We chatted a little more and then said our goodbyes. I hadn't seen Lyle Sankey in about five years.

In September, we had another University of Wyoming Rodeo team reunion during the college rodeo at Laramie because Pete Burns was retiring as the rodeo team coach after twelve years.

In October I announced the NIRA (college) rodeo in Sheridan, Wyoming. Zane Garstad was the college rodeo coach and hired me. It took me about six hours to drive to Sheridan. It was a little strange because I hadn't driven that far to participate in a rodeo for a few years. I was definitely out of practice.

During that rodeo I met another black rodeo cowboy from Chicago named Mike Moore, who was attending Casper Jr. College. At the time Mike was competing in the Bareback Riding as well as the Bull Riding events. He would later graduate from the University of Wyoming and qualify for the National Finals Rodeo in Bull Riding.

Mike and I got to be very good friends over the years. He became one of my MMCA clients and we played racquetball together on several occasions. I gave him a hard time when he didn't hit the rodeo trail hard. I told him he was the most talented bull rider I knew who refuses to travel. But Mike wanted to do things right. He took care of his education first so that he would have something to fall back on and then he hit the rodeo trail hard. It paid off.

I ended that year ranked seventh in the nation based on sales premiums for MMCA. I went home for Christmas to visit my family again for the holidays.

34

1997-1999

I judged the Bulldacious Bull Riding event in Torrington, Wyoming, for Byron in January. It was an annual big bull riding jackpot. I also attended the MMCA National Convention in Denver at which I was recognized along with a few other top agents at a special "Excellence in Achievement" awards banquet for finishing in the top ten for 1996.

In June, I announced the PRCA rodeo in Grover, Colorado. In July, I judged the Mr T. Classic Bull Riding event held annually in Laramie, Wyoming. Then, I acted as a broadcast commentator for Fox Sports Network along with Hadley Barrett for Cheyenne Frontier Days Rodeo again.

I announced two performances for the weekly PRCA rodeo in Steamboat Springs, Colorado, in early August. I went shopping for postcards and discovered one with a picture of a bucking bull on it and thought, *how cool, this will be perfect.*

As I stared at the postcard I kept thinking to myself that the bull looked very familiar. I finally realized why: the postcard was of me being bucked off of an NFR bull named Locomotion, owned by Mac Altizer (Bad Company Rodeo Company) at a major Bull Riding event in Steamboat in July of 1993.

I was wearing short pants and a T-shirt while I was shopping. I told the girl who was working as the cashier that the postcard was of me. I could tell by her reaction that she didn't believe me. I bought several of the cards and mailed them to my friends and family in New Jersey.

The rest of that year, I judged as well as announced a few Bull Riding events.

My father, the Reverend Abraham Jackson Morris, Sr., passed away on Saturday February 7th, 1998. My sister Janice called me at about 3:30 in the morning. He had had a stroke. I discovered that, no matter how old you are, the death of a parent is a very hard pill to swallow. I took it pretty hard.

I usually played in a racquetball league on Saturday mornings. I decided to go on and play anyway. When I got in my car, the first song that was playing was *Men in Black* by Wil Smith. I associated *"here come the men in black..."* with pallbearers. As a result I couldn't listen to this song for the next few years without my eyes filling with tears.

Jimmy Lee Walker called me on the telephone and all he said was, "Hello, Mr. Morris." I recognized his voice and immediately broke down and started crying. The same thing happened on several occasions over the next couple of weeks. My dad had been the lead singer on a 45 rpm record by the Morning Star Baptist Male Chorus entitled *Nearer My God to Thee*, and that song was palyed at his funeral. I absolutely could not listen to that song for the next four years.

Abraham Jackson Morris, Sr.

It was just too painful.

In May, I was back in New Jersey. I ran into Grant Harris at Cowtown on a Tuesday. He commented that if he'd known I was going to be in town, he would have asked me to announce the rodeo on Saturday night. We chatted a bit and made an agreement that I would announce the rodeo performance on May 30, 1998. It was indeed an honor to announce at Cowtown where I had initiated my entire rodeo career. I announced it with Dusty Cleveland who was a long time regular at the Cowtown Rodeo.

After I returned to Colorado, I had to study for my Series 6 (securities license for the financial services industry). I took and passed the test on June 24th. It marked yet another significant event that had happened on my birthday.

We were scheduled to do the telecast again at the Cheyenne Frontier Days Rodeo. It was cancelled after a contract dispute between the Cheyenne Frontier Days Rodeo committee and Fox Sports Network. Each side refused to budge on the issues. I was very disappointed. I looked forward to doing that rodeo every year. Cheyenne has always been my favorite and it was my one chance each year to be in the spotlight on a national and international television broadcast.

In September, I flew out to Sacramento to announce a black rodeo at the California State Fair. Bryan Riley, a black cowboy who had previously qualified for the National Finals Rodeo in Bull Riding, was the producer. Bryan paid for all of my travel expenses and on top of that, I was also paid very nicely for announcing. It was a fun event. I was able to visit with a few black PRCA cowboys such as Bryan Riley, Nick T. Buckley, Keith Louis and Ervin Williams whom I had not seen for a few years.

I sold my home in Fort Collins in September and moved to Denver. I really hated to leave Fort Collins and all the friends and acquaintances I had made during my twelve year stay in the city.

In October, I went to Fort Worth to attend a four day training

Morris Family Photo May 23, 1998 Left to Right: Rosalyn Rashel Hairston (Ft.Worth, Texas), Reuben Darryl Morris (West Deptford, New Jersey), Abraham Jackson Morris (Denver, Colorado), Janice Ellen Morris (Woodstown, New Jersey), Patricia Medina Morris (Woodstown, New Jersey), David Wayne Morris (Salem, New Jersey). Seated: Christine Morris (Woodstown, New Jersey)

session with a company called Farm and Ranch Healthcare. I already had a life and health insurance license and I wanted to broaden my horizons by selling health insurance which I knew would be a good addition for my rodeo cowboy market. I pursued some of my same MMCA clients for health insurance, as well. On some of my life insurance appointments I was able to sell health insurance and vice versa. My securities license meant I could also talk about mutual fund products. It made me better able to serve the friends and customers I had throughout the West.

In December I was again able to return to New Jersey to visit my family for the holidays.

I did not do as well selling health insurance and mutual fund products as I would have liked. I worked a Farm and Ranch Healthcare booth at the National Western Stock Show and Rodeo in Denver in January of 1999 and was able to generate a few leads but business did not turn out to be very rewarding.

I also was starting to get burned out on running all over the state of Colorado on sales appointments. Eating out in restaurants and staying in small motel rooms had started to get old because I was not making the money I had anticipated.

In early May, I announced a weekend rodeo in Lamar, Colorado, for the Senior Pro Rodeo Association. I managed to work in a few health insurance appointments in the vicinity as well.

In August, I gave up my career as a commissioned salesman and took on an office job as a telephone service representative for a variable annuity insurance company, Jackson National Life. A Series 6 securities license was a requirement for that position.

I didn't mind the office environment because I was ready for a change and it was nice to have a steady paycheck.

In November, I went back to New Jersey for my 25th High School Class Reunion. I attended the home high school football game in Woodstown on Thanksgiving Day. I ran into many former WHS students that I had not seen in years. The class reunion was nice. It was great to catch up with my former classmates.

35

A New Century

In the summer of 2001, on Friday, August 3rd and Saturday the 4th, Cowtown Rodeos, Inc. hosted a Cowboy and Cowgirl Reunion at the home of Grant and Betsy Harris. It was a very memorable celebration in which several cowboys and cowgirls from years gone by were in attendance. It was good to see so many of those who had competed at Cowtown on a regular basis. I had not seen many of them for several years.

During the festivities on Friday evening, Howard Harris, III, gave me one of the best compliments of my entire rodeo career: He said, "Abraham you have brought more dignity and class to our sport of rodeo than any other black man." I was shocked. Howard was not known for his compliments. He had really mellowed in his later years. And, even if he felt this way, I was flabbergasted that he would open up and tell me. The compliment really made me feel good because we'd had our differences during my years competing at Cowtown Rodeo. I knew that I would remember this extraordinary comment for the rest of my life.

BET Nightly News Studio with Monique Conrad
April 22, 2004 Washington, D.C.
Photo: David Morris

Abe Morris

Abe & Justin Morris, February 29, 2004   Woodstown, New Jersey
Photo: David Morris

36

In His Father's Footsteps

On Saturday, May 15th, 1999, my son Justin Abraham Morris was born. The doctor in the delivery room could not get him out of his mother's womb and had to purposely break his right arm. I was taping the delivery with my VHS camera and it was a very loud snap when Justin's arm was broken. When the doctor first said he had to break Justin's arm, I thought he was only kidding me. I couldn't tell if Justin was crying from the pain of a broken arm or the shock of birth like so many other babies. Poor little fellow, he hadn't even made it out of the chute and he'd already suffered a broken arm.

Due to several circumstances beyond my control I have not been able to spend as much time with my son Justin as I would like. But

I treasure our time together and really enjoy watching him grow.

After he was able to start talking I figured out that he loved to look at my VHS tapes and rodeo photo albums. Whenever I was around him he would say, "I want to watch Daddy ride bull on TV." Justin would watch my videos and become mesmerized. Then he would say, "Show again, show again, Daddy," or, "Slow Daddy, slow. I like to watch Daddy on slow." At the same time he would emulate my every move on a bull. He would wave his free arm and then stomp on the floor. When I asked him what he was doing he would say, "I'm spurring, I'm spurring like Daddy." Then he would throw his imaginary cowboy hat into the air and raise both arms over his head in a triumphant gesture.

I realized that he wanted to be just like his daddy. Whenever I would ask Justin what he wanted to be when he got bigger he would say, "I am going to be a bull rider like my Daddy." Once I realized how attached that Justin was to me and rodeo, I gave him my first trophy belt buckle that I won at the University Of Wyoming college rodeo in 1978. He was on cloud nine. He puts his daddy on a pedestal.

Sometimes I would ask him whose buckle was he wearing. Other times I would ask him, "Is that Daddy's buckle?" I always got the same response. "No, that's Justin's buckle." He had now claimed full ownership of that prized rodeo belt buckle. Then he would point to the buckle that I was wearing and say, "That's Daddy's buckle."

One time we were walking across the parking lot to the grocery store and Justin suddenly fell to the pavement. He got up holding his shoulder and said, "Ow, big bull stepped on me. Big mean bull get off of me. You hurt my shoulder." I had told him of my various injuries and he was mocking his favorite bull rider.

In September, I took Justin to a Woodstown High School football game on a Friday night and then to his very first Cowtown Rodeo on Saturday night. He loved them both. He was so excited to be going to the rodeo because he had heard me mention Cowtown Rodeo several times on my interviews and VHS tapes.

Justin Morris, February 2004, Cowtown Rodeo

He wore his cowboy hat and belt buckle and as we were walking through the parking lot he was loudly saying, "We are going to Cowtown Rodeo!" The people got such a kick out of his enthusiasm. He had a blast. During the calf roping event he would copy the ropers on the ground when they successfully tied up their calves.

In the fall of 2002, I took Justin to the playground at the park. He would ride the spring horse with his right hand and wave his left free arm just like a bull rider. When I would make the sound of the whistle, he would fall to the ground. Then he would jump up and run to the edge of the sawdust pit and throw his real cowboy hat into the air. Afterward, he would raise both arms to celebrate his successful ride...just like his daddy.

Since I finished writing this book I have become a free-lance writer for a couple of different publications. I have had stories published in the *Rocky Mountain Rodeo News*, Laporte, Colorado, *The Fence Post*,

Windsor, Colorado, *The Laramie Daily Boomerang*, Laramie, Wyoming, and *Humps N' Horns Bull Riding News* Chouteau, Oklahoma.

I've written a monthly column, *My Cowboy Hat Still Fits,* for *Humps N' Horns Bull Riding News*. In it I shared stories not included in my book from my rodeo career.

In the July 2004 issue of *Humps N' Horns* I wrote a story titled *Justin Is My Hero*. Here is a quote from that article.

If Justin decides to become a bull rider, I will be right there in order to coach him along, the same way that my first cousins Gene, Jimmy Lee and Willie Ed Walker coached me. I will not encourage him to be a bull rider, though. I want that to be his own decision. I already realize that he wants to be just like his daddy.

He knows that riding bulls is a very dangerous sport. I have shown him all of my bull riding battle scars. I constantly tell Justin that, "I don't want you to ride bulls just because Daddy rode bulls. I only want you to ride bulls because you want to ride bulls." Justin still maintains that he wants to be a bull rider when he grows up. If he does I predict that Justin Morris will be a world-class bull rider and all around good person just like his daddy.

Considering all of the challenges that Justin has had to endure and deal with in his early life, he has done very well. He is very competitive, loves to win and hates to lose. He is very polite and is well behaved and God could not have given me a better person to call my own son. Justin is so very proud to call me his daddy, and I am also extremely proud to call him my son.

Years from now, when he is able to read as well as comprehend this story, I want him to realize that he is loved very dearly. Not only is Justin Abraham Morris my best friend, but believe it or not, he is also my hero.

P R C A

I would say that the Professional Rodeo Cowboys Association is about ninety-seven percent white cowboys. They do not keep records and statistics on race. There are currently only a few African-Americans, Native Americans and Mexican-Americans. Of the minorities, I would say that there are more black cowboys than Mexican-Americans and even fewer Native-Americans on the rodeo trail.

There are a few cowboys from Australia who came over to the United States to further pursue their rodeo careers. In the 1970s Jimmy Dix from North Collie, West Australia, was a top bareback rider and qualified for the NFR on several occasions. Darryl Kong qualified for the NFR a few times in the Saddle Bronc Riding event.

Both cowboys did very well but have long since returned to their native country. Dave Appleton came over from Australia and won the World All Around Championship in 1988. He even had his own line of western wear with Roper Apparel. Dave now lives in Texas and is an announcer for a major horse race track.

Since then, other native Australians have come here and done very well. Troy Dunn, who would be considered one of the best bull riders of all time, is still competing in the PBR (Professional Bull Riders). Glen O'Neill won a World Championship in the Saddle Bronc Riding event in 2002. Greg Potter is still competing in both the PRCA and PBR. Brendon Clark is one of the newest stars from Australia to hit the trail on the PBR circuit.

Darren Clarke in the bareback and Scott Johnston bareback and saddle bronc riding have also qualified for the NFR. Scott Johnston was in the title chase for the All Around Championship in 2001 and the Saddle Bronc Riding World Championship in 2000.

There has been an influx of great bull riders that have migrated to the states from Brazil. Adriano Moraes will go down in history as one of the great bull riders of all time. Adriano qualified for the National Finals Rodeo several times and is a two time PBR World Champion. Ednei Caminhas was the PBR World Champion in 2002. Paulo Crimber qualified for both the PBR World Finals and the National Finals Rodeo.

To my knowledge only the countries of Canada, Australia and Brazil have produced any foreign cowboys who have had a significant mark on the upper ranks and echelon of the rodeo world.

In 1993, the last full year that I was very active in rodeo, the top winner Ty Murray, the All Around Champion, won over $297,000. In 1994 Ty repeated the feat by winning over $246,000. Trevor Brazile from Decatur, Texas, was the All Around Champion in 2003 and won over $294,000. Mike Lee from Paradise, Texas, clinched the PBR World Championship in 2004 and won $1,435,826.

The bull riders in the PBR Finals can win about forty-thousand dollars in one event now. The World Champion in the PBR wins a million dollar bonus. These figures were unheard of when I was competing.

Black Rodeo Cowboys
at Cowtown Rodeo

When I was growing up and competing in the Bull Riding event at Cowtown Rodeo there were several other black cowboys competing on a regular basis.

In the timed events there was Bud Bramwell and Billy Wilde from Connecticut. Both of them competed in the Calf Roping and Steer Wrestling events. Roger and Eddie Young from New York competed in the rough stock or riding events. Roger was a good bull rider and saddle bronc rider. Eddie competed in the Bull Riding event.

"C.R.," Charlie Reno Hall, was a great bareback rider until he bucked off of a horse named #55 Dark Moment in June 1968 and fractured his neck. I will never forget it because he lay injured and then left the arena under his own power. No one had gone out to assist him. It was a sad day for he was never able to ride again.

Rocky Mobley was a bull rider from Conshohocken, Pennsylvania. Ronnie Vails and Dave Brown were bull riders from New York.

Then of course there were us. It was like a huge family affair. Gene, Jimmy Lee and Willie Ed Walker were all exceptional hands and should have qualified for the National Finals Rodeo during their careers. Gene and Jimmy Lee competed in the Bareback Riding and Bull Riding events. Willie Ed competed in the Bareback Riding, Saddle Bronc Riding, Steer Wrestling and the Bull Riding events and by far, his best event was the Steer Wrestling or Bull Dogging events. All three of my cousins also fought bulls at one time or another. Gene even acted as Richard Pryor's stunt double in the bullfighting and rodeo scenes in the movie *Stir Crazy*.

Freddie and Stanley Thomas were brothers from Woodstown who competed at Cowtown Rodeo. Freddie only competed in the Bareback Riding a couple of times. Stanley was a regular and a force to be reckoned with in the Bull Riding and Bareback Riding events for many years on the East Coast. Their adopted younger brother, Tony Bouldin (Spaz), competed in the Bareback Riding and the Bull Riding events.

Our younger cousin Johnny Harp also lived right there at Cowtown and rode bulls very well for several years in the First Frontier Circuit of the PRCA. He was talented enough to qualify for the NFR but he never went down the road hard. His brother-in-law, Roland (JR) Shorter, married Vera Harp and competed in the Steer Wrestling and Bull Riding events. Roland's younger brother Charles "Chan" Shorter rode bulls for a few years.

Jerome "Buck" Howard was a very talented bareback rider and bull rider for several years. There were also other black cowboys who only competed for a few years in the Junior Bull Riding ranks and still dressed and played the role every Saturday night on a regular basis at Cowtown. I would put Eddie Shorter (no relation to Roland and Charles), Ike and Mark Redd into this category. David Walker did not compete in the rodeos but was a regular attendee, providing moral support for his brothers.

At one point in the late '70s and early '80s, the black cowboys practically dominated the Bareback Riding event at Cowtown Rodeo. Jimmy Lee, Stanley and Buck would place every week and it boiled down to who had drawn the best bucking horse for that evening.

We, the black cowboys, were the minority but we were very comfortable because we had numbers and were at the top of the talent pool on the East Coast. Even back East, not one of us won nearly as much money as we deserved to win. The older white judges slighted us on a regular basis. Among ourselves, we were always complaining about our scores from these "good old boy" judges who preferred that we get discouraged. But week after week we came back for more, until the judges finally gave in and gave us our due.

When I was growing up, Willie Ed would be there to pull my bull rope ninety-five percent of the time. Stanley Thomas was the only other person who pulled my rope on a regular basis. I relied on them to always be there for me. If Willie Ed was not around, I would feel very uncomfortable. I was used to him slapping me on the back right before I nodded for the gate. It really helped to pump me up.

We had a following of black women such as my cousins Barbara Jean (Walker) Gardner, Christine Walker and Vera (Harp) Shorter, Sara (Harp) Henson and Cindy (Harp) Brandjord, who attended the rodeos regularly. Willie Ed's wife, Rosemary (Taylor) Walker, was also a solid support system for us black cowboys.

I found it to be very encouraging to be around other black cowboys as we traveled on the East Coast. We were already family and good friends and had a lot of unity as if we were competing as a team. We took the word "camaraderie" to another level.

Abe Morris

Black Rodeos

There are two major black professional touring rodeo associations in the United States. The Bill Pickett Invitational Rodeo Association was initiated by Lu Vason in September 1984 and is based in Denver, Colorado. They produce ten to twelve rodeos all over the United States.

The association is named in honor of Bill Pickett, a black cowboy who is credited with starting the popular Steer Wrestling or Bull Dogging event in professional rodeo. You may find out more about Bill Pickett and this rodeo tour at www.billpickettrodeo.com.

The Cowboys of Color is another predominately black rodeo association that was founded and run by Cleo Hearn from Lancaster, Texas. Cleo, a calf roper and a member of the PRCA, produces most of these rodeos in the state of Texas. There is a National Cowboys of Color Museum and Hall of Fame located in Fort Worth that honors black cowboys. Interested parties can read more about them at www.cowboysofcolor.com.

There is also another black rodeo cowboys association called the Real Cowboys Association based in Longview, Texas.

Abe Morris